State and Laid-Off Workers in Reform China

In the 1990s, the Chinese government launched an unprecedented reform of state-owned enterprises, putting tens of millions of people out of work. *State and Laid-Off Workers in Reform China* is an empirically rich study combining quantitative data with qualitative interviews in its analysis of the variation in workers' collective action. Cai focuses on two sets of factors; the first is the difference in the interests of and the options available to workers that reduced their solidarity and the obstacles that prevented their coordination. The second, and perhaps the more important, is the Chinese government's policies that shaped workers' incentive and capacity for action.

Utilizing extensive interview and survey material, this book will appeal to those with an interest in Chinese politics, political sociology, and civil society.

Yongshun Cai is an Assistant Professor in the Division of Social Science at Hong Kong University of Science and Technology.

Routledge Studies on China in Transition
Series editor: David S. G. Goodman

1 **The Democratisation of China**
   Baogang He

2 **Beyond Beijing**
   Dali Yang

3 **China's Enterprise Reform**
   Changing state/society relations after Mao
   You Ji

4 **Industrial Change in China**
   Economic restructuring and conflicting interests
   Kate Hannan

5 **The Entrepreneurial State in China**
   Real estate and commerce departments in reform era Tianjin
   Jane Duckett

6 **Tourism and Modernity in China**
   Tim Oakes

7 **Cities in Post Mao China**
   Recipes for economic development in the reform era
   Jae Ho Chung

8 **China's Spatial Economic Development**
   Regional transformation in the lower Yangzi Delta
   Andrew M. Marton

9 **Regional Development in China**
   States, globalization and inequality
   Yehua Dennis Wei

10 **Grassroots Charisma**
   Four local leaders in China
   Stephan Feuchtwang and Wang Mingming

11 **The Chinese Legal System**
   Globalization and local legal culture
   Pitman B. Potter

12 **Transforming Rural China**
   How local institutions shape property rights in China
   Chi-Jou Jay Chen

13 **Negotiating Ethnicity in China**
   Citizenship as a response to the state
   Chih-yu Shih

14 **Manager Empowerment in China**
Political implications of rural industrialisation in the reform era
Ray Yep

15 **Cultural Nationalism in Contemporary China**
The search for national identity under reform
Yingjie Guo

16 **Elite Dualism and Leadership Selection in China**
Xiaowei Zang

17 **Chinese Intellectuals Between State and Market**
Edward Gu and Merle Goldman

18 **China, Sex and Prostitution**
Elaine Jeffreys

19 **The Development of China's Stockmarket, 1984–2002**
Equity politics and market institutions
Stephen Green

20 **China's Rational Entrepreneurs**
The development of the new private business sector
Barbara Krug

21 **China's Scientific Elite**
Cong Cao

22 **Locating China**
Jing Wang

23 **State and Laid-Off Workers in Reform China**
The silence and collective action of the retrenched
Yongshun Cai

State and Laid-Off Workers in Reform China

The silence and collective action of the retrenched

Yongshun Cai

LONDON AND NEW YORK

First published 2006
by Routledge
2 Park Square, Milton Park, Abingdon, Oxon OX14 4RN

Simultaneously published in the USA and Canada
by Routledge
711 Third Ave, New York, NY 10017

Routledge is an imprint of the Taylor & Francis Group

© 2006 Yongshun Cai

First issued in paperback 2013

Typeset in Times New Roman by
Newgen Imaging Systems (P) Ltd, Chennai, India

All rights reserved. No part of this book may be reprinted or
reproduced or utilised in any form or by any electronic,
mechanical, or other means, now known or hereafter
invented, including photocopying and recording, or in any
information storage or retrieval system, without permission in
writing from the publishers.

British Library Cataloguing in Publication Data
A catalogue record for this book is available
from the British Library

Library of Congress Cataloging in Publication Data
A catalog record for this book has been requested

ISBN 978–0–415–36888–9 (hbk)
ISBN 978 0–415–65191–2 (pbk)

For Wang Chen and Xinyu

Contents

List of tables	xi
Acknowledgments	xii
List of abbreviations	xiii

1 Introduction   1

Dismantling of moral arrangements and motivations for resistance 2
Reform and resistance: a dual interaction 4
Notes on the definition of laid-off workers and data collection 10
Structure of the book 11

2 The ending of a socialist contract and retrenchment   13

Budget constraints and the end of the socialist contract 14
The government's redress measures and limitations 18
Impact of layoffs 25
Conclusion 30

3 Retrenchment and laid-off workers' responses   32

Laid-off workers' responses 33
Statistical analyses of workers' responses 36
Conclusion 45

4 Fragmentation and collective action   46

Fragmentation and the difficulty of collective action 46
A means to the end: individual action 48
Alternatives and nonparticipation 55
Conclusion 60

5 Management and worker silence — 61

Dominance of management 62
Workers' ex ante resistance 68
Management and workers' ex post resistance 70
Constraints and management tactics 72
Management as a helpless patron 78
Conclusion 80

6 The government and the prevention of worker resistance — 82

Targeting the government 82
Belief and reaction of the government 83
Capacity, constraints, and government policies 85
Conclusion 99

7 The collective action of Chinese laid-off workers — 101

Constraints on the government 101
Mobilization and collective action 106
Scenarios for collective action 111
Scale of resistance and reform 115
Conclusion 119

8 Conclusion — 120

Shared interests and the potential of collective action 120
Coordination and collective action 122
Government and reform policies 124
Flexibility of the Chinese political system 125
*Evolution toward more institutionalized
  state–society interaction 128*

Appendix: data collection — 131
Notes — 135
Bibliography — 167
Index — 185

Tables

2.1	Laid-off workers by sector in 1997 ($N = 11.5$ million)	16
2.2	A linear regression of the number of laid-off workers on selected variables ($N = 31$)	17
2.3	Industrial SOEs in China by size (1995)	18
3.1	Collective appeals in China (compared to the previous year)	34
3.2	Number of instances of social unrest in China in selected years	34
3.3	Logistic regression of workers' participation in collective action on selected variables related to deprivation and discontent	38
3.4	Logistic regression of workers' participation in collective action on selected variables related to interests	42
3.5	Logistic regression of workers' participation in collective action on selected variables related to efficacy and cost	44
4.1	Logistic regression of the job search of laid-off workers on selected variables	54
4.2	Laid-off workers' attitudes toward collective appeals in Changchun ($N = 1,127$)	57
4.3	Unpaid retired workers (as of September 1997)	58
7.1	Backgrounds of organizers in Chinese workers' collective action ($N = 41$)	108
7.2	Situations in which unpaid or under-compensated laid-off workers take action	112
7.3	Laid-off workers' welfare provision ($N = 724$)	116

Acknowledgments

This book is based on my PhD dissertation for the Department of Political Science at Stanford University. I wish to thank my dissertation committee members: Jean Oi, Russell Hardin, Isabella Mares, Andrew Walder, and Doug McAdam. All of them were generous with their time and were always willing to provide help. During my graduate study at Stanford University, my chief advisor, Jean Oi, assisted me in more ways than I can count. She provided constant help and very insightful suggestions while writing the dissertation. Russell Hardin introduced to me some perspectives developed in the collective action literature. Isabella Mares was always ready to provide help and she also urged me to strengthen the comparative perspective of the dissertation. Andrew Walder's advice helped me restructure the dissertation in a more logical and effective way. Doug McAdam's comments helped me sharpen the perspective used in the dissertation. I also wish to thank the late Michel Oksenberg. Despite his very poor health at that time, he managed to read a large part of the dissertation and urged me to pay more attention to the variation in workers' reaction. When revising the manuscript, I received very helpful comments and suggestions from Jean Oi. I also wish to thank Dorothy Solinger, Elizabeth Perry, Lu Zheng, Yang Su, Yuen Yuen Tang, Peter Lorentzen, and two anonymous reviewers for their comments and suggestions on earlier drafts of the book. None of the above people is responsible for any errors in the book.

I am also grateful to those laid-off workers who were willing to accept our interviews and to share with us their unprecedented experiences in the reform process in China. I wish to thank the Graduate Opportunity Research Grant and the Center for East Asian Studies at Stanford and the Faculty of Arts and Social Sciences at the National University of Singapore for their financial support.

I wish to thank my wife, Wang Chen, who has always supported my research and assisted in my fieldtrips. I also want to thank my daughter, Xinyu, for, among many other things, not using the weapons of kids too often, one of which was to occupy the seat in front of the computer to prevent me from "playing with the computer." This book is dedicated to them.

Part of Chapter 7 originally appeared in "The Resistance of Chinese Laid-Off Workers in the Reform Period," *The China Quarterly*, 2002, 170, 327–44.

Abbreviations

ACFTU	The All China Federation of Trade Unions
LOWs	Laid-off workers
MICPC	Manager-in-charge under the leadership of the party committee
MRS	Manager responsibility system
RLS	Retaining the large and letting go of the small
RSC	Reemployment service center
SOE	State-owned enterprise

1 Introduction

Communism produced a class of workers with strong emotional ties to and material interest in maintaining that system,[1] so economic restructuring in the industrial sectors in communist states is very likely to invite labor resistance. The government would need to employ cautious measures to avoid strong resistance and possible social unrest. While there seems to be a "surprise of labor weakness" in post-communist societies, the reasons for labor quiescence are complex, including weak trade unions, limited worker solidarity, and prolonged economic downturns that produce discouragement and a kind of "learned powerlessness" among workers and their leaders.[2] But labor quiescence in some former socialist countries was also related to the modes of retrenchment. During the "shock therapy" of post-communist Poland, for example, the Polish government offered workers early retirement with generous compensation, which helped reduce laid-off workers' resistance. In 1990, the number of employees in Polish state-owned enterprises (SOEs) fell by 31 percent, with early voluntary retirement accounting for at least 70 percent of the net drop in employment. Voluntary retirement blunted the resistance to reform: "If the initial wave of job losses had been predominantly involuntary, a backlash might well have ensued; but the pattern that was actually observed in 1990 and 1991 posed far fewer risks, allowing much-needed reforms to take root."[3] In Russia, economic restructuring primarily involved privatization and did not lead to immediate large-scale layoffs. An overwhelming number of firms adopted the option of allowing workers and managers to hold a part or the majority of the firm's shares.[4] Privatization might not work to the advantage of Russian workers, but neither had it driven them to resist. Kramer writes: "Although in some cases privatization has indeed been a stimulus to worker mobilization, it has not in general proved to be such as workers have shown themselves to be too demoralized, divided and fatalistic to believe that they have the power to influence such major decisions."[5]

Unlike Poland and Russia, China initiated reform of SOEs in the 1990s by dismantling the lifetime employment system through massive layoffs. The number of employees in the state and collective sectors plummeted by more than 48 million from 1995 to 2000, a number equal to the population of South Korea.[6] Compounding the plight of laid-off workers is the absence of an inadequate welfare system, coupled with a difficult reemployment environment.[7] Facing the loss of jobs, decrease in income, and uncertainties about the future, some laid-off workers have acted collectively in defense of their interests.[8] Since the 1990s, numerous incidents of workers' collective action, with participants ranging from dozens to tens of thousands, have posed a serious concern for the Chinese government.[9] It has been claimed that "a more restive Chinese working class is in the making, as shown by the massive eruption of collective actions over the past two decades."[10] Hence, unlike in most other transitional economies, the issue of worker layoffs in China has been a serious challenge to the Chinese government.

Nevertheless, although worker resistance in China has stumbled the pace of economic restructuring,[11] it has failed to stop the government from carrying out reform measures. In 1995, the Chinese government began privatizing, closing, and declaring bankrupt small SOEs and collective enterprises. In 1997, the government officially promoted the privatization of small SOEs across the country. After 1999, the government applied these same policies to medium-sized SOEs and some large ones.[12] The continuation of the reform indicates that the retrenchment has not become an insurmountable challenge for the government. An important reason is that a majority of laid-off workers have remained silent.[13] This is puzzling given the fact that those who acquiesced may not fare better than those who resisted. The case of Chinese workers raises several questions: facing threat against their interests, why do some workers resist while many others do not? Why and when is collective resistance possible in China? What are the implications of worker resistance for reform and political stability in China? These are the questions that this book seeks to answer in order to understand collective action under an authoritarian regime and the relations between political institutions and economic transition.

Dismantling of moral arrangements and motivations for resistance

In communist states like the former Soviet Union and China, labor relations are claimed to be based on a "tacit agreement" or moral arrangement between the state and labor that protects workers' interests.[14] Where such contracts are fulfilled, labor movements are rare.[15] Cook describes state–labor relations in the former Soviet Union in this manner:

> [T]he regime provided broad guarantees of full and secure employment, state-controlled and heavily subsidized prices for essential goods, fully socialized human service, and egalitarian wage policies. In exchange for such comprehensive state provision of economic and social security, Soviet workers consented to the party's extensive and monopolistic power, accepted state domination of the economy, and complied with authoritarian political norms. Maintenance of labor peace in this political system thus required relatively little use of overt coercion.[16]

Similarly, prior to the reform era, labor relations in SOEs in China were characterized as "organized dependence" of workers on firms. In this arrangement, workers depended on their work units or employers for highly secure jobs as well as cradle-to-grave welfare coverage, although provisions of welfare varied across firms. As Walder suggests, "the extraordinary job security and benefits, the goods and services distributed directly by the state enterprise in a situation of scarcity that affects other sectors of the workforce more severely, is an important source of the acceptance of the system."[17]

The implicit moral agreement functions on the assumption that workers are willing to sacrifice their rights to effective and meaningful political participation in exchange for economic and other welfare benefits.[18] The corollary, moral economists would suggest, is that ending the moral arrangement will make workers angry and drive them to take action.[19] It is thus maintained that workers become intolerant when their sense of justice—composed of both illusion and truth with regard to ethos, dignity, well-being, and freedom—is violated.[20] For example, Posusney suggests that Egyptian workers protested out of anger when the status quo was disrupted, namely, that they lost their salary and other benefits.[21]

Loss and anger have also been suggested as the motivation for worker resistance in China. For example, Chen writes: "Labor protests by laid-off Chinese workers are largely motivated by a crisis in which workers find their subsistence ethic violated. Managerial corruption in factories that workers perceive as exacerbating their economic plight intensifies their sense of injustice and further inflames their militancy."[22] Indeed, the situation of laid-off workers in China also fits what Ted Gurr calls "decremental deprivation," whereby people are angered over the loss of what they once had or thought they could have. They experience relative deprivation by reference to past circumstances. One implication is that discontent "arising from the perception of relative deprivation is the basic, instigating condition for participants in collective violence."[23] This has also been claimed to hold true for China: "Most protest actions taken by workers have been driven by economic grievances, mostly over the cracking of their 'rice bowl'."[24] Lee suggests that Chinese workers' resistance amounts to a "revenge of history"; that is, the collective memories of Maoist socialism, under which workers' interests were protected, motivate action.[25]

It may be true, as prospect theory also suggests, that when facing loss, as opposed to gains, individuals tend to be less averse to taking risks and are thus more likely to take action.[26] Yet, motivation may not be a sufficient explanation. Studies also find that Chinese laid-off workers take action because the structural barriers (i.e., workers' dependence on their firms) against labor movements are lowered, and thus the risk of retaliation is diluted.[27] In the pre-reform period, dependence on SOEs for almost all their basic needs and a lack of alternatives gave management powerful leverage over workers. Walder writes: "This complex web of personal loyalty, mutual support, and material interest creates a stable pattern of tacit acceptance and active co-operation for the regime that no amount of political terror, coercion, or indoctrination can even begin to provide."[28] Crowley points to the same reason for labor silence in the former Soviet Union: "While workers everywhere face the problem of collective action, workers in Soviet enterprises have run the risk that an unsuccessful strike would likely deprive the initiators not only of wages, but of housing, day care, summer vacations, and the rest."[29]

4 *Introduction*

Reform of SOEs in China implies a possible end to traditional labor relations and welfare provisions. Workers who will be laid off no longer depend on their firms as before, and their collective action is thus less risky. Chen points out that laid-off workers were only nominally affiliated with SOEs and were entitled to minimal living allowances. Many actually received no assistance whatsoever from their enterprises and were left to fend for themselves. "But this also means that they now have less to fear by engaging in collective action—for they have already lost everything from benefits to jobs.... In short, the constraints on collective action largely evaporated once the dependence of laid-off workers on enterprises was ruptured."[30] If this were true, one would expect collective resistance to be widespread in China.

Nevertheless, other studies argue that it is not common for laid-off workers to take action, because they lack the motivation for resistance. Blecher's research suggests that workers fail to take action because "many—probably most—of China's workers have come to accept the core values of the market and of the state as legitimate."[31] This may be the case for some workers but not others. For example, Hung and Chiu find that many laid-off workers belong to the "lost generation" whose "life histories bear witness to a series of state policy changes, each of which had disadvantaged them in some way."[32] These workers believe that the state is responsible for their problems, especially when they failed to receive the minimum allowance after being laid off.[33] Therefore, they fail to resist perhaps because of causes other than their acceptance of the core values of the market and of the state as legitimate. In fact, there is evidence that other factors, such as a lack of confidence in taking action, are responsible for workers' silence. In Blecher's own research, some workers he interviewed reported that they did not take action because "there's no use in doing so."[34] In other words, the possible costs involved in resistance and the slim odds of success may dampen workers' incentive to resist, although they may not accept the core values of the market or are resentful of the state.

The aforementioned explanations of workers' reaction have no doubt promoted our understanding of workers' reaction to reform measures in China. Yet they have not adequately addressed the variation in workers' reaction. Explanations of worker resistance tend to focus on those who act but fail to explain those who do not. Hence, while "accelerated reforms have triggered both a proliferation and a deepening of labor activism," it is unclear who has taken action.[35] On the other hand, the explanation of worker silence based on market hegemony focuses only on those who remain silent. This approach thus needs to show that the numerous incidents of collective action have been taken by those who refused to accept the hegemony of the market. But it is also possible that workers may take action because they lack alternatives, regardless of whether or not they blame the state.[36]

Reform and resistance: a dual interaction

In examining collective resistance to reform, it is imperative to analyze the solidarity and coordination among those seeking redress as well as the target at which their action is directed. People negatively affected by reform should not be seen as a group with much solidarity. Specifically, in China, while tens of millions of workers have been laid off, they should not be regarded as a group ready for collective action. How do the different degrees of suffering affect workers' attitudes toward and thus participation in collective action? Equally important, when workers intend to take action, what mechanisms are needed to translate their intention into action? As individuals are interdependent in collective action in the sense that "one's participation tends to encourage others' participation by making collective action more likely to succeed,"[37] how can individuals know one another's interest in taking action?

Reform is a dynamic process in which reformers interact with affected individuals. Hence, reform policies shape individuals' incentives or perceptions of costs as well as their ability to resist. The interactive nature of reform requires any explanation of reactions to reform to take into account the power and policies of the reformers. The targets of Chinese laid-off workers' action include the management of their firms and the government, especially local governments,[38] so it is imperative to analyze their policies toward workers.

Given the need for sufficient participants and mobilization in collective action as well as the interactive nature of reform, this study shows that Chinese workers' resistance is better understood as a result of a dual interaction: one among workers and the other between workers and the targets of action. It argues that workers' collective resistance is possible because the political space in the Chinese political system creates opportunity for action and workers are able to mobilize themselves. Collective action becomes difficult when fragmentation occurs among workers and when the enterprise management and government adopt policies that increase the cost of action.

Solidarity and coordination in collective action

Collective resistance requires cooperation among prospective participants. From the perspective of an individual, collective action can be understood as the interaction between one prospective participant and a group of other prospective participants.[39] Although rational choice theory stresses individuals' propensity to maximize benefits or minimize costs through free-riding or defection, cooperation among individuals is not lacking.[40] As Lichbach summarizes, there can be dozens of solutions to the collective action problem in rebellious actions.[41] Such mechanisms include selective material incentives, coercion, effective monitoring, and credible future punishment.[42] Others point out that factors unrelated to the collective goal may motivate people to participate. These factors, called private benefits, include friendship, expectations of others, and altruism.[43]

Collective action based on voluntary participation is conditional. First, in the absence of incentives such as those mentioned above, individuals either have a tangible stake in taking action or believe that collective action is a more effective means to achieving their goal and thereby, "it pays to participate."[44] Second, prospective participants take action only when they know others will.

Hence, information dissemination and preference disclosure are preconditions for participation.[45] Third, given the possible costs or risks, individuals should have confidence in taking action. In other words, people will be reluctant to take action if the odds of success are too slim to justify action or if the risks involved in the action are perceived to be sufficiently high.

These conditions also point to the difficulties of organizing defensive collective action. First, such action is usually goal oriented. If some people have access to other alternatives, they will not see collective action as a desirable means to an end. Thus, solidarity among the deprived should not be assumed.[46] Charles Tilly suggests that the most organized type of collectivity is possible in a group that combines both "catness" and "netness," called "catnet" for short. Catness ("category") refers to the strength of shared identity in a group, whereas netness ("network") refers to the density of networks among group members created by interpersonal bonds.[47]

A group that lacks "catnet," or that is fragmented, faces more barriers against taking collective action. It has long been found that fragmentation prevents workers' collective action in various contexts.[48] Yet, in her analysis of workers in pre-1949 Shanghai, Perry suggests that there may be "a positive link between workers' fragmentation and their activism."[49] These seemingly conflicting conclusions are not in fact contradictory. The difference lies in the unit of analysis. One type of fragmentation is *within* a group, and the other is *across* groups. Perry's argument focuses on fragmentation across groups, in which case people of one group use other groups as a reference point to achieve greater group solidarity.[50] In contrast, collective action among Chinese laid-off workers during the reform period is difficult because they are in a group of low or limited solidarity. The asymmetries of suffering among workers produce fragmentation in two ways, reducing their "catness." One is the lack of solidarity between laid-off workers and those still employed. Second, different degrees of access to alternative jobs either before or after retrenchment produce different stakes in collective action. That some and not all Chinese workers have taken action indicates a fragmented response in light of specific circumstances and needs rather than class action.[51]

Second, collective action becomes difficult because mechanisms of mobilization are lacking. Laid-off workers who have the intention to resist should be able to communicate and organize. Research on social movements, such as resource mobilization theory, points to the importance of organizations in collective action.[52] Yet such organizations are nonexistent in communist states like China.[53] Students of communist systems therefore point out that resource mobilization theory may not be suitable for explaining collective action in communist regimes,[54] although this does not imply that resources are irrelevant in people's collective action in communist states.

Given these constraints, how is workers' collective action possible in authoritarian China? What affects their solidarity and ability to mobilize? Instead of assuming that all who are laid off face the same situation, this study will discuss the asymmetry of suffering among workers and its impact on their incentive to resist. For this purpose, it will examine the factors that affect workers' search for alternatives both before and after retrenchment and thereby their incentive to participate. It will also explore the mechanisms for overcoming fragmentation among workers. Specifically, it will analyze the way layoffs are carried out and its impact on the degree of fragmentation among workers and their mobilization. In doing so, it will compare workers who are simultaneously laid off with those who are sequentially laid off.

On the mechanisms for coordination, this study will explore two crucial factors that influence the way workers organize a course of action or achieve mobilization. One is the microenvironment within which individuals interact;[55] the other is the emergence of coordinators or organizers. The microenvironment bears on communication and preference disclosure, which are preconditions for collective action. For example, are workers who live in close proximity better able to interact and communicate with one another? The other factor that affects workers' mobilization is the emergence or absence of organizers.[56] Although the importance of political entrepreneurs in collective action has been well recognized,[57] limited efforts have been expended to examine empirically why and how such people emerge. The case of China provides a good opportunity to address how organizers, who do not benefit more from an action than an average participant but often bear more risks, may emerge. While existing studies highlight moral forces that inspire some individuals to become leaders of collective action,[58] this study eschews simplistic assumptions and explores the conditions for the emergence of leaders as well as the constraints they face.

Target and collective action: power and constraints of reformers

The existence of solidarity and coordination mechanisms does not necessarily mean that collective action will occur or succeed. When people adversely affected by reform consider whether and how to respond, they think about the odds of success and potential costs or risks. In doing so, they take into account the reformers' intentions, power, and constraints. Group action is more likely to occur and be sustained when the reformer is believed to be unwilling or unable to deny demands. For the same reason, action is less likely to occur or be sustained when those affected believe that they have little chance of success or that the potential costs are too high to justify participation.[59] Confidence in the ability to achieve success through action positively affects participation when individuals believe that the reformer is constrained either in a moral sense or in terms of capacity.

In China, SOE management and local governments are the targets of laid-off workers' action. To understand the variations in collective action, one must take into account the power and constraints of SOE management and local governments that oversee the SOEs. Both management and local governments are embedded in the administrative hierarchy of China's political system. Chinese SOEs used to be production units as well as social and political organizations responsible for their employees' welfare.[60] This study will analyze how the power and financial resources of the management shaped its interaction with workers. Yet it must be stressed that what distinguishes worker resistance in the recent reform period from previous actions is the target to which their action is more frequently directed. Layoffs often mean the end of the work-unit socialism, so workers now confront the state, as opposed to their firms, much more frequently than before. Hence, this book will also examine the responses of the government, usually at the local level.

State responses and the prevention of resistance

The reform experience of transitional regimes like post-communist Russia points to the importance of state power, as it determines whether and how reform policies are carried out.[61] Given the fact that reform often provokes resistance, the government needs to adopt policies to reduce or prevent it. Current studies of a regime's responses to nonconventional action tend to focus on the strategies of repression and concession. For example, in their study of regime responses to protests, Goldstone and Tilly point out that the scenarios or outcomes of the interaction between the state and protestors vary, depending on the balance of power between them. Yet, they largely focus on repression and concession on the part of the regime.[62] As later chapters of this study will document, the Chinese government has often employed means that fall between concession and repression.

Chinese laid-off workers often take action to achieve concrete economic goals, so their participation is determined by estimations of success and the risks or costs involved. The question for the government becomes, what could be done to dampen workers' incentives to take action, so as to continue reforms. The Chinese government may resort to repression, but it also has a choice as to which participants to punish. The government may also make concessions. Which participants are likely to obtain concessions? What kind of concessions would they receive? This study shows that in addition to partial concessions and selective repression, the Chinese government has adopted a wide range of other policies, from consensus building and blame avoidance to peaceful confrontation without giving concessions. These multiple strategies combine to erode workers' confidence in taking collective action and to increase the costs of participation.

Constraints on the government and opportunities for action

Despite the obstacles to workers' collective action discussed above, some have taken action and succeeded. How do workers overcome these obstacles? As for the government, why would it allow such action and even make concessions to the workers? Research on social movements suggests the necessity of a political opportunity structure for collective action.[63] Although students of social movements do not agree on a unified concept of "political opportunity structure," many suggest that it has two important dimensions. One is the formal legal and institutional structure of a given polity, and the other is the informal structure of power relations characteristic of a given system.[64] Collective action becomes possible when changes occur in a polity. As McAdam suggests, "proponents of the political process model sought to link the initial development of insurgency to an 'expansion in political opportunities' beneficial to the challenging group."[65] Similarly, Tarrow points out that opening up political access, unstable alignments, influential allies, or divided elites may encourage "unrepresented groups to engage in collective action."[66]

Protests in some post-communist countries seem to confirm the importance of new opportunities for collective action.[67] In post-communist Russia, workers sometimes organized strikes to demand back pay, salary increases, and jobs, because a new political environment created opportunities for collective action.[68] For one, the risk of retaliation largely evaporated with the collapse of the communist system.[69] For another, unleashed political freedom pushed the rise of independent trade unions. As Cook writes: "Militant independent trade unions had emerged out of early strikes, providing an organizational infrastructure (and creating an organizational imperative) for renewed strikes when conditions worsened."[70]

Studies of collective action in China have likewise suggested the importance of elite politics and government policies in collective action. Zhou concludes that in China, "collective action has often grown out of political campaigns initiated and organized by the state or has stemmed from cleavages created by the relaxation of state political control."[71] Perry points out that a significant number of worker strikes in the 1950s were permitted or even encouraged by the central government and Mao.[72] During the Cultural Revolution, worker participation was initiated, permitted, and encouraged by the elites.[73] Indeed, "the Cultural Revolution's guiding credo—'to rebel is justified'—presented an opportunity for people who felt deprived by the system to articulate their accumulated resentment."[74] The 1989 Tiananmen incident has been regarded as a political event of unprecedented significance because it was spontaneous action by the Chinese people.[75] While many immediate and long-term social and economic problems motivated citizens, like workers, to voice their discontent,[76] they did not suffice to drive them to action in 1989.[77] An obvious reason why workers took action in Beijing and other cities is that they recognized the opportunity created by the split or hesitation among central leaders and that other activists, like students, had not been repressed in early actions.[78]

Compared with the situations during the Cultural Revolution or the Tiananmen incident, political opportunities, as defined by students of social movements, are absent in China today—at least for laid-off workers. Yet, the lack of political opportunities does not preclude collective action. Elsewhere, it is found that threats may also contribute to mobilization: "In polities where there is some expectation of state responsiveness and few formal barriers to mobilization, we should expect perceived threats to group interests to serve, along with expanding opportunities, as two distinct precipitants of collective action."[79] This, however, is premised on the expectation of a positive response from the state.

Why do Chinese workers have such expectations of positive responses from the authoritarian state? In this study, I will put forth the argument that there is political space embedded in the Chinese political system. This political space provides a latent opportunity structure for collective action, which can be exploited by citizens.

Thus, despite its authoritarian nature, to borrow Herbst's words in describing regimes in Africa, the Chinese state is not always "a forbidding monolith dedicated to exploiting the powerless."[80] In China, local governments are responsible for social stability and are allowed to crush actions that pose a political threat to the regime. Yet, they cannot use force at will when dealing with people whose claims are legitimate and whose action is peaceful, although the leaders of such action may be punished. This is because the local government is not supposed to damage the legitimacy of the state by repressing people without justifiable reasons.[81] This is a significant constraint on the state's response to laid-off workers and has significant implications for workers' collective action because it makes mobilization possible. In other words, the constraint creates an opportunity that can be exploited if workers achieve coordination among themselves.

A better understanding of workers' collective action also entails an analysis of the impact of resistance. For analytical convenience, in relation to the state, people's collective action can be divided into contentious (i.e., regime-threatening) and non-contentious ones (i.e., acceptable to the regime). According to Tarrow, "contentious collective action" is often sustained and fundamentally challenges government authority.[82] In China, the power of the government and its policies determine that workers' collective action is non-contentious. As this study will show, most laid-off workers' action is individual firm based, often peaceful, non-political, and short-lived—far from posing a political threat to the central state. In fact, appealing to the government has been the most important mode of action on the part of laid-off workers, and violent action, such as attacks on the government, are the exception rather than the rule. Hence, to the government, the importance lies not in the occurrence of collective resistance, but in the nature of resistance.

Given the nature of worker resistance in China, the existence of channels through which people are more or less able to pursue their interests, even using noninstitutionalized modes, reduces the possibility of backlash that would otherwise happen in an entirely repressive regime.[83] Workers' collective action may thus indicate flexibility rather than weakness of the Chinese regime. Equally important, workers' non-contentious collective action does not imply the futility of their action. Indeed, even the weak have power.[84] The many actions of Chinese laid-off workers not only lead to concessions from the government but also become a pressure that prompts the state to institutionalize its interactions with the society in China.

Notes on the definition of laid-off workers and data collection

The initial official definition of "laid-off workers" (*xiagang zhigong*) was those employees who were temporarily off duty but still maintained their labor relations with their firms; they were supposed to resume work if their firms needed them. Hence, the term "laid-off workers" is unique to the Chinese context during the 1990s, and this practice was not common before the reform of SOEs. As the reform proceeded, the category of "laid-off workers" not only covered workers as previously defined but also included workers who were laid off due to bankruptcy, mergers, or privatization, in which case the labor relationship was often terminated. Workers retrenched in these ways were also included in the government's count of laid-off workers.[85] As this study aims to examine workers' reaction to reform, it adopts a broader definition of "laid-off workers" to include workers who were laid off with or without their labor relations maintained with their firms. Moreover, as layoffs have affected some managerial personnel, they have also participated in collective action as other workers or have even become the leaders. It is thus reasonable to include them into those who took action to pursue their interests. Finally, layoff is a continual process in terms of the change of a worker's status from an employee to a laid-off worker; worker resistance is also a continual process that may start by resisting layoffs first. Hence, this study regards pre-layoff resistance as part of laid-off workers' defense of their interests.

This study is based on secondary sources, survey research, and in-depth interviews. Secondary sources include government documents, Chinese newspapers, magazines, and academic journals. I surveyed 724 laid-off workers in 27 cities in eight provinces in China in June and July of 1999. The sample includes five provinces that had the most laid-off workers, two provinces that had a medium number of laid-off workers, and one that had the least laid-off workers in 1997 (see Appendix). It must be acknowledged that the sample size is limited compared with the large number of laid-off workers. Data collection was also compounded by some constraints, in particular the sensitive nature of the study and thereby the access to interviewees. But this study is not entirely based on the survey. Secondary sources and my interviews serve as check on the survey outcomes. I interviewed 33 laid-off workers in one city in 1998 and 44 more in two cities in 1999. To gain a better understanding of the layoff process and management–labor relations in state enterprises, I also conducted 21 interviews with enterprise leaders, including managers, party secretaries, chairpersons of trade unions, and department managers in 1999. I also interviewed four officials at the provincial and city levels in 1998 and three in 1999. The multiple sources allow me to examine the complex interaction between the state and workers and its implication for civil resistance and economic restructuring in China.

Structure of the book

Chapter 2 describes the background of layoffs in Chinese public enterprises, pointing out the reasons for massive layoffs and describing the inadequate welfare system. By discussing the many problems layoffs have caused for workers, I demonstrate that layoffs amount to dislocation for a majority of workers and become a source of resentment. Chapter 3 examines laid-off workers' different responses to retrenchment in terms of collective action. It shows that while numerous incidents of workers' collective action have become a serious concern for the central and local governments, many more workers have not taken action, although they have not fared better than those who acted. Using the data collected from my survey, I test two approaches—deprivation theory and cost-benefit calculations—and show that the data suggest that Chinese workers' resistance is motivated by material interests in taking action, as well as the perception of costs and risks.

While Chapter 3 presents a logic for the collective action of Chinese laid-off workers, this study does not reduce the complexity of state–labor interactions to mere statistical outcomes. Chapters 4 through 6 analyze the reasons for the collective *inaction* of laid-off workers by looking at interactions among laid-off workers and between the workers and the management or the government. Specifically, Chapter 4 discusses the factors that undermine worker solidarity. It suggests that fragmented interests among workers significantly reduce the scale of their resistance, thus explaining why workers may use individual action rather than collective resistance to pursue their interests.

Chapter 5 analyzes the interaction between laid-off workers and the firm. It explains why collective action is difficult at the firm level by examining the power, strategies, constraints, and financial abilities of the firm. In those firms that are able to provide subsistence subsidies, the management occupies a stronger position than laid-off workers. In firms that have difficulties surviving, workers take action against the government instead of the firm, because they realize that a firm that can hardly survive cannot provide benefits. This chapter also examines the importance of other management strategies undertaken to prevent worker resistance. Chapter 6 discusses the interaction between laid-off workers and the government and provides an explanation for why collective action directed at the government is also difficult. This chapter explores the multiple policies adopted by local governments for dealing with laid-off workers. It shows that collective action is difficult because governments impose various costs on different types of participants and dampen their incentive to act.

Chapter 7 turns to the other side of the puzzle to explain why collective action has occurred despite the many hurdles. It argues that laid-off workers' collective action takes place because Chinese local governments face constraints embedded in the political hierarchy. These constraints provide the leverage that allows laid-off workers to act and to succeed. This chapter also explores how coordination is achieved among prospective participants by showing when and why organizers appear, and how the mode of layoffs influences mobilization. The last chapter concludes by pointing out the implications of the case of Chinese laid-off workers for our understanding of collective action. It also discusses the relationship between the flexibility of a political system and reform and its implications for China's political development.

2 The ending of a socialist contract and retrenchment

In restructuring a state economy, regardless of the political system, the government may play an important role in addressing the issue of layoffs. For instance, in the mid-1980s when the Japanese government privatized the national railways, it reassigned about 90,000 redundant employees by encouraging early retirement or by providing alternative jobs or training.[1] Cao, Qian, and Weingast have likewise suggested that the Chinese local government has employed an *ex ante–ex post* arrangement in dealing with laid-off workers in the course of privatization. As an *ex ante* measure, the government provides laid-off workers with credible compensation for a given period of time; *ex post*, the government helps laid-off workers find new jobs, thereby reducing resistance. Hence, this mode of reform "not only buys workers" but also "buys them out."[2] Yet, this *ex ante–ex post* arrangement is premised on a number of assumptions about the government and workers. One is that the government assumes responsibility for the firms and has the financial ability to provide subsidies to laid-off workers *ex ante*. A second assumption is that, with the help of the government, laid-off workers are able to find new jobs and more important, that these new jobs provide similar insurance benefits.

This chapter shows that these assumptions fail to hold in many cases because of the budget constraints faced by SOEs and the government. As the moral arrangement between the state and labor in communist countries benefits both parties, neither side should have an incentive to break it. Yet, this arrangement cannot be sustained without sufficient financial resources. Many SOEs retrenched workers because of their failure to obtain financial support; therefore, they could pay only limited compensation, if any. The dramatically decreased income led to "absolute deprivation" for a significant number of laid-off workers.[3] Worse still, the lack of insurance benefits in the private sector, simultaneous layoffs of millions of workers, and the abundance of peasants searching for jobs in urban areas created a difficult reemployment environment.[4]

While the Chinese government adopted a variety of measures to address the problems faced by laid-off workers, their effectiveness was limited, at least in the 1990s, by the shortage of financial resources. Some measures like the establishment of reemployment service centers (RSCs) posed a new problem for laid-off workers, because joining an RSC required that they terminate labor relations with their firms, in an absence of an adequate welfare system. The economic plight and uncertainty about the future were an unprecedented experience for most laid-off workers. It was thus common for laid-off workers to be depressed and frustrated especially during the initial period of the reform. Perhaps more important, as moral economists would suggest, laid-off workers were resentful of retrenchment.

Budget constraints and the end of the socialist contract

In China during the Mao period, SOEs faced no hard budget constraints, nor was welfare a concern for workers. But in the transitional period, two important factors placed unprecedented budget constraints on many SOEs and drove them to undertake layoffs. One was that the government withdrew its financial commitment to many SOEs, and the other was the reduced ability of SOEs to generate profits. Consequently, budget constraints became a fundamental cause of massive layoffs and impacted the distribution of laid-off workers across industrial sectors, regions, and SOEs of different sizes in the 1990s.

Ailing SOEs as a burden on the government

Since the early 1990s, increasingly unprofitable SOEs in China have posed a serious problem for the government in that they are responsible for about 80 percent of the nonperforming loans in state banks.[5] By the end of 1996, the nonperforming loans of the four state banks accounted for 19 percent of total loans, and the proportion of loans in default was at an estimated 11 percent.[6] By 1997, the total amount of nonperforming loans reached 1,360 billion yuan, accounting for 25–30 percent of total loans, or four times the assets of state banks, which might still have been underreported.[7]

Potential problems, such as the collapse of the financial system, arising from bad loans, demonstrated by the Asian financial crisis in the late 1990s, forced the government to reform the banking system and impose restrictions on state banks. Chinese local governments tended to see banks as their "second source of revenue."[8] In the late 1990s, the central government, which owns the banks, established nine cross-regional bank headquarters to strengthen control over its branches across the country and to reduce the intervention by local governments in the banking system. In order to make state banks operate more like those in market economies, the government also allowed these banks to write off old debts and required them to assume responsibility for future performance.

To ensure that these new rules would be followed, some banks regulated that the persons who grant loans to firms would, for the rest of their lives, guarantee repayment. In some places, banks at the county level or below needed the approval of their higher-level counterparts when granting loans.[9] This new development in the banking system since the second half of the 1990s has, more or less, placed constraints on state banks in China, although it may not have entirely removed intervention by local governments.[10] As a result of the new measures, banks are more discriminating in granting loans, and loss-making SOEs (especially small- and medium-sized ones) face more difficulty in obtaining financial support.[11] As a manager of a machinery factory said in an interview:

> Just like people in today's China, better firms are getting better and poor enterprises are getting worse. The reason is simple: the more profitable a firm is, the more likely it will receive various forms of support from both the government and financial institutions. In our city, banks now keep visiting profitable firms, urging them to borrow money; in contrast, they never look at us. In our city, the textile sector was the first to lay off workers, and now it is the turn of the machinery industry. In our factory, we have laid off one-third of the workers because we do not have other choices.

In addition, as government support is highly selective and often provided to several hundred of the largest SOEs in the country, most other SOEs have to "sing the *Internationale*"—"There has never been a savior, and we need to be entirely self-dependent."[12] In other words, most SOEs have to generate profits in order to survive. This, however, is not an easy task. Due to complex reasons such as government policies, social burdens, accumulated debts, redundant employees, outdated technology and equipment, and mismanagement,[13] SOEs' abilities to generate profits keep declining. The proportion of loss-making SOEs increased from 9.7 percent in 1985 to 46.5 percent by September 1997 when nationwide massive layoffs began. This is especially true for small- and medium-sized SOEs. In the 1990s, over 60 percent made losses, accounting for over 80 percent of the total number of loss-making SOEs.[14]

Budget constraints and layoffs

Given the budget constraints, layoffs were perhaps the only way to reduce the cost of operations for loss-making SOEs, at least in the initial period of streamlining. A study of 10 large SOEs in northeast China suggests economic failure as the major reason for the occurrence and magnitude of layoffs.[15] Similarly, among the 724 laid-off workers surveyed in my fieldwork, more than 63 percent reported that they were laid off because macro- or micro-level factors prevented their firms from generating enough profit. About 23 percent reported that they were laid off because of their firms' reform measures (e.g., ownership reform). The rest reported reasons such as mismanagement or corrupt managers, low educational level, older age, and poor relationships with managers.

National statistics, although not detailed, illustrate the relationship between budget constraints and the scale of layoffs in industrial sectors. Under China's work-unit system, workers' salaries are often tied to the financial resources of their firms. Hence there should be a correlation between the level of salary and the degree of layoffs. In other words, those sectors that provide lower salaries tend to have fewer financial resources and thus lay off more workers, and as a consequence, the percentage of laid-off workers in those sectors is larger. Sector-based statistics show this pattern. For example, the average salary of workers in the wood processing and transportation sector was the lowest among all industrial sectors in 1997, and the percentage of laid-off workers in this sector was also the highest (Table 2.1). The textile industry was also a severe loss-making industry, and the average salary of workers in the sector was one of the lowest. Correspondingly, its layoff rate was about 31 percent, the second highest among all industries. In contrast, in a sector with an average salary exceeding 8,000 yuan, the layoff rate was less than 7 percent. For example, employees in the finance and insurance sector, which is also state-owned and managed, received the highest salary, or 48 percent higher than the national average of state employees. The layoff rate in that sector was the lowest, or 0.8 percent.[16]

Budget constraints also help to explain the regional distribution of laid-off workers. It is not surprising that the number of laid-off workers varies across provinces, and there could be many reasons for the variation. The first possible factor is the number of state employees in the province, based on the assumption that, other things being equal, provinces that have more state employees would also have more laid-off workers. Yet, the situation may be different when the financial resources of the government are taken into consideration. Hence, a second factor that may affect the number of laid-off workers is government revenue. It is a reasonable hypothesis that provinces with more revenue (i.e., measured in 10,000 yuan) are better able to prop up their firms, and thus the number of laid-off workers would be smaller. As discussed above, SOEs' performance also affects the likelihood of layoffs. Therefore, a third factor that may affect variation in layoffs across provinces is the amount of losses made by SOEs in each province. It is assumed that provinces whose SOEs incur more losses (i.e., measured in 10,000 yuan) would also have more laid-off workers.

Table 2.1 Laid-off workers by sector in 1997 ($N = 11.5$ million)

Sectors	Proportion of LOWs (%)	Salary (yuan)
Wood-cutting, transportation	39.08	4,304
Manufacturing	20.48	6,008
Textile	30.94	
Construction	15.08	7,388
Mining	12.60	7,091
Social service	12.36	7,425
Retail, restaurant	11.00	5,134
Transportation, storage, postal service	6.25	9,303
Real estate	5.50	8,570
Scientific research and service	2.87	8,974
Electricity, coal, water	2.73	9,541
Finance, insurance	0.79	10,012
Miscellaneous	11.64	6,891

Source. Compiled from Fan Qin, "Who Were Laid off?" *Zhongguo guoqing guoli* (The situation and strengths of China), 1998, no. 5, pp. 20–22, and *Chinese Labor Statistics 1998*, pp. 241–42; LOWs: laid-off workers.

While the determinants of layoffs may be complex, it is possible to test whether the variables outlined earlier can account for the variation in the regional distribution of laid-off workers. The following presents a statistical analysis based on the data published in Chinese statistical yearbooks.[17] The dependent variable is the number of laid-off workers in each province in 1997, when the first peak of layoffs occurred. The statistical outcome presented in Table 2.2 suggests that the proposed relation between the three factors and the number of laid-off workers is valid insofar as the correlations are statistically significant. First, the amount of losses is positively associated with the number of laid-off workers in a province. This may imply that an increase in losses made by SOEs would mean a harder budget constraint and thus an increase in the number of laid-off workers. Second, local government revenue is negatively associated with the number of laid-off workers, which may suggest that if the government had more revenue, it would be able to provide help to SOEs that would in turn avert more layoffs. Third, the number of state employees is also positively associated with the number of laid-off workers. This may imply that, other things being equal, a province with more state employees also has more laid-off workers. In 1997, Heilonjiang, Liaoning, and Jilin were among the top five provinces with the largest number of laid-off workers.[18] This should not be surprising because these provinces had been the industrial bases of China and had a large number of loss-making SOEs and workers. But at the same time, the local governments of these provinces lacked the financial resources to provide help.[19] Henan and Hunan were the remaining two provinces with the highest number of laid-off workers; they faced the same situation of limited financial resources.[20]

Budget constraints also affected the distribution of laid-off workers across SOEs of different sizes in the 1990s. This distribution has a significant implication for worker resistance as will be discussed in Chapter 7. As Table 2.3 shows, as of 1995, about 87 percent of industrial SOEs were small sized, about 9 percent were medium sized, and 4 percent were large sized. Although large and medium-sized industrial SOEs accounted for only 13 percent of all industrial SOEs, their workers constituted about 71 percent of the total worker population. This may imply that workers at larger SOEs constitute a significant segment of the total number of workers in China. Yet, this segment does not have the majority of the laid-off workers, as their firms suffered fewer budget constraints. As indicated in

Table 2.2 A linear regression of the number of laid-off workers on selected variables ($N = 31$)

Selected variables	Coefficient (standard error)
Constant	−116.86 (64.58)*
Loss	3.593 (1.671)**
Fiscal revenue	−1.843 (0.6170)***
Number of employees in the state sector	0.175 (0.0200)***
R^2 (adjusted R^2)	0.784 (0.759)

Note
* $p < 0.1$, ** $p < 0.05$, *** $p < 0.01$.

Table 2.3 Industrial SOEs in China by size (1995)

Categories	Large	Medium	Small	Total
Number	4,685	11,000	102,315	118,000
Number (%)	3.97	9.3	86.7	100
Employees (%)	46.9	24.5	28.6	100
Debt–asset ratio	62.34	71.82	71.87	65.81
Profits (100 million yuan)	723	−18	−39	666
Profits and taxes (%)	79.2	20.8[a]		100

Source: Compiled from the State Statistical Bureau, *Dayoushi* (Perspective), Beijing: Zhongguo fazhan chubanshe, 1998, pp. 214–15, 218, 222, 227.

Note
a For both medium-size and small SOEs.

Table 2.3, large SOEs are more profitable and generally perform better than smaller ones. The government's policy of "retaining large SOEs and letting go of the small" also benefits large ones because the government tends to provide the large ones with more support.[21] Although national statistics have not been disaggregated based on the size of SOEs, available ones provide some evidence. In China, the scale of an SOE often corresponds to the administrative level of its owner. SOEs owned by the central government are often larger, although not all of them belong to the category of large SOEs.[22] In 1998, laid-off workers from SOEs under the central government accounted for only about 9 percent of all laid-off workers.[23]

While the number of laid-off workers varies across regions, sectors, and SOEs, layoffs have become a nationwide phenomenon in China since the mid-1990s. The official count of laid-off workers increased from 5.6 million (or 5 percent of all state employees) in 1995 to 16.5 million (or 20 percent of all state employees) in 1999.[24] The actual number, however, could be larger. A sample survey of about 3,000 enterprises in 190 cities of 30 provinces in 1999 by the Ministry of Labor and Social Security revealed that the number of laid-off workers had been under-reported.[25] The magnitude of layoffs has inevitably increased the government's difficulty in addressing the problems faced by laid-off workers.

The government's redress measures and limitations

Massive layoffs have occurred before in socialist China. For example, as a consequence of the Great Leap Forward, between 1958 and 1960, the net increase in the number of employees in the urban sector reached 28.7 million, with 75 percent originating from the countryside. Overexpansion of the industrial sector and shortages of production materials and food supplies presented serious problems for the government and forced it to send workers recruited from the countryside back to their villages. Although the process proved difficult,[26] about 20 million of those workers were eventually sent back to the countryside.[27] The most important reason for the success of this policy was that those peasants-turned-workers were provided with an alternative—returning to work in their villages—although it was not a desirable one.[28]

Layoffs are a thorny issue today because it is beyond the ability of the Chinese government to provide laid-off workers with alternatives or even compensation. Although the government has enacted policies to address the problems faced by laid-off workers, success has been limited. Layoffs have largely been conducted in the absence of an adequate welfare system and a favorable reemployment environment, or as Chinese people put it, "draining the water before the tunnel is ready," thereby adversely affecting tens of millions of people and putting them in a serious economic plight as Solinger has pointed out.[29]

Problems with welfare provisions

Over the years before the reform of SOEs, China adopted a welfare system based on individual work units. Like all other work units in the public sector, SOEs assumed full responsibility for employment, welfare provisions, and subsidies-in-kind for their workers. Unemployment arising from layoffs had been rare. Indeed, before 1994, official propaganda did not use the term "unemployment." It is not surprising that the Chinese government did not issue a pooled or cross-work-unit policy on unemployment insurance to complement the work-unit-based welfare system until 1986. It was then that the labor contract system, which was aimed at replacing the lifetime employment system, was introduced. As stipulated by the 1986 policy, each firm paid insurance based on 1 percent of the wage bill of its workers, while the workers paid nothing. According to the policy, four types of workers who were laid off or fired were entitled to the insurance.[30]

Yet this system was only able to support about 2 percent of those who joined the program or 600,000 workers.[31] In 1993, the government issued another policy that extended the system to cover seven groups of workers instead of four. Similar to the 1986 system, the amount of insurance paid by the firm was between 0.6 percent and 1 percent of the wage bill of its workers. Again, workers paid nothing. After large-scale layoffs began in 1995, the insurance system could hardly meet the demands of tens of millions of laid-off workers. By September 1995, unemployed people in urban China, not including laid-off workers, exceeded 4.8 million, but only about 29 percent received unemployment insurance. For this reason, the government issued a new policy in 1998 to increase the portion of unemployment insurance paid by firms from 1 percent of its wage bill to 3 percent. The policy, which took effect in 1999, stipulated that the firm should pay 2 percent, and workers should pay 1 percent.[32]

Nevertheless, it takes time for this system to accumulate enough funds to support a large number of unemployed people. In 1998, only about 10 percent of the unemployed received unemployment subsidies.[33] In addition, firms without adequate financial resources were unable to pay the insurance premium for their employees. By 1997, about 73 percent of urban employees had joined the unemployment insurance program.[34] However, this figure might be exaggerated. A survey of 14 cities by the State Planning Commission found that in 1999, only about 15 percent of urban employees surveyed were covered by the insurance system.[35] Another survey of 137,000 households in that year by the National

Statistical Bureau suggested that less than 12 percent of employees were covered. Both surveys found that only about 40 percent of employees were covered by the pension system, and about 14 percent were covered by medical care.[36]

Reemployment service centers

As the pooled unemployment insurance system was far from adequate when massive layoffs began, the Chinese government began to establish a threefold welfare system in the second half of 1998, which included layoff subsidies, unemployment insurance, and the minimum allowance.[37] These three welfare-provision mechanisms were designed to function in sequence. The reemployment service center (RSC) required in SOEs was supposed to provide subsidies and job opportunities for laid-off workers for 2–3 years after they were laid off. In 2–3 years, laid-off workers would leave the RSC and receive unemployment insurance for up to a maximum of two years if they failed to secure employment. After that, they would receive the minimum allowance from social welfare agencies if they were still unemployed.

RSCs were first established in Shanghai. In 1996, the municipal government required its industrial bureaus to set up RSCs to help manage laid-off workers and provide them with subsidies, training, and jobs. The funds were provided by the industry bureau, the firm, the government, and other social welfare agencies.[38] In 1998, the central government viewed this arrangement as a practical solution to the issue of laid-off workers and fully promoted it. It then made it compulsory by requiring SOEs that intended to lay off workers to establish such centers. Funding for this program was provided on the basis of a "three one-third" principle, that is, each of the three parties—the firm, the government, and welfare or insurance agencies—provided one-third of the funds needed.

Urged by the central government, local governments began to establish RSCs in the second half of 1998, and many RSCs were brought into existence at an extremely rapid pace. In June 1998, less than 22 percent of laid-off workers had entered the RSCs, but three months later, the percentage reached almost 99 percent. In one province, there were 154 RSCs in June, but by August, the number increased to 3,786.[39] However, as one might expect, not all RSCs operated as required. A lack of contribution by the local government, the firm, or the insurance organization would pose a problem for the system.

Many SOEs laid off workers precisely because they could not pay them, and some firms even required their employees to take unpaid leave. The local government's ability to provide funds also depended on its financial resources. In one province, for example, SOEs could only provide less than 10 percent of their one-third share, the insurance departments could only raise one-third of their due, and the government could provide only one-half of its part. Total funding for the RSCs of the province was thus only one-third of the required amount.[40] In another example, in a city of Hunan province in 1998, SOEs under the city government needed 1.2 million yuan to pay their laid-off workers. According to this program, the government, insurance organizations, and SOEs should each have contributed

40 million yuan. By the end of November, the three parties together provided only 40.5 percent of the required amount.[41]

To resolve the shortage of funds, some local governments tried to find additional sources. For example, one county government regulated that those employed in work units that were able to provide stable salaries donate 2 percent of their salaries each month to pay laid-off workers. In addition, the work units were also required to donate money as collectives. However, when those measures failed to raise enough funds, some local governments tried to reduce their portion of contribution and to increase that of the firm.[42] In one example, the city government provided 25 percent of the fund, and required each firm to provide 40 percent. Others regulated that only after the firm allocated its one-third portion would the government and the insurance organizations provide their shares.[43]

Not surprisingly, given the budget constraints, not all RSCs were able to provide help to laid-off workers. My survey suggests that more than 33 percent of the 724 laid-off workers did not receive any payment or only received it for a period of time much shorter than the 2–3 years mandated by the government. National statistics indicated that the shortage of funds plagued RSCs across the country.[44] By the second half of 1998, the shortage was so severe that the central government finally stepped in and paid about 47 percent of the total amount of subsidies for laid-off workers, whereas local governments, insurance organizations, and SOEs paid 25 percent, 14 percent, and 14 percent, respectively.[45] To make up for the shortfall, in that same year, the central government imposed a tax on bank deposits in order to raise funds to subsidize laid-off workers, unpaid retirees, and the poor.[46]

Reemployment service centers as a problem

Not only did RSCs fail to provide substantial help for a significant number of laid-off workers, they created new problems because of the regulations on laid-off workers' labor relations with their firms. It was stipulated that laid-off workers who entered the RSC would have to terminate their labor relations with their firms within 2–3 years. That placed tremendous pressure on laid-off workers. In China in the 1990s, layoffs initially meant that workers were off duty for a period of time and would resume work when their firms performed better. Severance of relations with their firms thus created uncertainty about the future, especially because of the inadequate welfare system and the difficult reemployment environment. A survey of employees in 15 provinces in 1997 by the All China Federation of Trade Unions (ACFTU) found that only about 21 percent reported that the existing pension system could provide a basic guarantee for life after retirement.[47] In 1998, about 67 percent of laid-off workers nationwide were aged 36 or older.[48] Retirement and medical insurance became the most serious concerns of these people.[49]

One might ask why laid-off workers did not simply buy insurance on their own. The reasons were complex. First, at least in the 1990s, many public insurance organizations only dealt with public work units instead of with individuals. The municipal government in Beijing, for example, admitted that this had been a very serious problem for those who wanted to be self-employed.[50] Second, without any experience with insurance, many workers lacked confidence in private insurance agencies. Third, according to the policy adopted in the late 1990s, the insurance responsibility was divided between the firm and individuals, with the firm bearing more. As firms were still responsible for the insurance of laid-off workers, it was in the interest of laid-off workers to keep their memberships in their firms to receive benefits.[51] Fourth, as some SOEs had not paid insurance premiums for their workers in years, laid-off workers would face empty insurance accounts and would not be able to receive pensions if the problem of overdue insurance premiums was not resolved. Laid-off workers believed that by maintaining labor relations with their firms, they would be better able to handle the insurance problem.[52]

Finally, some laid-off workers wanted to keep their memberships in their firms, because they hoped to return to work once their firms started performing better. But entering RSCs would rule out this possibility and forced them to find work in the private sector or become self-employed, because the chance of securing jobs in other public enterprises was almost negligible.[53] Yet, working in the private sector in China was not desirable for some practical reasons. Compared with work units in the public sector, private firms were characterized by the "Two Nos"—no labor contract and no welfare provision. For example, in 1997, over 95 percent of SOEs joined the retirement insurance program (although not all of them paid money), as opposed to only 27.5 percent of the private firms, including foreign and joint ventures.[54] In Harbin, the capital city of Heilongjiang province, only 74 private firms out of 8,000 joined the pension program in 1998. While the number of employees in private firms totaled 88,000, only 450 joined the program, and none of those who were self-employed joined.[55] Hence, those working in the private sector were extremely dissatisfied with the existing social security system.[56]

Worse still, the tight labor market also weakened laid-off workers' bargaining position. Some private employers even claimed that "we cannot find a frog with three legs, but we can easily find a person with two legs." Private firms in China are notorious for their maltreatment of employees.[57] For instance, some firms adopted a system under which newly hired people had to work for a trial period that lasted for a few months. During this period of time, the salary was extremely low; when the trial period expired, the employers would use various pretexts to fire those people, and then recruit and exploit new employees. Some laid-off workers interviewed said that after so many years of socialism, they were now experiencing exploitation under capitalists, as did their counterparts in other countries in the seventeenth and eighteenth centuries. In other cases, private employers required newly hired people to pay a certain amount of money as a bond. Conflicts often arose when the employers laid off these people but failed to return their money. Other hurdles to employment in the private sector included poor labor protection revealed by numerous accidents and discrimination (e.g., same job with unequal pay).[58] Some laid-off workers complained that they were often assigned heavy or coarse work. But unlike other employees, they usually failed to receive welfare benefits or bonuses.[59]

All these problems made laid-off workers reluctant to join RSCs. Some of them had not received subsidies but still refused to be transferred there. A survey of 100 large- and medium-sized SOEs by the ACFTU found that unwillingness to enter the RSC was common among laid-off workers.[60] Some workers viewed joining an RSC as a "death penalty," albeit delayed for 2 or 3 years. They complained: "The government has gone too far. Why should we be required to terminate our status as a state employee? Is this what the Party can give us after we have worked for our whole lives?"[61]

Sympathetic factory managers also acknowledged the difficulties faced by laid-off workers:

> Some workers have worked for the factory for many years and will be close to or over fifty years old in two or three years. By that time, there is almost no possibility that they will be able to find jobs that will provide them with pension and medical care. In my factory, over a fourth of laid-off workers will face that situation if they enter the reemployment service center. Although the government may provide a subsistence subsidy, there is no guarantee that they will be able to receive it. It is unfair for them to lead that kind of life after working for so many years.[62]

However, while the reasons for laid-off workers' reluctance to terminate labor relations and take jobs in the private sector are clear, it does not mean that, given the difficult reemployment environment, they would be able to find employment in the private sector when they went to look for it.

Government and laid-off workers' reemployment

By design, RSCs were supposed to help laid-off workers find jobs, but they were limited in effectiveness. Among the 724 workers surveyed, almost 67 percent replied that the RSC never provided them with help in their job search or only provided "spiritual help." In Beijing in 1997, only 6 percent of those who entered the RSC were reallocated. This situation not only increased the economic pressure on the reemployment center but also made those who had not entered it skeptical and reluctant to join.[63] In Shanghai in 1998, less than 20 percent of those who entered the RSCs became self-employed or found jobs through the labor market.[64] As the difficult reemployment environment was beyond the RSCs' ability to address, governments at both the central and local levels enacted numerous policies to help laid-off workers secure new jobs.

One common practice was to offer a tax reduction or exemption to those firms that hired laid-off workers and to self-employed laid-off workers. For example, the central government regulated that those firms with 60 percent of their labor force comprised of employees formerly laid off or unemployed would enjoy a three-year income tax exemption. In addition to implementing this policy, many local governments also gave such firms favorable treatment, such as cheap or free access to business sites and electricity.[65] In almost every city and even in some counties, such favorable policies were adopted. In one example, the county government regulated that only laid-off workers could drive pedicabs to prevent peasants from competing with laid-off workers.[66]

Another favorable policy concerned the business activities of laid-off workers. Some local governments allowed laid-off workers to engage in previously prohibited businesses and simplified the application procedure; others provided direct help. In a city in Henan province, for example, the labor bureau, the city construction bureau, the industrial and commercial bureau, and the tax bureau worked together to set up a trading market for laid-off workers to conduct private businesses. Laid-off workers who operated in that market were exempted from management fees and income tax for 1–2 years.[67] A third type of policy was the provision of reemployment capital. Some local governments established reemployment foundations based on contributions from the government, loans, donations, and other sources, to help train and compensate laid-off workers, as well as to help them set up enterprises. Other policies included free or subsidized use of state assets such as land. Laid-off workers were also encouraged to work on farmlands, forests, and barren land in rural areas.

Yet, the effectiveness of these policies varied significantly across regions, largely depending on local economic development and the financial resources of local governments.[68] Thus, not all local governments succeeded with these policies. For example, in 1998, the People's Congress of Wuhan in Hubei province refused to approve a report on reemployment work presented by a city government official. The Congress claimed that the report was too ambiguous and had equated making favorable policies toward laid-off workers with achieving success.[69] Another important reason for the government's limited success in creating jobs for laid-off workers was the lack of coordination among government agencies. Many policies were poorly implemented because those who made the policies and those who implemented them did not cooperate with each other, nor did they ensure that laid-off workers would know that special policies were available to help them. One survey found that 7.3 percent of laid-off workers knew nothing about favorable policies regarding laid-off workers, whereas another 69 percent did not know the content of those policies.[70] Self-employed laid-off workers often complained bitterly about how government agencies, including the tax bureau, the industrial and commercial bureau, the city hygiene department, and the market management department, failed to implement favorable policies like tax or fee reduction or exemption. While the government wished to create a favorable environment for the retrenched, the pressure on those agencies, especially the tax bureau, to generate revenue remained. Tax collection was a major source of revenue and neither the central nor local governments were willing to reduce their quotas. Because of such pressures, local tax bureaus might fail to implement the tax exemptions issued by the same level of government.

Some laid-off workers thus gave up their private businesses because the numerous fees, some of which should have been exempted, made it impossible for them to make a profit.[71] Others engaged in retail businesses complained about the city management department that often prohibited people from setting up business in the streets, for the sake of keeping the city clean. One laid-off worker reported that doing retail business on the streets was just like being a thief:

> When the people from the city management department come by, we have to escape. After they leave, we return and resume business. Sometimes, when we get caught, we have to pay a fine. I did not apply for a license for my business, because in addition to the charge for a license per se, the taxes and fees from the nine government departments would render it impossible for me to make any money.[72]

All these obstacles undermined the government's efforts to help retrenched workers secure reemployment. A survey of over 1,000 laid-off workers across 55 cities in 1997 suggested that only 4.5 percent reported that the government's efforts to help them find employment were of some help.[73] In Changchun, the capital city of Jilin province, a survey in 1998 by the National Statistical Bureau suggested that only 2.7 percent of laid-off workers found jobs through governments' direct help.[74] Aggregate statistics point to the limitations of the government's efforts to create a favorable reemployment environment at least, and to their failure to keep pace with the increasing number of laid-off workers. In 1997, nationwide, the reemployment rate was about 50 percent, but that decreased to 40 percent in 1998, and 27 percent in the first half of 1999.[75] It may not be an exaggeration that the government's efforts to help workers secure jobs were a dismal failure in many places.[76]

While some laid-off workers had found jobs, the dominant mode of reemployment was self-employment.[77] In 1997, on average, 387 private businesses and over 4,300 individual industrial and commercial households were set up every day, and more than 16,500 people took jobs in the private sector, with about 63 percent being laid-off workers.[78] In 1998, about 45 percent of those who secured reemployment were self-employed, and another 30 percent worked in non-state firms.[79] In Hunan province in 1998, about 70 percent of laid-off workers who found jobs were self-employed.[80] Due to the lack of skills and funds, most self-employed laid-off workers ran the same type of business. For example, in one city, a survey of 260 self-employed laid-off workers found that 86 percent engaged in restaurant and retail businesses, and many fared poorly because of intense competition.[81]

Impact of layoffs

The limitations of the government's redress measures had significant impact on laid-off workers, both financial and psychological. Many laid-off workers failed to receive subsidies after being laid off. Their economic plight and uncertainty about the future made them feel depressed and betrayed by the state.

As a result, workers' plight has important implications for their attitudes toward SOE reform and the government.

Workers' economic plight

The most important and direct impact of layoffs on workers is the decrease in income, which has been the unanimous conclusion of numerous studies and surveys.[82] Although everywhere in the world, unemployment insurance tends to be much less than one's salary, it is more so in China. In Chinese work units, including SOEs, salary is only part of one's income, and various subsidies and bonuses can be of equal or higher value. Some research suggested that in 1987, there were as many as 113 subsidies in public work units, including SOEs, and the number had increased, although not all the subsidies were available in every SOE.[83] A survey by the National Statistical Bureau found that the subsidies received by employees in the public sector accounted for 8 percent of income in 1978 and 50 percent in 1994. In some work units, it was 100 percent or more. These subsidies contributed significantly to the income gap in urban China. It was estimated that in the 1990s, welfare benefits paid to high-income families were 87 percent higher than those received by low-income families.[84] When workers are laid off, they no longer receive most of their welfare benefits.

The 1990s witnessed a surge of workers suffering from reform measures. A survey of 23 provinces suggested that by the end of 1994, about 2.9 million workers failed to receive full salaries, and another 2 million received none at all.[85] The situation became more serious after the mid-1990s.[86] In 1997, half of the 12.74 million laid-off workers failed to secure new jobs, and over 3 million received no subsistence subsidies.[87] In that same year, the number of poverty-stricken employees reached almost 11 million, with over 27 percent failing to meet the subsistence level of their localities.[88] In 1999, the poverty-stricken population increased to 30 million, or 8 percent of the urban population in China. Laid-off workers and unpaid retirees comprised the majority of that population.[89] Some poverty-stricken laid-off workers died of illness because they could not afford medical care. In one reported case, an old laid-off worker suffered liver cancer and could not afford medication. He had only painkillers. When the painkillers did not help, he would dig at the bricks in the wall with his fingers in order to distract himself from the pain. He once removed one-third of a brick with his fingers in an attempt to "forget" his pain.[90]

In my survey of 724 laid-off workers, only about 5 percent reported that being laid off did not negatively impact their family income, whereas almost 57 percent reported that it had a big negative effect, and about 38 percent reported some negative impact. The decrease in income made laid-off workers worry that they could not afford expenses incurred by illness, children's education, gift exchange, and housing reform.[91] A laid-off worker stated in an interview:

> We are a family of three. My wife still has a job, and her salary is more than 400 yuan per month. When I was laid off, my subsidy was about 200 yuan. But because my factory is close to bankruptcy, our subsidies have been

suspended for months. Life is hard and I am now trying to find a temporary job because stable jobs are almost impossible for me. What we are most concerned with is the lack of a stable source of income and our son's education. He is now in a high school, and both my wife and I are worried about his future. If he is able to pass the college entrance exam, we may not be able to afford to pay the tuition. If he fails the exam, he will have difficulties finding jobs in the future. We want to save some money for him. But as you know, because we even have difficulties making ends meet, how can we save money?

Similarly, a middle-aged woman reported how decreased income affected her family:

We fare worse than peasant workers. For people at my age, it is very difficult to find a job. I received a 200-yuan living subsidy from my work unit, a decrease of almost 400 yuan compared with my previous salary. And I am not sure whether I will be able to receive it in the future because the enterprise is getting worse now. My husband also works in a money-losing enterprise, and he can only receive a salary of about 400 yuan. But some expenditures are inevitable. We spend about more than 100 yuan on house rent, gas, electricity, and water each month. We have a son in school, and the tuition as well as other charges in the school keep rising each year. I am eager to find a job. The thing that worries us most is medical care. It is true that "You can have anything but illness." I have no place to get reimbursed for the medical expenses, and we cannot afford to see a doctor on our own. Although we can manage to make ends meet, we feel that nothing is readily affordable.

Another laid-off worker reported in an interview that the first thing he did after receiving his subsistence subsidy was to buy rice. Buying vegetables, not to mention meat, depended on whether he had money left. The dismantling of the lifetime employment system and the socialist welfare regime adversely affected some people more than others. Those who once enjoyed enterprise subsidies because of special problems like poor health tended to experience more difficulties.[92] Such cases have been widely reported in the media. As a woman said:

After I was laid off in 1995, I worked as a salesperson in a store, a waitress, and a newspaper seller. But I have not worked for two months. My husband passed away last year. I have a child in school. Although I receive a 150-yuan living subsidy from the factory per month and 1,000 yuan from the city trade union per year, life is still very hard. My child has bad health, and I have spent 3,000 yuan on her medical care. But I have no place to get reimbursed, and I borrowed it. I have a heart disease, but I cannot afford to see a doctor. Sometimes, I borrow the medical certificate from someone else and try to get some medicine. Our house leaks whenever it rains, but no one takes care of us. I cannot overcome all these difficulties by myself. How should I raise my child? What can I do when I get old.[93]

The difficulty for and despair of unpaid laid-off workers is reflected in the words of a laid-off woman:

> I was laid off in 1997 and received subsidy only for two months. After that, we could not even find the manager. The whole family [which includes her husband, her son, her mother-in-law] could only subsist on my husband's 500-yuan salary. You can imagine how difficult our life was. To be frank, it once occurred to me that it might be better to die.[94]

Workers' depression and resentment

Layoffs are common in market economies, but were simply beyond the experiences and expectations of state workers in socialist systems like China, which made the economic and psychological impact more intense. Some laid-off workers admitted that they never "dreamt that this could happen." As Solinger suggests, "[u]nemployment means much more than being out of work on an individual level."[95] Reportedly, frustrated laid-off workers committed suicide, and helpless workers became beggars or criminals.[96] Divorces also occurred because of the deteriorating economic situation.[97] In some places, because of hardship, "most laid-off workers turn their loyalty and expectations from the collective (i.e., the work unit) to the god of Buddhism. They display unprecedented loyalty and enthusiasm to temples, and their sense of religion has been promoted. As a result, a number of temples have received surprisingly frequent visits from these people, which has never happened before."[98]

Frustration and depression were common among these people. A survey of 2,000 laid-off workers in Hunan province in 1998 found that over 97 percent felt depressed and worried after being laid off, and about 74 percent were pessimistic and felt hopeless.[99] Both the media and my interviewees reported on laid-off workers' difficult experiences and their attitudes toward layoffs. A woman who claimed to have been an optimistic person described the impact of being laid off:

> If any laid-off person claims that the layoff does not affect him at all, he is not a normal person and must have mental problems. Optimistic people like me even cried several times. But tears do us no good, and we still need to find ways out after crying.[100]

Another woman interviewee reported her frustration:

> I used to work in a factory of about 1,000 employees. Due to the poor performance of the factory, I was laid off in 1996. I was dismayed at first. My daughter was twelve years old at that time and was in school. My mother-in-law had poor health. My husband was also in a money-losing work unit. How could we make ends meet? After I received the layoff

notification, I lay in bed for a few days, eating almost nothing. We were in a difficult time and even had no money for fresh vegetables, not to mention meat. For days, my daughter could only eat the rice mixed with salted vegetables. But she did not complain and said, "Mum, I will not compare our life with that of other students. I do not need anything else and just want to go to school." I was deeply shocked, and I wept. It was my love and sense of responsibility for my daughter that woke me and made me pull myself together and try to find a job.

Such experiences are not confined to female workers. A male worker in a shoe factory experienced the same frustration after being laid off:

I was laid off in 1997 because our factory stopped production. When I received the notification, I could hardly believe it. Although we had not received any salary for months, I still believed that factory leaders or the government would help us work out some solutions. In any case, our factory was a state-owned one. Worse still, my wife was also laid off at the same time. We have a daughter in a primary school. How could we afford to pay her tuition in the future? In addition, my mother has poor health, and we need to pay the medical expenses for her. My wife cried, and I felt stifled. I wept silently for a whole night. And for quite a period of time I did not have any appetite. For several days, I went back to the factory, sometimes unknowingly. Only after I had repeatedly seen its locked gate did I fully realize that the factory was finished. Whenever I think of this, it seemed like it just happened yesterday.

The reform of SOEs thus spelled the end of socialism *per se*. For example, a survey of about 10,000 people in Shaanxi province in 1996 found that only 15.5 percent of workers and less than 24 percent of Party members agreed that the current socialism "is to get rid of exploitation and polarization and to achieve a rich life for all."[101] As moral economy theorists suggest, violation of a moral order tends to raise discontent.[102] Many workers believed that they were being victimized for the sake of reform and were thus angry with both the firms and the government. The end of work-unit socialism in some but not all work units, and the immunity of corrupt managerial personnel became another target of discontent and anger.[103] As a worker stated in an interview:

The factory requires us workers over forty-five years old to leave, but no enterprise cadre was told to leave. Are there any government officials at our age asked to leave? Being a cadre makes one better off regardless of the type of work place. The government has always said that the reform would cause short-term pain. For the government, it is short-term; but for us, the pain will not end. Some officials often fail to keep their promises, and the reemployment program has not benefited us. They even think that we cannot find jobs because we are not hardworking people. In their words, the market economy does not starve hardworking people. But they seldom think of the fact that even capitalists know that it is wrong and inhuman not to pay their employees. Why did we not receive our salary for months?

Another woman recalled her experience of frustration and discontent after being laid off:

> After being laid off, for several times, I woke up weeping. The change was so dramatic that I was in a trance. A few times, I sent my child to my mother-in-law's and hurriedly rode to the factory on a bike. But when I saw that the once noisy factory was deserted and no single person was there, I realized that I no longer needed to come back again. But this was the place where I had worked for more than ten years, and I felt attached to it. We were workers of a state enterprise, how could we suddenly be left unattended? The government was too cruel. After the trance came worry, and after worry was complaint. At that time when a few of us in the same workshop gathered, we sighed and made endless complaints. We complained that we were unfortunate to be in such a small enterprise, that the society was in disorder, and that we were living in the wrong time. When complaining, we had to face the fact that our subsistence subsidies were decreasing as time went on. Worries about subsistence made me understand that complaints did not help. If we wanted to change our situation, we needed to find work.[104]

Among the 724 laid-off workers I surveyed, almost 90 percent were dissatisfied with their economic and employment status. As an interviewee complained, "The state wants to reform the enterprises, but it should not ignore our basic right to live and work." Other research has yielded similar findings. A survey by the National Institutional Reform Commission in 1997 found that about 53 percent of the laid-off workers surveyed could not accept being laid off.[105]

Conclusion

Over the years, SOEs in China have provided lifetime employment and a range of welfare benefits to their workers. This arrangement is based on sufficient financial resources. As inefficient SOEs put increasing pressure on the banking system, the Chinese government finally decided to adopt unprecedented reform measures to withdraw its financial commitment to most SOEs and their workers. The government's reform measures, as well as the SOEs' failure to make profits, made it impossible for a significant number of SOEs to keep their workers. Consequently, the lifetime employment system lost its economic foundation and tens of millions of SOE workers were laid off. Budget constraints also put laid-off workers in economic jeopardy because not all of them received unemployment subsidies. Abundant evidence suggests that many laid-off workers had difficulty in making ends meet after being laid off.

Given the inadequate welfare provisions, the government attempted to help workers by establishing RSCs. But RSCs became another source of problems because workers who registered with the RSC would have to cut off labor relations with their firms in two or three years. In other words, they would have to be self-sufficient after they left the RSC in search of jobs. Because of the inadequate insurance system, laid-off workers were very reluctant to take up jobs in the private sector or become self-employed. Hence, laid-off workers not only suffered from the loss of jobs and decreased income; they also faced an unprecedented dilemma. As moral economists would predict, layoffs became a source of resentment among laid-off workers. Yet, although frustration and discontent were common among laid-off workers, they do not imply that laid-off workers would take action against the government or the management, as Chapter 3 will show.

3 Retrenchment and laid-off workers' responses

Chapter 2 shows that the Chinese government failed to live up to its earlier socialist contract. It also underscores the finding of others that many Chinese workers experienced deprivation and became resentful after being laid off.[1] Theories on collective action differ in their assessment of the impact of deprivation and discontent. Frustration–aggression theory and the moral-economy approach suggest a causal link between discontent and participation in collective violence, whereas resource-mobilization theorists contend that grievance is not the decisive factor.[2] Extant research presents evidence to support both assertions. Some studies suggest that there is no correlation between grievance and collective action. It is argued that people "who are *only* dissatisfied with the provision of public goods but otherwise do not expect that rebellion will be successful and/or do not believe that their participation is important, have little potential to participate in rebellious action."[3] Yet other research maintains that in some cases grievance can be as important as resources,[4] because "it is precisely the salience of 'cause'—be it grievance or remedy—which appears at the forefront of appeals to join and decisions to participate."[5] Hence, dissatisfaction with government provision of public goods motivates participation in collective action.[6]

Similarly, in explaining worker resistance during the reform period in China, some studies hold that the dismantling of the lifetime employment system and the resulting subsistence crisis motivated resistance.[7] Yet, others claim that "the vast majority of Chinese workers, including the unemployed, remained politically passive."[8] Existing research therefore alerts us to the fact that Chinese workers have reacted differently toward reform measures such as layoffs. But the existing literature either focuses on action or its absence. There needs to be a coherent explanation for variations in workers' responses to layoffs. Specifically, the determinants of workers' participation in collective action remain unaddressed. This chapter examines the possible factors that affect workers' reactions and shows that factors related to deprivation or dissatisfaction are not sufficient to drive individuals to take action. More important to consider are factors that affect workers' incentive to resist, such as individual benefits (i.e., economic interests) derived from taking action, belief in the chance of success, and the perception of possible costs.

Laid-off workers' responses

During China's SOE reform, laid-off workers have taken various modes of collective action to pursue their rights, or they have failed to resist at all.[9] As defined in the Chinese trade union statistical yearbook, an act that is taken by three or more people is regarded as "collective action."[10] Hence, collective action in my study is also defined as an action taken by three or more people.[11] My survey and secondary sources reveal that workers' collective actions include letter writing, lawsuits, appeals (*jiti shangfang*), demonstrations, protests, traffic blockades, government-office blockades, and attacks on the government or its agencies. Some actions, such as letter writing, are peaceful, while others, like protests, are more disruptive.

Appeals, or *jiti shangfang*, are the most common mode of collective action among laid-off workers.[12] About 77 percent of laid-off workers' collective actions in my survey consist of appeals, and the rest are made up of other actions such as letter writing, lawsuits, and arbitration. Collective appeals include both peacefully approaching the government and more disruptive action such as blockades of government offices.[13] In some cases, workers' action may begin as a peaceful appeal to the government but end up as a traffic blockade or demonstration. The participants and their demands remain the same even as the mode of action changes. Some workers thus report protests or demonstrations as appeals to the government.[14]

As Tarrow has pointed out, collective action takes many forms: brief or sustained, institutionalized or disruptive, humdrum or dramatic. Some are not destructive, whereas others are contentious in that they challenge others.[15] In this book, the analysis of laid-off workers' collective action includes both disruptive and peaceful action for two reasons. First, both types of action are undesirable to local governments and have prompted them to prevent such actions. For example, it has become a rule that lower-level governments should prevent the practice where people appeal to higher-level governments especially at the central and provincial levels.[16] Second and more important, laid-off workers need to solve the problem of coordination in both cases.

Workers' collective action

Since the mid-1990s, massive layoffs have become a serious concern for the Chinese government. President Jiang Zemin cautioned, "Workers are the ruling class of our country and are the fundamental force promoting social stability. The Party committee and government at each level must take great care of the lives of laid-off workers and their reemployment. This is a serious political task and should be done by all means."[17]

This concern is shared by local governments who also believe that possible resistance from laid-off workers will conflict with the government policy of "stability taking precedence over anything else."[18] For example, in 1998, the Party secretaries of Shaanxi province and Chongqing municipality commented that an increase in the number of laid-off workers was the most significant factor affecting social stability.[19]

Government concern over social stability during the reform period is well-founded given the significant increase in collective action in China. In China, the most frequently used method by citizens to defend their interests against state or other public actors is making appeals to the authorities concerned, either individually or collectively.[20] As Table 3.1 suggests, the number of collective appeals (*jiti shangfang*) increased over the years.[21] During the first half of 1996, for example, collective appeals in 20 provinces to the governments at the county level and higher totaled 42,300, with the number of participants standing at over 2 million.[22] In 1998, collective appeals to the complaints bureau of the central government increased by almost 80 percent compared to the previous year.[23]

Collective appeals are often peaceful, but some of them may escalate into more disruptive modes of action, such as demonstrations, protests, traffic blockades, and even attacks on state agencies. As Table 3.2 reports, such instances increased

Table 3.1 Collective appeals in China (compared to the previous year)

Year	Increase in cases (%)	Increase in participants (%)
1993	28.5	40
1994	26	30.8
1995	27.4	31
1996	43.2	27.54
1997	—	13.64
1998	42.8	52.4
1999	—	—
2000	36.8	45.5
2001	36.4	38.7

Sources: For 1993–1996, see Wei Lei "Methods to Solve Peasants' Collective Appeals to the Government," *Lilun tantao* (Exploration of Theories), 1999, no. 4, pp. 94–98; For 1996–1998, *Banyuetan* (Biweekly Forum), February, 1999, pp. 54–55; For 2000–2001, see Chen Hao, Huang Weiping, and Wang Yongcheng, "A Study on the Interest Groups of China," *Guanli shijie* (Management World), 2003, no. 4, pp. 63–74.

Table 3.2 Number of instances of social unrest in China in selected years

Year	Number of instances of unrest
1993	8,700
1998	25,000
1999	32,000
2002	51,130
2003	58,500

Sources: Murray Scot Tanner, "Protests Now Flourish in China," *The International Herald Tribune*, June 3, 2004; "Layoffs: A Big Shock at the End of this Century," *Shandan* (Mountain Flowers), 1999, no. 5–6, pp. 4–20; "China's Economic Reform Causing Social Unrest and Crime," http://www.mabico.com/en/news/20040609/foreign_exchange/article4589/ (accessed September 6, 2004).

by 6.7 times in China from 1993 to 2003. While not all of them were taken by workers, their actions constituted an important part.[24] The Ministry of Public Security admitted that in 1998 and 1999, about a third of collective actions took place in China because SOEs failed to pay salaries, subsidies, or pensions to their workers, including those who were laid off.[25] For example, over 10,000 workers from a factory surrounded the manager and the Party secretary for hours in a city in Liaoning province in 2000 because of their subsistence problem. The local security department sent police to disperse the crowd. But because of the lack of equipment and training, the few hundred police were also surrounded by the workers. The Public Security Bureau of Liaoning province issued an urgent order, and several hundreds of riot police from nearby cities went to the city immediately. "Their equipment like the shield enabled them to resist the attack from all directions. Using the method of segregation and subjugation, the riot police succeeded in rescuing those surrounded. In the whole process, no one was hurt."[26]

In Shandong province in 1998, the number of collective actions—including demonstrations, traffic blockades, and attacks on the government—reached 575 and involved about 9,600 people. The most important reasons for these events were encroachment on the interests of workers, housing demolition in city construction, and financial problems of banks and other financial organizations.[27] In Jilin province, the governor acknowledged in 2001:

> Recently, collective action has occurred across the whole province. The number of appeals to high-level governments has increased. The action is often large-scaled, intense, and well organized. It is common for the compounds of the Party and government organs or the traffic to be blocked. The impact of this kind of action is severe. The reasons for the actions are mainly poor implementation of social security, stoppage of salary payment, and unauthorized fee collection, among others.[28]

Some local governments report that they have become "fire brigades" in that time and again, they need to put out the "fire" of collective action like protests.[29] It is not just the increasing number of actions that is of concern to authorities but the growth of cross-firm collective action. For example, representatives of laid-off workers from different firms may act as a collective to negotiate with the government.[30] In a city of Liaoning province in 2001, workers from 28 firms jointly elected 64 representatives to go to Beijing to appeal. In Inner Mongolia that year, over 20 firms jointly made appeals to higher-level governments.[31] Also in 2001, the governor of Jilin province cautioned:

> More effective measures should be adopted to curb coordinated appeals. Appeals to the central government are not tolerable. Some people disseminated information of collective action in the form of "thanks letters," and others even raised money for collective action. We must educate those who organize cross-firm, cross-sector, or cross-region action. We must be on guard for those who intend to engage in destructive activities.[32]

The government is reluctant to accept cross-firm collective action for a simple reason—if cross-form negotiation with the government is allowed, cross-firm disruptive action is also possible. One such example occurred in Liaoyang in Liaoning province in 2002, where over half of the city's factory workers had lost their jobs and many had failed to receive subsidies for months or years. In March, when the chairman of the city People's Congress told a local TV reporter in an interview that workers were well cared for, thousands of workers from a ferroalloy factory, who had not received subsidies for about two years, decided to protest. On March 11, 2002, workers from six factories, including the ferroalloy factory, took to the streets and marched to the city hall, demanding back pay and punishment of corrupt managers. A few days later, workers from over 20 enterprises took to the streets. They demanded to "Fire Gong Shangwu [the chairman] and Liberate Liaoyang City" and claimed that "the army of workers must have food and jobs." An organizer of the ferroalloy factory was detained and his release became an important goal of protestors in subsequent days. Reportedly, between 10,000 and 50,000 people participated in the protests. The protests ended with the city government making partial concessions and the four leaders being charged with leading illegal protests.[33]

Yet, in spite of the high profile and press attention that appeals and protests have generated, many laid-off workers have remained silent,[34] and more important, reform in China continues. My survey of 724 laid-off workers bears out the variation in workers' responses to layoffs. While about 23.8 percent (or 172) of the surveyed laid-off workers participated in collective action, most of them did not. In other words, many laid-off workers did not organize to resist. The varied responses of laid-off workers call for an explanation for both their resistance and their silence. Such an explanation will not only promote our understanding of collective action in an authoritarian regime, but will also illustrate the possibilities and difficulties of economic reform in China.

Statistical analyses of workers' responses

Explaining the variations in response to layoffs is to identify the factors that affect the workers' behaviors. As explained in Chapter 2, many laid-off workers experienced deprivation and became discontented after being laid off. Hence, one possible explanation for workers' response is, as suggested by the depression–aggression approach and moral-economy theory, the factors such as deprivation and resentment arising from the severing of a moral arrangement. Yet, as discussed in Introduction, such explanations tend to pay undue attention to the possible motivation for resistance like discontent or its absence thereof. And it is also possible that workers' responses are determined by the factors that affect their incentive and ability to act. Workers take action to address their concrete economic needs, so their incentive to resist may be shaped by the possible benefits and costs involved in resistance.

My survey contains data on factors related to workers' discontent and deprivation as well as factors concerning the possible benefits and costs arising from participation in collective action. It is thus possible to test which of the two types of factors can account for laid-off workers' participation in collective action. In the tests, I treat the deprivation–aggression approach and moral-economy theory similarly because both approaches emphasize motivation arising from deprivation and discontent.[35] In the following tests, the dependent variable is dichotomous: laid-off workers' participation or nonparticipation in collective action. The purpose of the tests is to identify which approach is more appropriate in explaining the behavior of Chinese laid-off workers, not which approach is wrong.

Deprivation, discontent, and collective action

"People who take part in acts of civil obedience or political violence are discontented about something. That is a truism."[36] As discussed in Chapter 2, layoffs inevitably make laid-off workers experience deprivation and give rise to resentment. According to moral economists, "an outrage to these moral assumptions, quite as much as actual deprivation, was the usual occasion for direct action."[37] Hence, frustration-induced action can be a possible explanation for their reactions. The following statistical analysis examines whether factors related to deprivation and dissatisfaction affect individuals' participation in collective action.

Four variables were chosen to measure laid-off workers' deprivation and dissatisfaction: decrease in income, the type of firm, perception of the decrease in income, and dissatisfaction. Laid-off workers no longer receive their full salary after being laid off; instead they receive a limited amount of un-guaranteed subsistence subsidies. Therefore, the first variable indicating their deprivation is the decrease in income after layoffs (i.e., the gap between income before and after layoffs). It is a continuous variable measured in Chinese yuan. It is hypothesized that the larger the decrease, the more likely that an individual will participate in collective action.

As the moral-economy approach assumes that the violation of a tacit agreement invites resistance, a second variable measuring discontent is the type of ownership of the firms that lay off workers. As workers in SOEs are likely to receive more benefits than workers in collective firm,[38] they are thus more likely to participate because they lose more benefits when they are laid off, all other things being equal. My sample contains about 18 percent of laid-off workers who worked for collective enterprises (i.e., enterprises owned by government agencies or SOEs rather than by the state), and we can examine whether those workers behave differently from those who worked in SOEs. This is a dummy variable. Those who used to work in SOEs were coded "1," and those who used to work in collective enterprises were coded "0."

As the degree of decrease in income is also determined by workers' subjective perception, it is necessary to "focus directly on the perceptions of individuals."[39] Thus, a third variable is laid-off workers' perceived degree of decrease in income after being laid off. Perceptions were classified as big decrease, small decrease, and no decrease. It is assumed that the larger the perceived decrease, the more likely an individual will take part in collective action.

A fourth variable measuring laid-off workers' dissatisfaction is their answers to the question on whether or not they were satisfied with their economic and employment status after being laid off. Their answer choices were "no," "yes," or "indifferent." In the statistical analysis, those who answered "yes" were included with those who answered "indifferent," because the number who answered "yes" was very small.[40] It is hypothesized that an individual who is dissatisfied with his or her situation is more likely to participate in collective action.

Table 3.3 reports the statistical outcomes of a logistic regression of worker participation in collective action. Failing to confirm the hypotheses, the two variables measuring decrease in income and that measuring dissatisfaction are not statistically significant. This may imply that laid-off workers' participation is not dictated by deprivation or dissatisfaction. In addition, the variable of the types of ownership is not statistically significant either. This suggests that laid-off workers from SOEs may not differ from those from collective enterprises in terms of their participation in collective action. The test shows that motivation alone is insufficient for taking action in the case of Chinese laid-off workers. This finding fails to lend support to the claim that grievance or discontent is the most accurate predictor of collective action. Instead, it supports the view that "psychological attributes of individuals, such as frustration and alienation, have minimal direct impact for explaining the occurrence of rebellion and revolution *per se*."[41]

Other sources also suggest that discontented or frustrated laid-off workers may fail to take action. A survey by two research institutions in Beijing found that the average monthly income of laid-off workers decreased from 434 yuan before being laid off to 190 yuan after being laid off, or by 56 percent. Because of decreases in income as well as those welfare issues, as discussed in Chapter 2, discontent was common among these laid-off workers. Through questionnaires and interviews, the researchers found that the common response among laid-off workers was that "they could not accept being laid off, and they were resentful, helpless, depressed, and eager to get re-employed." Many laid-off workers thought that the economic failure of their enterprise was not their fault, and so it

Table 3.3 Logistic regression of workers' participation in collective action on selected variables related to deprivation and discontent

Selected variables	Coefficient (standard error)
Intercept	−3.82** (1.738)
Absolute income decrease	0.00117 (0.0013)
Ownership type	0.2105 (0.1514)
Perceived income decrease	
No decrease (reference group)	
Big decrease	0.2465 (0.4232)
Small decrease	0.1893 (0.2326)
Dissatisfaction with their situation	0.1364 (0.3667)

Notes
$N = 724$; percentage predicted correctly: 33.7; ** $p < 0.05$.

was wrong to be laid off. As the researchers conclude:

> Many more people showed their strong discontent. First, they were angry with the managers, for they believed that it was the manager's incompetence, poor management, and corruption that led their enterprises to stop operation. If anyone should be laid off, these managers should be the first. Second, they were angry with the government.[42]

But despite their resentment, few laid-off workers ever took action.

Both the police department and government officials in Beijing seemed to confirm that laid-off workers there seldom took action against the government.[43] Claiming that the issue of laid-off workers had been blown out of proportion in the mass media, a vice mayor of the municipal government gave his own evidence:

> I have two channels to obtain the information about reemployment. One is people's appeals to the government, through which I find that very few people come to the government for reemployment. Most approach the government for the reallocation of their houses due to city construction. The other channel is the mayor's telephone. Among the over 100 telephone calls each day, very few are about reemployment.[44]

Discontented people elsewhere also remain silent for various reasons. In postcommunist countries, labor quiescence was common even though workers found their situation unacceptable.[45] For example, in Russia, as Clarke *et al.* write:

> Workers were almost universally dissatisfied with their condition, but without any institutional channels through which they could articulate and express that dissatisfaction, and without any easily identifiable agents of their exploitation and oppression, they tended to accept their condition with a fatalistic resignation.[46]

Ekiert and Kubik's comparative study of workers' protests in four postcommunist countries—East Germany, Hungary, Poland, and Slovakia—between 1989 and 1993 suggests that the deprivation theory cannot provide a valid explanation for workers' variations in protests. For an average year in the period under study:

> Poland had a higher magnitude of protest than Slovakia and Hungary, although its economy performed better than the economies of the other two countries and although *Poles were far more satisfied* than were Slovaks and Hungarians with the results of the post-communist economic reforms.[47]

My study does not posit that motivation is irrelevant; instead, it suggests that motivation is not sufficient for action.

Individuals and collective action: a cost-benefit analysis

Discontent or frustration-based explanations have been criticized for, among other things, their insufficient attention to the capacity or resources of the discontented. Capacity is the power (institutionalized or otherwise) that the discontented can use to influence the target of their action, and it affects their odds of success and the likelihood of being punished. This is an important reason why discontent may fail to lead to action. In former East Germany, for example, "the East German populace was by and large discontented with its standard of living and lack of political freedoms, and it grew increasingly so in the period 1975–1989." Despite the discontent, there had been little action taken until 1989 because "the violent suppression of the 1953 mass uprising with the help of Soviet military forces rendered the cost of anti-regime protest prohibitive for all but a small minority."[48]

As Chinese workers' action is aimed at addressing their concrete economic problems,[49] an alternative explanation of their reaction is based on variables related to the benefits they will receive by participating in the action and the costs they might incur. The benefits of participation for laid-off workers are mainly economic, like compensation or subsistence subsidies. The costs of participation include both risks and opportunity costs, which are assessed in light of the odds of success and the time to be spent. In addition to incurring punishment from the government, slim odds of success may also undermine workers' confidence and their incentive to take action. Participating in a hopeless action involves opportunity costs.[50] It is in this sense that estimations of the chances of success and the time to be spent taking action enter workers' calculations.

Hence, for collective action to take place among laid-off workers, in addition to having sufficient participants, there should be a possibility of success given the possible costs. In other words, laid-off workers' collective action can be viewed as a result of two types of interaction. One is the interaction among workers themselves that affects the number of participants, and the other is interaction between workers and the target of their action (e.g., the government). As I will show, in the interaction among workers, it is one's concrete benefits derived from action that motivates participation; in the interaction between laid-off workers and their target, an individual's confidence in group action and the possible costs affect participation.

Benefits and individuals' participation

Collective action can be seen as cooperation between a prospective participant and a group of other prospective participants. Its difficulty lies in individuals' propensity to free ride.[51] While there can be a number of methods to overcome the collective action problem,[52] one solution is shared interests in the action and intention to make collective action a success. Shared interests create a situation where it is in the individuals' best interests to act collectively,[53] especially when prospective participants realize that success is more likely when acting together rather than individually. By the same token, when individuals have little shared interests (i.e., benefits) in a collective goal, they lack the incentive to participate, other things being equal.

The following presents a statistical test of the relationship between individual stakes or benefits (i.e., economic needs) and participation in collective action. The goal of most laid-off workers is to obtain economic benefits, including subsidies or salaries (63 percent), jobs and subsidies (21 percent), only jobs (12 percent), and others (16 percent), including medical insurance and bonds.[54] Hence, a direct way of measuring their stake in collective action is to see whether they received such benefits after layoffs. The information was obtained by asking them whether their needs were met before participating in collective action, the answer being either "yes" or "no." It is assumed that those who have received benefits do not have an incentive to participate.

Individuals' stakes are relative to their access to alternatives, which measures their opportunity cost of participating in collective action. Three variables are included to measure laid-off workers' access to options other than collective action. As the most important option for laid-off workers is new jobs, the degree of difficulty finding a job is the first variable. It is assumed that the more difficult an individual feels it is to find a job, the more likely he or she will participate in collective action. In this case, the opportunity cost of participation is lower. This variable is measured by their answer to the question of whether they felt it difficult to secure a job after being laid off. Survey participants chose one of the three responses: "very difficult," "difficult," and "not difficult." A second variable is whether the RSC provided help to the laid-off workers. If the answer is positive, it means that the worker has another alternative and is less likely to participate; if negative, the worker lacks an alternative and is more likely to participate. Finally, some laid-off workers may have other sources of income. A third variable—family income level—is included as another indicator. This is a continuous variable measured in Chinese yuan. It is hypothesized that the higher the income level, the more likely a person has other sources of income and the less likely he or she will participate in collective action.

The statistical outcomes of a logistic regression are reported in Table 3.4. As hypothesized, compared with those who have had their needs met, those who have not are 4.6 times more likely to participate.[55] This implies that the action of laid-off workers is strongly interest-driven. In other words, participating in an action from which a laid-off worker does not benefit (e.g., receive subsidy or salary) increases his or her opportunity costs. Confirming what was hypothesized, those who felt it is difficult to find jobs are more likely to take part in collective action. Compared with those who reported that it was not difficult to find jobs, those who reported "very difficult" were about twice as likely to participate. Similarly, those who reported "difficult" were almost 65 percent more likely to participate. Although the RSC may not dispel the dissatisfaction of laid-off workers, it does reduce their odds of participation. Compared with those who received help, those who did not were more likely to participate.[56] This suggests that government efforts, as limited as they might be, help reduce the scale of collective action.

Table 3.4 Logistic regression of workers' participation in collective action on selected variables related to interests

Selected variables	Coefficient (standard error)	Exp (coefficient)
Intercept	−2.873 (1.443)**	
Needs un-met	1.724 (0.5236)***	5.607
Difficulty in job search		
Not difficult (reference group)		
Very difficult	0.7186 (0.2398)***	2.051
Difficult	0.5012 (0.2825)**	1.650
Failure to receive help from the RSC	0.3286 (0.1509)**	1.389
Family income level	−0.1038 (0.2965)	0.901

Notes
$N = 724$; percentage predicted correctly: 77.8; ** $p < 0.05$, *** $p < 0.01$; RSC: reemployment service center.

The influence of family income level is not statistically significant. This may imply that people with higher family income levels may still participate in action to pursue their individual interests, such as finding other jobs or receiving subsidies. The statistical outcomes suggest that it is plausible to regard laid-off workers' participation in collective action as being driven by concrete benefits.

Confidence, costs, and participation

Workers' incentive to resist is affected not only by benefits derived from the action but also by the possible costs and the odds of success. My analysis assumes that rational action means that "given the beliefs of the agent, the action was the best way for him to realize his plans or desires."[57] Individuals who face losses often see collective action as a means to an end, and mull over their chances for success before taking action. As Chong suggests, group members

> are enthusiastic about contributing to collective action or are pressured to do so, only when such collective action has a realistic opportunity to achieve the desired public good. When collective action is widely regarded as futile, or as an ineffective symbolic protest, these social and psychological incentives vanish.[58]

In my analysis, benefits (e.g., compensation) are thus weighed against the possibility of a successful action. An action is defined as costly when it incurs the risk of suppression, consumes too much time, or fails despite the effort.

The following test considers the factors related to action efficacy and costs affect the action of laid-off workers. Four types of variables are chosen: participants' expectation of action efficacy, perceived costs, perceived importance of individual participation, and the locality where a laid-off worker is from. The efficacy of action is measured by whether they, based on their experiences before layoffs, thought group action was helpful in addressing problems. Survey participants chose one of the three responses: "helpful," "maybe helpful," and "not helpful." The hypothesis is that the more an individual thinks collective action is helpful, the more likely he or she will participate, and the inverse is also assumed to be true.

As noted above, success is weighed against possible costs or risks involved. In the Chinese context, collective action incurs two types of costs: potential punishment imposed by the target and the time spent. Given the sensitive nature of this study, risk is measured by a less direct question of whether workers thought that their action would be acceptable to the target (i.e., the government or firm), based on previous experience. If they believed that it was unacceptable to the target, the risk would be higher and they would be less likely to participate, and the inverse is hypothesized as true. As for the cost of time, they were asked whether or not they thought their action would be time consuming, and their answers were either "yes" or "no." It is hypothesized that those who believe it is time consuming are less likely to participate.

As individuals tend not to participate if they believe that their individual participation will not affect the outcome of the collective action,[59] it is also necessary to measure the belief in the necessity of individual participation. To examine whether Chinese laid-off workers feel that their participation is important, I used the question "Based on your previous experience, did you believe that if more people, including yourself, participated in a group action, the more likely your problems would be addressed?" Their answers were either "yes" or "no." It is hypothesized that those who believe in the importance of individual participation are more likely to participate than those who do not.

Finally, as the data includes laid-off workers from different places, they were classified by the income level of their localities (i.e., the cities to which they belong). This is based on the assumption that governments in higher-income regions may have more resources, and that workers may be more confident in receiving help from the government if they take action and thus are more likely to take action, other things being equal. In the analysis, laid-off workers are divided into three groups: high-income regions (mainly in the eastern area), middle-income regions (mainly in the middle region), and low-income regions (mainly in the western area).

The statistical outcomes of the logistic regression are reported in Table 3.5. As hypothesized, confidence in group action has a positive effect on the odds of one's participation. Compared with those who did not think it would be helpful, those who, based on their previous experience, thought so were more than twice as likely to participate. Similarly, those who thought it might be helpful were also more likely to participate. Their perception of the importance of individual participation is also statistically significant. Those who thought their individual participation was useful were more than twice as likely to participate as those who did not think so.[60] In other words, individuals may perceive individual participation as having some influence. Hence, the assumption that "no average contributor could significantly affect the likelihood that the public good would be produced" is only conditionally

Table 3.5 Logistic regression of workers' participation in collective action on selected variables related to efficacy and cost

Selected variables	Coefficient (standard error)	Exp (coefficient)
Intercept	−0.3543 (0.1667)**	—
Confidence in group action		
Not helpful (reference group)		
Helpful	0.7659 (0.3212)**	2.151
May be helpful	0.4416 (0.2234)*	1.555
LOWs in low-income regions (reference group)		
LOWs in high-income regions	−0.3224 (0.2085)	0.7244
LOWs in middle-income regions	0.1150 (0.2471)	1.12
Individual participation	0.8234 (0.3553)**	2.27
Potential risk	−1.026 (0.3194)***	0.3584
Time	−0.5237 (0.2265)**	0.5923

Notes
$N = 724$; percentage predicted correctly: 82.5; * $p < 0.1$, ** $p < 0.05$, *** $p < 0.01$; LOWs: laid-off workers.

true.[61] Laid-off workers understand that a small number of participants often fails to put enough pressure on the target, and their contribution may be perceived as necessary. In addition, they usually do not know how many people are enough.

The two variables measuring the cost are also statistically significant. Compared with those who thought action was unacceptable to the target, those who did not think so were almost more than twice as likely to participate.[62] Similarly, compared with those who thought it was time consuming, those who did not think so were about 70 percent more likely to participate.[63] This implies that the potential opportunity costs arising from participation may prevent participation. But the variable of locality is not statistically significant. There can be a number of reasons for this result. One possibility is that laid-off workers in more developed areas are better able to find alternatives. Another possibility is the difficulties of mobilization in both developed and less developed areas, which will be discussed in Chapters 6 and 7.

Yet, it must be acknowledged that using recall in data collection may introduce inaccuracy in the analysis, especially when some variables are subjective. However, as this study stresses that collective action is only a means to an end for laid-off workers, this proposition can be tested using a more objective indicator. For example, it was not surprising that some laid-off workers had also taken individual action to pursue their interests, and some of them had also participated in collective action later on. It can be assumed that such people were more likely to participate in collective action than those who had never taken individual action (or had not taken individual action before the collective action). This proposition is substantiated by a statistical test. Compared with workers who had never taken individual action, those who had were more than 2.3 times more likely to participate, other things being equal.[64] This finding has important implications for participation in collective action.

Individuals do not always want to be free riders. As Tarrow suggests, "For people whose lives are mired in drudgery and desperation, the offer of an exciting, risky, and possibly beneficial campaign of collective action may be a gain."[65] In other words, it is reasonable to contribute one's efforts in order to achieve something rather than "free riding" on nothing, especially when the cost of participation is smaller than the possible loss from inaction. Some laid-off workers are more willing to participate in collective action because it is a more effective means than is individual action. According to my survey, while about 29 percent of those who participated in collective action reported that their action was helpful, only less than 9 percent of those who took individual action reported so.

Conclusion

This chapter illustrates that responses to layoffs varied significantly among Chinese laid-off workers. A large number of incidents of collective action have occurred since layoffs were carried out in the 1990s, and such resistance has been seen as a threat to social stability in China. But on the other hand, many workers have remained silent. There are two possible explanations for workers' resistance or its absence thereof. One is based on the motivation arising from deprivation and resentment. And the other is based on factors related to workers' benefits and confidence in an action in light of the costs and odds of success. This chapter presents statistical tests and finds that factors related to deprivation and resentment are not the best predictors of Chinese laid-off workers' action. Factors related to the benefits of collective action, their confidence in success, and their perception of costs significantly affect the likelihood of participation in collective action. As discussed in Chapter 2, this finding is not surprising in that laid-off workers suffered tremendous economic pressure after being laid off. Activities that cannot bring benefits incur high opportunity costs because they must work to support their families. This implies that in the interaction among laid-off workers, workers who have access to alternatives will lack an incentive to participate. Also, as workers' action is aimed at achieving concrete goals, if they lack confidence in exercising influence on the target of their action, they will also lack the incentive to take action.

The statistical outcomes can by no means capture the richness of workers' responses to layoffs. In the following chapters, I analyze the difficulties and possibilities of workers' collective action by examining the contexts under which workers, factory managers, and the government operate and interact. By looking at the interaction among workers, I show empirically how one's benefits in collective action affect his or her participation. Workers' action is often directed at their firms or the local government, so it is also necessary to explore how the policies adopted by firms and the government shape workers' behavior by influencing their estimation of costs, confidence, and opportunity costs. On the other hand, collective action requires cooperation among individuals with shared interests. I also discuss the mechanisms that contribute to the coordination of workers and that promote their confidence in taking collective action.

4 Fragmentation and collective action

"Collective action is collective,"[1] and it does not occur without the cooperation of sufficient participants. However, individuals tend to maximize benefits and minimize costs by free-riding or defecting, even if cooperation would lead to greater benefits for all.[2] This assertion is based on the assumption that the collective good is beneficial or valuable to prospective participants. In some circumstances, this assumption does not hold, and collective action becomes more difficult when the solidarity of prospective participants is weak or nonexistent.[3] Specifically, collective action is difficult when some people do not view it as a desirable choice and do not face coercion of participation. Hence, fragmented interests in collective goals or the availability of alternatives reduces the scale of collective action or even prevents it.

Chapter 3 finds that Chinese laid-off workers' participation in collective action is interest driven. This chapter explores the interaction among workers and shows how fragmented interests have prevented Chinese workers from taking concerted actions. It demonstrates that fragmented interests reduce solidarity among workers because some workers do not regard collective action as a necessary or desirable means to an end. Workers not only differ in their attitudes towards reform measures,[4] but also in their access to alternative employment before or after being laid off, depending on their personal networks, level of education, skill, and former occupation. Over the years, some Chinese workers have chosen to act individually rather than collectively to pursue personal interests. Hence, the shared identity of laid-off workers does not necessarily imply that they will act as a group.[5] While individual action of finding alternative jobs undermines worker solidarity, the lack of alternatives helps bind workers together and enhances their solidarity.

Fragmentation and the difficulty of collective action

Fragmentation in terms of age, gender, skills, and the like has long been viewed as an obstacle to workers' collective action. In the United States, for example, members of the working class come from different national, racial, and religious backgrounds. The working class was formed successively rather than simultaneously through immigration, which created hierarchies that fostered hostility among these groups and prevented concerted responses to common problems.[6] In a discussion of workers in Detroit in the early nineteenth century, Richard Oestreigher suggests that "workers were different from each other: work experience, skill, background, nationality, attitudes, ambitions, religion. While they faced common problems, their perceptions of the meaning and importance of these problems were filtered through different cultural and social visions. Different perceptions could mean very different responses."[7] Charles Sabel also holds that different groups of workers, categorized by skills and status in a factory, tended not to cooperate with each other because they had their own ideas of what was worth fighting for.[8]

Barrington Moore also uses the differentiation of skills among workers to explain their differing militancy—"all the obstacles to collective action against the dominant groups come from the acts and policies of the authorities...the fragmentation that arises from a complex division of labor is especially important."[9] Hence, although coal miners faced a similarly undesirable situation as did iron and steelworkers in Germany in the early twentieth century, the former tried to take action while the latter largely remained silent. The most persuasive reason for the difference in response between these two groups of workers is that the division of labor among steelworkers was much more elaborate and workers were more severely differentiated based on skills and the types of work. As steel workers lacked shared interests, they were much less receptive to union organization than were the coal miners and thereby were far less active in defending their interests.[10]

Research on Chinese workers in the pre-1949 period yields similar findings. In her study of women mill workers in Shanghai, Emily Honig points out that "those aspects of factory work that might theoretically have brought women together were overshadowed by forces keeping them apart."[11] Women workers in the mills, most of whom were peasant daughters, had lower expectations of career advancement. While management–labor relations were overshadowed by Chinese–foreigner relations, the "divide-and-rule" strategy of the capitalists also prevented worker participation. All these factors combined to prevent the building of solidarity and thus curtailed labor movements. Similarly, Gail Hershatter suggests that before 1949 the Tianjin working class was "deeply fragmented," for its members consisted of handicraft workers, freight haulers, casual laborers, and millhands. "The fragmentation of the working class into a number of different sectors with widely varying experiences made the development of any unified working-class activity unlikely."[12] Rural ties might give workers less of a stake in urban workplace struggles and might even bind workers to owners.[13]

Despite the negative impact of fragmentation on collective action, two points need to be mentioned. The first is that fragmentation does not preclude collective action. As Elizabeth Perry suggests, there can be a "positive link" between fragmentation and labor militancy within a distinctive group.[14] Second, despite fragmentation, collective action is possible in the long run when people realize that organized action is an effective means to protecting common interests. Indeed, regardless of fragmentation, workers protest and strike in almost all countries. As Oestreigher has shown, regardless of the everpresent fragmentation among workers of different nationalities, a subculture of resistance exists among them when faced with similar situations of encroachment on their interests.[15] Fragmentation is more likely to be overcome when workers lack alternatives because that helps bind them together. For this reason, Harry Braverman suggests that as long as the degradation of working people continues, divisions will not be important and more homogeneous factors among workers may lead to a more consolidated class.[16]

There is also evidence that shared interests or a common situation may promote coordinated action among people in China. During the reform period, peasants-turned-workers organize associations in their struggle against both domestic and "imported" (i.e., foreign) bosses, more or less pointing to potential solidarity of people with common interests. It is a well-known fact that peasants-turned-workers have been ill treated in private enterprises in China.[17] Some of them have realized that it is to their benefit to organize. A number of organizations have thus emerged, such as The Peasant Workers' Association, The Association of Brothers, The Association of Friends, and The Strike Committee. By the late 1990s, there were more than 200 strikes in Fujian province, and some of them were organized by such associations.[18]

Yet things are different for Chinese laid-off workers for two reasons. First, layoffs are the beginning of the dismantling of the lifetime employment system, and it takes time for homogeneous factors to emerge in order to unite workers or for them to realize the necessity of unity. Second, not all laid-off workers are bound together because some of them can find alternatives. As discussed in Chapter 3, workers' stake or shared interests (such as jobs or subsidies) in collective action is an important motivation for participation. Their collective action is thus frustrated by the fact that workers with alternatives may not see collective action as the most desirable means to an end.

A means to the end: individual action

As elsewhere, state workers in China have long taken individual action to pursue their interests. Over the years, the social and economic status of Chinese state workers has declined as the planned economy gives way to a market one.[19] This decline created a strong incentive for workers to find alternatives before massive layoffs began. Although many workers were unable to do so and had to find new jobs after being laid off, still, they differed in their access to alternatives. When some workers find alternative jobs, the "catness" or solidarity of the worker community will be undermined.[20] As a result, different access to new jobs compounds workers' collective action.

Workers' declined status and ex ante *job search*

While Chapter 2 discusses workers' suffering in recent layoffs, the decline of workers' economic and social status was a gradual process that had started much earlier.[21] Although the Chinese government has claimed that the working class is the "master of the firm," few SOE workers believe it. As early as 1982, some SOE workers pointed out that they had been cheated by a state that was "socialist in appearance, on a capitalist road, and cast in a feudal shadow."[22] Others admitted in the mid-1980s: "We were the masters, but we are not now. In the 1950s, when we walked in the streets in uniform, even the police would show their respect, and we felt proud of ourselves; but now if you walk in the streets in your uniform, even the salesperson is reluctant to talk to you, and we feel inferior to others."[23] In the 1990s, workers also began to complain about the lack of job security and an increasing income gap in society.[24]

The decline of workers' economic and social status has also been reflected in public opinion. A survey of the citizens of 38 cities in 24 provinces in 1997 revealed that SOE workers were regarded as the group that had benefited the least from reforms, which was also admitted by higher-level officials.[25] Being a worker is thus not viewed as a respected occupation.[26] A survey by the Beijing Labor Bureau in the 1990s found that only about 1 percent of junior high-school graduates and 0.5 percent of senior high-school graduates were willing to be factory workers. The social status of workers has fallen to that of peasants. Some students and their parents believe that in the future only marginalized members of society should be workers or peasants, such as the illiterate, those with poor academic records, people indulging in dissipation, former criminals, beggars, and those whose parents are workers or peasants.[27]

In an undesirable situation, people may choose to exit or remain silent, if they cannot change it.[28] To improve their social and economic status, some Chinese workers have tried looking for jobs that are better paid, more secure, or both. SOE workers have a stronger desire to switch jobs than other groups of employees in urban China.[29] A survey of blue-collar workers in the machinery industry in 1996 suggested that about 46 percent of the workers admitted that they were unwilling to be laborers but had no choice, whereas another 21 percent reported that they were unwilling to be laborers and were looking for alternatives.[30]

According to a national sampling survey of over 3.4 million employees by the All China Federation of Trade Unions (ACFTU) in 1997, regardless of their occupational status (i.e., workers, technicians, or cadres), a good salary and job security were the two most important criteria in their choice of jobs.[31] Since the beginning of the reform, SOE workers have tried various ways to secure better jobs or to increase income. Specifically, they may choose to stay in SOEs while moonlighting elsewhere, keep their unpaid membership in SOEs while working elsewhere, or simply to leave for better jobs.[32] The emergence of job opportunities in the non-state sector and reform of the traditional employment system, which prevented people from leaving their work units, have made it possible for some people to "exit." Because of their skills or personal connections or both, some state workers have been able to secure jobs outside their original work units.[33]

Yet, given the many advantages of working in the state sector, there are two characteristics of state workers' job transfers. First, many people often leave for other public work units instead of private ones. According to the ACFTU survey in 1997, over 34 percent of those surveyed had switched employment at least once but often within the public sector.[34] Second, those who leave for private firms believe that their higher income will offset job insecurity in the private sector. These two characteristics also suggest that the number of people who were willing and able to transfer to positions outside the state sector was limited in the 1990s. Therefore, as job transfer in China usually entails personal connections or skills or both,[35] for some people, the emergence of a labor market poses a threat rather than an opportunity in that there is an oversupply of labor in the market. But voluntary job shifts suggest that state employees with marketable skills can fare better by leaving poorly performing firms.

Keeping unpaid membership in SOEs

In 1983, the former State Labor Bureau (renamed the Ministry of Labor and Social Security in 1998) and the State Economic Commission issued a policy that allowed workers in state sectors to retain unpaid membership with their work unit while working elsewhere for a maximum of two years.[36] The purpose of this policy was to encourage people to become self-employed and to streamline the state employee workforce. This policy allows people to return to their work units if their private businesses fail. Some people in the public sector have taken advantage of this policy, many of whom have strong family backgrounds, personal networks, or marketable skills. As a manager reported on a worker in his firm:

> That worker was a porter of our company who applied to retain an unpaid membership in 1985. His father's business of selling fried chicken had been quite good. As the worker did not have a job with good prospects in our company and his father needed a hand in the business, he left while retaining his membership with our company. We require him to turn in 80 yuan per month as a management fee while we continue paying the insurance for him. This worker has been faring quite well. But recently, most enterprises have stopped this practice of unpaid membership, so has our company. We have asked him to resign and plan to terminate our labor relations with him.[37]

Workers may also keep their unpaid membership in other ways. For example, in some loss-making firms, despite prohibition from the government, there exists a phenomenon called shift selling and buying. Some workers sell their work shifts to other people, including colleagues, peasants, students, and other unemployed people, while taking jobs elsewhere.[38] Sometimes, lower-level managers found shift selling and buying an acceptable way to increase productivity because those who bought shifts were more likely to be disciplined and were easier to manage. The head of a work group admitted in an interview that as long as nothing was wrong with worker safety, higher-level managers would pretend that shift selling was not practiced. But as in the case of unpaid membership practice, with the reform of the employment system, firms tend to lay off people rather than allow them to sell shifts.

Compared with the above methods, a safer bet is to obtain an early retirement when possible. Feigning illness to secure early retirement has been a severe issue for some firms. For example, among the 270 workers of a textile factory who obtained early retirement based on claims of poor health, only two fulfilled the criteria for early retirement. In another factory of about 430 people, more than 160 applied to retire citing poor health. Many left because they found better jobs while securing pension and welfare benefits from the firms they left. "Few workers who have skills or expertise would be willing to lead a life of poverty, so many of them resort to feigning illness."[39] My interviewees also reported such cases. For instance, a salesperson well known for his abilities and social network received a basic monthly salary of only about 300 yuan due to the poor performance of his factory, an SOE. He managed to obtain a doctor's verification of failing health and was granted early retirement and then accepted a job with a private firm that paid a monthly salary of 3,500 yuan. When the retirement pension is paid by an insurance organization instead of the firm, the management would have an incentive to offer early retirement to workers because it reduces the firm's expenses.[40] In 1993, about a third of all retirees retired early.[41]

Leaving firms

While some workers have tried to maintain labor relations with their firms, others have simply sought employment elsewhere. In Beijing in the late 1990s, it was estimated that more than 60 percent of those who looked for jobs in the labor market were from public work units, while those from SOEs accounted for 44.5 percent.[42] The emergence of joint ventures and private businesses provides skilled workers with alternatives. As a manager reported in the late 1980s, "The mobility of the lifetime workers is high. From 1986 to 1989, we hired 4,597 workers, but meanwhile 1,607 people left... 129 resigned or left voluntarily, 56 found jobs in foreign joint ventures, and 226 went abroad...."[43] Job shifts have created a serious problem for non-profitable businesses where a shortage of qualified workers has plagued a number of SOEs.[44]

Yet job transfers are mostly confined to better educated or skilled and often young employees in SOEs. Comparably, average workers who lack marketable skills or personal connections are less disposed to changing jobs than are technicians, and are less likely to pose a problem for the firm. Some people say that those who remain in loss-making SOEs "are staunch but incompetent supporters of socialism."[45] In contrast, the brain drain has been a serious issue for a number of SOEs. A survey shows that in Beijing, about 77 percent of those workers with high- or middle-level technical skills have left their factories. Similarly, the textile industry of Shanghai, which had over 300,000 workers and was once well known for its technical personnel, retained only six senior engineers in 1996. The brain drain also seems to be common in inland provinces where talented employees leave SOEs for non-state local firms or coastal areas.[46]

In a factory I visited, 11 designers, or half of the staff in the design department, had left the factory since the early 1990s. These people had found jobs at universities, professional schools, foreign companies, and other businesses. The department head complained, "In fact, staff in my department are better paid than those from the workshops. They get commission for their designs in addition to their salary. Although they earn more than 10,000 yuan per year, which is considerably high in our city, they still want to leave." Those who left the factory had their reasons. A person who left for a position in a university told the department manager, "It is true that I can earn a little more here than at the university, but I have to consider the future. If I do not take up the offer now, I will lose it forever. The job at the university is stable and respectable. I cannot afford to wait until the factory goes bankrupt." Hence, despite the efforts of factory leaders, the technician left after serving the factory for 10 years. Another person who left for a well-paid job in a foreign company admitted that his monthly salary there was more than six times that at this factory. Indeed, many SOE managers also want jobs in the public administrative sector,[47] but it is very difficult for factory cadres to secure those jobs. Some managers seek well-paid jobs in the private sector instead. In a loss-making factory with about 1,800 workers, for example, a deputy manager in charge of the sales department left with about 30 salespeople and department managers for a foreign company. This created strong resentment among those factory leaders and workers left behind.[48]

Able people in failing companies are more likely to leave. Firms usually do not make losses suddenly but gradually. Economic failure serves as advance notice of layoffs that prompts workers to find other jobs. For example, in 1994, among the 173,580 laid-off workers in Shanghai, over 15 percent left their firms voluntarily.[49] Another survey of 1,000 laid-off workers also indicated that about 17 percent left their factories voluntarily, and about 70 percent of whom were below the age of 35 and believed that they could find better-paying jobs.[50] A department manager reported job shifts in his company in an interview:

> In the past, very few people would leave our company because it performed very well, and some people even transferred here. We began making loss a few years ago, and the situation has persisted since then. Employees became dispirited, and many of them began to look for alternatives. Some of them were able to do this because of their personal connections, whereas others relied on their personal abilities. Young people are more likely to find jobs elsewhere, and they are usually the people a firm most needs. The financial and insurance companies in our city have recruited quite a few people from our company. Although the insurance business faces intense competition, these people are still willing to work for it, because they think that our company will fare even worse.

One interviewee reported that after his loss-making firm ceased production, almost half of the 1,000 workers left with or without maintaining labor relations. Another interviewee reported that within a year after their factory stopped production, about a hundred people had secured other employment. As others have also observed, "in those firms that persistently lose money or are to go bankrupt, many people, including those with skills, have left for other jobs or retired ahead of time to pursue other business opportunities, which is not good for the production."[51]

Employees' job shifts have led some SOEs to adopt different policies toward different groups of employees. To retain qualified employees, SOEs provide both incentives and disincentives. They may require those people they need to sign long-term contracts (e.g., 10 years), withhold their personal files, or impose a large fine on them for leaving.[52] Yet such disincentives are not necessarily effective. Some people simply leave their firms without the file if their request is denied. Others may resort to violence. Reportedly, in the mid-1990s, a desperate technical worker in a chemical factory, whose application for a transfer was denied, bombed the factory. Sixty-one people were killed and 21 injured.[53] Some SOEs have thus begun to provide more incentives to retain the people they need by offering high salaries and generous benefits, including housing. As a matter of fact, while SOEs are laying off employees they do not need, they are enhancing the lifetime employment system to attract those they need.[54] Hence, workers with different skill levels within an SOE may receive different treatment in the reform period.

Ex post *job search*

While some workers found other jobs before their firms ceased production or began layoffs, many more were forced to look for work after being laid off. Not surprisingly, not all laid-off workers have equal access to new jobs. Chen points out that "massive layoffs and the subsistence crisis have affected or threatened the majority of the workers in many factories and therefore have erased past division and united large numbers of workers in a common discontent and shared demands."[55] But it is also true that not all laid-off workers see collective action as the only means to their end. As discussed in Chapter 3, only those who fail to receive regulated benefits or secure jobs are more likely to participate in collective action.

To identify those factors that may affect laid-off workers' odds of a successful job search, the following presents a statistical analysis. The dependent variable, which is dichotomous, is whether or not they had found jobs after layoffs. The impact of four types of variables on the job search of laid-off workers are analyzed. The first variable, age, is included because people of different ages are more or less competitive in the labor market. Following the categories used in the *Chinese Labor Statistical Yearbook 1998*, laid-off workers are divided into three groups: those below 35 years of age (35 included), those between 36 and 46 (46 included), and those over 46. It is hypothesized that the older a person is, the less likely he or she will secure a job. The second variable is gender. It has been widely reported that women are discriminated against in securing jobs after layoffs,[56] so this variable is included to test whether women face more difficulties in finding work. It is thus hypothesized that women are less likely to secure employment after being laid off, compared with males. Education, the third variable, has become increasingly important in China and is included to examine whether the educational level, measured in terms of the number of years of schooling, affects an individual's chance of securing new work. It is assumed that laid-off workers with higher education are more likely to find new jobs. The fourth variable, the previous occupation, is divided into three categories: workers, technicians, and cadres. It is

Table 4.1 Logistic regression of the job search of laid-off workers on selected variables

Selected variables	Coefficient (standard error)	Exp (coefficient)
Intercept age	3.127 (1.712)*	
Below 35 (reference group)		
Between 36 and 46	−0.3218 (0.1467)**	0.7248
Over 46	0.2134 (0.1792)	
Gender	0.1424 (0.0741)*	1.153
Education	0.2170 (0.064)***	1.242
Occupation		
Workers (reference group)		
Technicians	0.4287 (0.1983)**	1.535
Cadres	0.7544 (0.2365)***	2.126

Notes
$N = 712$; percentage predicted correctly: 87.2; * $p < 0.1$; ** $p < 0.05$; *** $p < 0.01$.

hypothesized that, due to their skill level and connections, cadres are more likely to find jobs than are average workers.

The statistical outcomes of a logistic regression are reported in Table 4.1. Age matters to the group between 36 and 46. Compared with the group between 36 and 46, those below 35 years old are about 38 percent more likely to find jobs.[57] But this is not the case for those over 46 years old. Age does not seem to affect the job search of those over 46 years old, probably because older workers are qualified for early retirement that provides a pension. Hence, they may be willing to accept jobs that others would not, such as one that does not provide insurance. While the effect of gender is statistically significant, its influence is rather limited, perhaps because women are equally competitive in the tertiary sector, an important channel of reemployment. As hypothesized, laid-off workers' previous occupations impact their job search. Compared with workers, technicians are about 54 percent more likely to find jobs, whereas cadres are twice as likely.

As expected, education significantly impacts laid-off workers' probability of finding a job. An additional year of education increases one's odds of finding reemployment by about 24 percent. Most laid-off workers who reported that it was difficult to find jobs did not have any higher education. According to my survey, about 88 percent of them received a high-school education or below. In 1998, among laid-off workers nationwide, only about 7 percent received college or higher education, about 57 percent received a high-school education or its equivalent, and over 35 percent received an education of junior high school or below.[58] Education is a proxy for one's skills. Other research also points to the importance of skills in the job search of laid-off workers. A survey of 20,000 laid-off workers in three cities of Hebei province found that 39 percent possessed one skill and secured jobs within five months, while about 16 percent who possessed two skills found jobs within two months. The 192 laid-off workers who had three or more skills were hired by other employers and offered higher salaries soon after they had been laid off. In contrast, most of those who failed to secure jobs had no marketable skills.[59]

In China, however, education is not always a decisive factor. It has long been found that personal connections often play an important role in a job search.[60] This is also an important factor affecting the job search of laid-off workers. As a laid-off worker reported in an interview, "I am now working in a bank as a temporary worker and am responsible for doing the cleaning, boiling tea water, and distributing mail and newspapers. It is really difficult to find jobs these days because of the oversupply of labor. We have to turn to our friends and relatives. I got this job because of my relative who is an official and knows the head of the bank."

Among the 724 people surveyed, personal connections were cited as the most important channel for finding jobs. Among the 341 people (or 47 percent) who found jobs, about 67 percent secured them on their own or with the help of family members, relatives, or friends. A survey of over 1,230 laid-off workers in 17 provinces in 1997 yielded the same finding. Help from one's family and friends was the most important factor in a successful job search. While about 47 percent reported that this network was helpful, about 7.6 percent reported that employment agencies had provided some help.[61]

Alternatives and nonparticipation

Different access to reemployment has an important implication for collective action because it affects the solidarity of workers. Fragmentation caused by mobility is not conducive to group action. For example, Sombart attributed the lack of socialism in the United States to mobility. "The newness of the society, its democratic character, the smaller gap between the employing class and the workers... and many other things, all worked together to let a far from insignificant number of ordinary workers ascend the rungs of the ladder of the capitalist hierarchy to the top or almost to the top."[62] Others also suggest that mobility impacts class solidarity: "As the instability of classes grows, the intensity of class conflict is bound to diminish."[63] Hershatter likewise points out that the high degree of mobility "decreased the likelihood of long-term clandestine organizing" in factories in pre-1949 Tianjin.[64]

Fragmentation of Chinese laid-off workers is a result of mobility or unequal access to alternatives. It implies that workers may resort to individual instead of collective action to pursue their interests. There is "mutual evasion" (*liang bu zhao*) between the firm and laid-off workers—workers do not approach their original firm or the government for help, and the firm does not bother with them, premised on the condition that the firm retains labor relations with workers. As an official explained:

> Laid-off workers consist of two types. Some of them are more capable and are thus more disposed to independence. "Hidden employment" is very common among these people, and some of them have even become "small bosses." They neither approach the government nor turn to the enterprise for help. The other group is less able to become self-dependent due to factors such as age, ability, and health. They are most afraid to terminate their relations with the firms.[65]

"Hidden employment" (*yinxing jiuye*) means that laid-off workers have found jobs and do not report it to the government or the firm and continue to receive subsidies from the RSC or the government. This mode of employment was common in the initial period of reform in the 1990s. A survey of 3,000 laid-off workers in Shanghai in 1999, for example, found that almost 70 percent of 971 people who found jobs did not report their employment status.[66] As "hidden employment" is often temporary, it is clearly not in the interest of laid-off workers to report their employment status and terminate labor relations.[67] But the government criticized such workers as they were no longer entitled to RSC subsidies. Indeed, hidden employment was an important factor in the government's decision to disband RSCs in the early 2000s.[68]

"Hidden employment" is an important alternative to turning to the government or the firm for assistance. Some laid-off workers who secured other jobs did not even return to their firms when requested. As a department manager said in an interview:

> Sometimes when we do not have enough orders, we would ask workers to return home to wait for orders to come in. But time and again, when we have orders, some of them do not come under various pretexts despite repeated phone calls because they have found other jobs.

According to an investigation by the State Institutional Reform Committee in 1997, about 15 percent of the more than 20 million people engaged in trading stocks were laid-off workers. In Shanghai the percentage was as high as 22 percent. For example, when several workers from the same workshop ran into each other at the stock exchange, they asked their former group leader to continue to lead them to wealth in this market. When their factory asked them to return to work, they rejected the request unanimously.[69]

The importance of "hidden employment" and "mutual avoidance," however, should not be exaggerated. "Hidden employment" benefits laid-off workers because it brings extra income and allows them to maintain labor relations. But this is not the case for all. When workers are laid off, not all are certain that they would be able to find jobs, given the tight labor market. Among the 724 laid-off workers surveyed, more than 80 percent reported that they were eager to find jobs after being laid off and more than 84 percent reported that it was difficult or very difficult to find jobs. It took an average of nine months to find a new job.

Although not all laid-off workers were able to find reemployment, the fact that some had, hidden or otherwise, fragments laid-off workers as a group. Collective action is no longer a means to an end for reemployed laid-off workers. As an interviewee reported of his colleague:

> Many of us wanted to find jobs after being laid off. Our subsidy is very limited, especially because our factory usually fails to pay us on time. One of the salesmen in our factory found a job at an insurance company and was assigned the job of selling life insurance. To be true, these companies are learning from

Table 4.2 Laid-off workers' attitudes toward collective appeals in Changchun ($N = 1{,}127$)

Attitudes	Frequency	Employment status (%)	
Sympathetic but no participation	73.8	With jobs	79.1
		Without jobs	72.2
Willing to participate	13.7	With jobs	6.2
		Without jobs	15.9
Not opposing and not participating	9.8	With jobs	—
		Without jobs	—
Opposing	2.7	With jobs	3.3
		Without jobs	2.6
Total	100		

Source: Compiled from Song Baoan and Wang Yushan, "Changchun shi xiangang zhigong de wenjuan diaocha" (Questionnaire About the Laid-Off Workers in Changchu), in Lu Xin, Lu Xueyi, and Shan Tianlun (eds), *1999 nian zhongguo shehui xingshi fenxi yu yuce* (An Analysis and Prediction of Chinese Society), Beijing: Shehui kexue wenxian chubanshe, 1999, pp. 282–83.

capitalists and using any possible means to exploit their workers. The company does not provide a basic salary for people like my colleague who is not a formal employee. His salary depends on the commission earned, which means if he cannot sell any insurance, he will receive nothing. But he has been doing quite well. By last month, we had not received the subsidy for three months. When we decided to demand our subsidies, this person was too preoccupied with his business to come with us although we told him about our plan.

Other research has also found that the availability or absence of alternative jobs may significantly affect laid-off workers' participation in collective action. According to a survey of over 1,120 laid-off workers in Changchun, the capital city of Jilin province, one of the provinces with the most laid-off workers in China, regardless of their job status, most of them were sympathetic to those who appealed to the government for help (see Table 4.2). On the question of whether or not they would participate in an appeal if there were one, the rate of participation was low for both groups (i.e., with and without jobs). However, whereas about 6 percent of those who had jobs intended to participate, about 16 percent of those without jobs desired to do so. This suggests that job status may affect individuals' propensity to take action. While the availability of alternatives prevents participation and coordinated action, the lack of alternatives may bind individuals together. As will be discussed in the following section, individuals without alternatives are more willing to pay the price of taking action, even if their chances for success are slim.

The case of unpaid retired workers

In the early 2000s, a central government official admitted that labor unrest in China in the late 1990s had two most important sources: unpaid retired workers

Table 4.3 Unpaid retired workers (as of September 1997)

Province	People affected	Province	People affected
Heilongjiang	486,639	Anhui	29,099
Jilin	191,000	Qinhai	28,248
Xinjiang	182,300	Guangdong	13,550
Liaoning	169,900	Zhejiang	10,648
Hunan	156,451	Fujian	8,647
Hebei	120,250	Hainan	8,100
Jiangsu	115,000	Ningxia	5,768
Sichuan	110,714	Yunnan	4,500
Shanxi	77,466	Shanghai	2,086
Henan	69,824	Tibet	1,912
Jiangxi	52,545	Guangxi	1,023
Shaanxi	43,729	Chongqin	950
Inner Mongolia	36,503	Beijing	—
Shandong	30,265		
		Total	1,957,117

Source: Adapted from Mo Daquan, *Gongzhi anquanwang* (Establishing the Safety Network), Beijing: Jingji kexue chubanshe, 1998, p. 57.

and unpaid laid-off workers.[70] That the lack of alternatives may drive people to take action has been fully reflected in the case of unpaid retired workers. Economic failure has forced a number of SOEs to suspend the pensions of retired workers, either because they cannot pay the workers directly or because they have failed to pay the insurance for them. Due to the poor performance of SOEs, retirement insurance collected by the state insurance organization decreased in the 1990s. Nationwide, the collection rate decreased from 95.7 percent in 1992 to about 80 percent in 1997.[71] The issue of pension payment is a daunting challenge to Chinese governments at both central and local levels not only because of the inadequate welfare funds accumulated, but also because of the increasing number of retirees. From 1997 to 2001, the number of retirees increased from 25 million to 31 million.[72] In the 1990s, it was a nationwide phenomenon that retired workers did not receive their pensions or did not receive them on time (Table 4.3).

Stories of unpaid and underpaid retired workers abound in the media. A retired female worker of a bankrupt factory stated:

> I do not know where to get the 150 yuan in retirement pension next month. The factory no longer exists, and I do not know who will take care of us in the future. Now what we are most worried about is ill health. For a less serious illness, we cannot afford to buy medicine; for serious ones, we wait for death.[73]

An interviewee recalled the case of his father:

> My father worked in a state factory his whole life. The factory had about 700 employees, but most of them were asked to leave due to its poor performance. As the factory did not join the pooled insurance system, retired

workers received their pensions from the factory. At first, the factory managed to pay retired workers before it paid the other workers. But gradually as it could no longer make any profits, pension payments were suspended. As a last resort, retired people appealed to the government. Sometimes they succeeded in receiving some money, but at other times they did not. The aged usually suffer more because of poor health. In my father's factory, reimbursement for medical expenses has been suspended for almost five years. He even sent gifts to the manager in order to have his medical expenditure reimbursed. Who expected that they would be in such a situation after working their whole lives in a state enterprise?

In Liaoning province in 1991, 272 SOEs owed 29,810 workers 11 million yuan in retirement pensions. In 1997, 3,590 SOEs owed pensions to 471,980 workers. Among the 2.1 million retired workers in this province, about 22.4 percent did not receive their pensions. As loss-making SOEs could no longer provide medical care either, a number of retired workers troubled by both ill health and poverty had to borrow money, sell properties, or even collect garbage to survive.[74] In Shanxi province, a once nationally acclaimed model worker frustrated by his pension suspension wrote a doggerel that became a popular slogan. Retirees in other provinces used it in their actions against the government: "We contributed our youth to the Party, but no one takes care of us when we are old; when we want to turn to our children for help, they have also been laid off."[75]

Unless a retired worker has a wealthy family, his or her retirement pension is the most important or the only source of income. Collective action of unpaid retired workers has been widely reported.[76] For example, in Wuhan, 181 retired factory workers appealed to the government several times because of suspended pension payments. They even applied to the local government to stage a demonstration in 1995. In a mining factory of Heilongjiang province, more than 1,500 retired workers approached the government and its agencies for aid because of the suspension. About 500 held sit-in demonstrations and blocked traffic.[77] In a district of Shenyang, the capital city of Liaoning province, between January and April of 1997, there were 36 cases of collective action directed at the government by 3,250 participants, most of whom were between 60 and 80 years old. Indeed, such events occurred across the whole province. In the first half of 1997, there were several hundred collective appeals to the government by retired workers, with each petition involving 50 or more participants. The total number of participants reached tens of thousands.[78]

Against this background, the Chinese central government has repeatedly demanded that local governments guarantee payment of retirement pensions and subsistence subsidies to laid-off workers. Local governments also recognize seriousness of this issue and have tried hard to solve the problem. In some places, the labor bureau sent its officials to SOEs that failed to pay retirement insurance, and the officials could not return until the SOEs paid the insurance.[79] In one case, in a meeting attended by managers of 410 SOEs in a city that failed to pay pensions, the mayor said, "No matter how many reasons you have for your owing workers pensions, it is inhuman to stop paying retired people. If you have no money, sell your car; if you do not have a car, sell your office building; if you refuse to pay, turn in your 'hat' [i.e., resign]."[80] By 1999, the situation had become so serious that the central government paid the overdue retirement pensions for more than 20 provinces and required local governments to make the payments afterwards.[81]

Conclusion

This chapter discusses the factors that affect the solidarity of laid-off workers by pointing out the importance of an individual's stake in collective action. The impact of the reform of the lifetime employment system on workers has been profound but varied among firms and workers. While statistical analyses presented in Chapter 3 point to a stake-driven participation of Chinese laid-off workers, this chapter substantiates this claim with empirical cases. The reform of SOEs has been gradual, as is the declining performance of these firms. Workers with marketable skills and connections looked for alternative jobs before the layoffs. Depending on their education, skills, and previous occupations, some laid-off workers were more likely to secure jobs than were others. As collective action is a means to an end, those who secured jobs lacked the incentive to participate in collective action.

Yet, there are always a significant number of people who are unable to find work. Indeed, due to a flooded labor market, most people face great competition when looking for work. As noted earlier, in 1997, the reemployment rate of laid-off workers was about 50 percent; it fell to 27 percent in the first half of 1999.[82] This, however, does not mean that laid-off workers will take collective action against the firm or the government. If collective action is viewed as an interaction between prospective participants and an intended target, the overcoming of fragmentation at most solves the problem amongst prospective participants. Whether or not collective action occurs and succeeds also depends on the capacity-based strategies of the party at which the action is directed. Chapters 5 and 6 respectively discusses the polices that firms and the government have adopted to avert or mitigate group action.

5 Management and worker silence

In a reform, the emergence and success of resistance depend not only on the interaction among the individuals affected, but also on their interaction with the reformer. Hence, the capacity, intention, constraints, and strategies of both parties determine the confidence of the defensive party when it considers whether and how to respond. Collective action may fail to occur because the offended lack confidence in their ability to influence the target.[1] Hershatter thus suggests that workers in Tianjin in pre-1949 China took action because there was a "concrete possibility of doing something about the immediate conditions for their working lives."[2] The converse is also true. In explaining the labor quiescence in Germany, Dick Geary suggests that workers' failure to organize may not "denote satisfaction with the status quo, or absence of class consciousness. Both industrial and political passivity may indicate 'a correct assessment of objective possibilities'."[3]

The success of collective action should also be weighed against the costs that may be exacted by the target. For example, Marx once claimed that the proletariat would have nothing but chains to lose if they rose to oppose the capitalist system. Yet, repression may deter action, "when it is a choice between losing their chains or their lives, people will mostly choose to keep their chains, a fact which Marx seems to have overlooked."[4] Similarly, Piven and Cloward point out that workers in the United States often failed to organize protests until the first half of the 1900s largely because of state repression. "Whatever force workers mounted against their bosses, whatever their determination and their unity, they could not withstand the legal and military power of the state, and the power was regularly used against them."[5]

Chinese laid-off workers also base their action on the perceived odds of success and possible costs, which are influenced by the target to which their action is directed. Laid-off workers thus need to consider the power and constraints of their target which is SOEs or local governments. SOEs are targeted because they handle layoffs directly, and the government is chosen because it is involved in reforms or is believed to be able to resolve problems faced by laid-off workers. In their action directed at firms, workers may face two different types of targets: a powerful management and a helpless one. In SOEs that are still able to provide jobs and welfare benefits, the management retains power over workers. The reform of SOEs, while failing to promote efficiency, has granted great autonomy to the management.[6] This autonomy enables the management to exclude workers from decision making and reduces the opportunities for workers to protect their interests *ex ante*. Most actions taken by laid-off workers are thus *ex post* after decisions are made. But powerful management also undermines workers' confidence in *ex post* action. While the structural barrier (i.e., workers' dependence on firms) generally served as a credible deterrent to worker resistance in the pre-reform period, laid-off workers' continued dependence on the firm for welfare insurance remains a barrier to action. Management, however, also faces constraints when dealing with workers. Pressure from higher authorities and other informal constraints may induce the management to be tactical when executing layoffs in order to defuse potential resistance.

Equally important, the lack of collective action directed at firms may also reflect the fact that the management is not able to help workers. In those firms that have very limited financial resources and can hardly survive, laid-off workers may lack the incentive to take action because it is likely to be futile. In this circumstance, they either remain silent or direct their action at the government. This is why, according to my survey, the majority of laid-off workers' collective action was directed at the government rather than at their firms.

Dominance of management

In Chinese SOEs, a number of parties may affect workers' interests—such as the management, the Party organization, the trade union, and the workers' council. Government policies and reform measures have significantly shaped the power structure within SOEs, producing an ineffective Party organization, a persistently weak trade union, and token participation of the workers' council. "In most advanced capitalist countries, enterprises find their discretion in effecting large-scale layoffs curtailed by national legislation, collective agreements, or both."[7] This is not true in China because the trade union and the workers' council not only fail to protect workers' interests *ex ante* but also fail to organize collective action *ex post*.

The Party and management

A possible way of protecting workers' interest is to grant some power to the Party organization (i.e., the Party committee) within SOEs. Yet reform in SOEs has reduced the power of the Party organization and increased that of the management. Over the years until the late 1990s, two major management systems had been adopted in Chinese SOEs—the manager-in-charge under the leadership of the Party committee (MICPC) and the manager responsibility system (MRS).[8] Under the MICPC, the decision-making power resides in the Party committee, whose members include the manager. As the Party secretary heads the committee, this system can be turned into a Party-secretary responsibility system. In the MRS, the decision-making power, at least for administrative and production issues, is wielded by the manager. The reform of SOEs has led to the adoption of the MRS, resulting in increased power of management.[9]

In the early 1980s, the Chinese government began trials of the MRS for the following reasons:

> The labor division in modern enterprises is very delicate, and production is a continual process that entails more qualified technology. Also due to the complexity in coordination, the enterprise must have a unified, strong, and efficient production guidance and management system, and only the manager-responsibility system can meet these requirements.[10]

In 1986, the central government issued a number of policies that formally promoted the MRS and granted SOEs managers decision-making power with respect to important issues, including production, management, finance, and personnel. The profound impact of these measures became more obvious in the 1990s. For example, some surveys found that after the mid-1990s, about 98 percent of managers or chairpersons of the boards of directors personally controlled the financial affairs of their firms. Some appointed relatives as the firms' accountants, paving the way for corruption.[11]

In contrast, the Party committee has been assigned abstract tasks, such as Party affairs and other political work, aiding management with production and management, and supervision of policy implementation. In the late 1980s, the government further expanded the role of manager as director and legal representative with full responsibility for the SOE. He or she should be placed in a central position and function as the "brain."

> The manager and the Party secretary should proceed according to this new regulation and fulfill in cooperation their responsibilities. As to those managers and Party secretaries who fail to meet their job requirements, the authorities concerned should actively but cautiously switch their jobs.[12]

The status of the manager was made official in the Enterprise Law enacted in 1988.

Due to the 1989 Tiananmen incident and obvious decline of the Party status in SOEs, the Party has tried to balance relations between the Party committee and the management. In the 1990s, the Party specified two types of work for the SOE Party organization: (1) the implementation of Party and government policies, laws, and regulations; and (2) recommending, selecting, and sending representatives or managers to manage state assets, and ensuring that these people are "revolutionary, young, knowledgeable, and professional." In practice, however, the manager is selected by higher-level authorities and is not checked by the SOE Party leader. As follow-up national surveys in 1993, 1994, 1997, and 1998 suggested, SOE managers appointed by higher-level authorities accounted for about 90 percent of the total number.[13] As the priority of higher-level authorities has shifted to economic development, managers who make profits win their trust and support. A Party secretary reported what SOE Party secretaries commonly complained about:

> Nowadays, when choosing cadres, their integrity and work style do not receive enough attention. Some higher-level leaders take a biased attitude toward the manager and the Party secretary. They treat the manager as the leader and the Party secretary as a subordinate. They only ask the manager to support and cooperate with the Party secretary, but they do not educate and discipline the former. If the manager has a single merit, their misconduct is overlooked. As long as the firm operates and workers do not take to the streets, the manager is deemed a good cadre; or as long as the manager is not corrupt, nothing is serious. Because of the lack of basic protection, the Party secretary is usually relegated to the position of a "daughter-in-law," but he or she is asked to perform tasks that should be carried out by the "mother-in-law." If there is a tension between the Party and the management, higher-level leaders usually transfer the Party secretary elsewhere rather than investigate the cause. In some small firms, the manager can even remove the Party secretary.[14]

Although the relationship between the Party secretary and the manager varies, the decline in the power of the Party secretary is widespread.[15] According to a survey of almost 10,000 workers in 100 SOEs between 1991 and 1992, workers tended to approach the manager rather than the Party secretary for requests and demands.[16] Some interviewees reported that their Party secretaries now assume marginal responsibilities, such as preparing for government hygiene inspection and implementing the family-planning policy, although they may still receive token respect from the manager.[17] In some SOEs, one person assumes the roles of manager, Party secretary, and in some cases chairperson on the board of directors. This aggregation for roles is usually undertaken to reduce conflict between the Party and management, not to strengthen the Party organization.

The trade union

Trade unions are important organizations for workers in capitalist systems, although their power varies. It is found that two important factors determine the power of a trade union:

> first, the extent to which unions, as a broad national pattern, are integrated into the process of managerial decision making, especially concerning work reorganization; and second, the existence of laws or corporatist bargaining arrangements that regulate firm-level union practice from outside the firm.[18]

In communist systems, neither condition holds. In their 1970 strike, Polish workers cried "Where are the unions? Why aren't they leading the workers?"[19]

Indeed, communist systems are characterized by weak mass associations like trade unions. In the former Soviet Union:

> prior to a take-over, communists inside the trade union movement strive unceasingly and by all means available to generate hostility to the capitalist state. Once in power, with the state now supposedly on the side of workers, the relationship is totally changed. This apparently signifies the trade unions' almost total surrender of their position as independent institutions to promote and defend the workers' interests and welfare.[20]

What happened in the former Soviet Union also holds true in China.[21] Until the early 1950s, the Chinese Communist Party had encouraged the trade union to fight against private business owners. But soon after nationalization, the trade union was deprived of its independence and kept under the control of the Party. The subordination of the trade union was determined in the 1950s after two leaders (i.e., Li Lisan and Lai Ruoyu) of the ACFTU were purged for attempting to establish an independent trade union.[22] Indeed, as early as 1955, in a report to the central government, the ACFTU admitted that "the phenomenon that the trade union demands independence from the Party has largely disappeared. It is now focused on production matters."[23] Consequently, as defined in the trade union charter, the major task of the trade union is to help management fulfill production goals.

Chinese workers have long realized the weakness of trade unions. In the mid-1980s, some workers pointed out that "the trade union should be disbanded or at least reorganized."[24] According to a survey of about 10,000 workers conducted by the ACFTU in 1986, about 60 percent thought that the trade union seldom resolved practical problems faced by workers. Instead, it only collected membership fees and operated like a government organ rather than a workers' organization.[25] Things have not changed much since then. Another nationwide survey of about 10,000 workers in 100 enterprises conducted between 1991 and 1992 showed that about 50 percent did not care about trade union activities, and those with higher education were even less interested. The negative relationship between education and political activism can be attributed to people's recognition of the limited role of trade unions.[26]

While the trade union was subordinate to Party leadership in the pre-reform period, it is subject to management in the reform era, which has undermined its status in a firm. Although trade unions try to advance the economic interests of workers at both the central and local levels,[27] their institutional weaknesses severely limit their effectiveness. In most cases, it is the higher-level trade union that is able to exercise some influence on lower-level firms. At the firm level, the chairperson of the trade union is often recommended or even appointed by management, which often places him or her in a difficult situation when he or she tries to protect workers' interests.

For example, in one factory, the manager retired in 1997, and the higher-level authority sent a new manager to the factory. Not long after the new manager arrived, he began to streamline the departments in the factory, which was not unreasonable. But he proposed to disband the trade union and to merge it with the Department of the Party and Masses Work. The chairperson of the trade union opposed his proposal and pointed out that, according to the Trade Union Law and other regulations, the trade union should be independent and could not be disbanded. The manager was quite angry at the chairperson's objection and said that it was not up to the chairperson to decide whether to keep the trade union. Instead, it would be decided by the votes of factory leaders. The voters failed to pass his proposal, and the trade union was maintained. But the chairperson was eventually removed because of his opposition to the manager. The chairperson recalled:

> Another confrontation between me and the manager was our disagreement on the reform plan of the factory. Last October (1998), our factory adopted the share-holding system, and the factory asked all workers to buy shares. But it was regulated in the reform plan that "As to those who refuse to buy shares, the enterprise has the right to switch their jobs, require them to leave their posts to await re-allocation, or lay them off." I told the manager that this regulation should not be included, as he had promised that shares would be purchased voluntarily. He replied that that policy was not to force workers to buy shares. Several days later, when the workers' assembly discussed the plan, they unanimously agreed to remove the regulation of the compulsory purchase of shares. To help the factory, at my suggestion, the assembly encouraged and mobilized workers to buy shares. In the end, almost all the workers did that, and the factory raised enough funds. I assumed that my conflict with the manager was over, but the manager believed that I was pitting myself against him by amassing the support of workers... I was removed from the office, and the notification was issued by the Party committee of the factory.[28]

Given the weaknesses of the trade union, while workers often complain about its incompetence, staff of the trade union have their own difficulties. The chairperson of a trade union made a bitter complaint in an interview: "People always complain that the trade union does not protect their interests, but few of them have considered the issue of who protects us." Given the limited autonomy of this organization, it is less likely for its people, including the chairperson, to ignore the top leaders within a firm. Some chairpersons of trade unions were laid off even without *ex ante* notification.[29] Hence in the reform period, although the trade union has tried to fight for workers and has become the "most important source" for negative news of high-level governments,[30] it can hardly function as an independent organization or assume the role of organizers for workers' collective action against the management, not to mention against the government.[31]

Workers' council

Another organization set up by the Chinese government to grant power to workers in state or collective enterprises is the workers' council (*zhigong daibiao dahui*).

Reinstituted in 1981, this organization has the right to participate in almost all enterprise decisions. Yet in practice, it often has no final say in important issues. As a matter of fact, as early as in 1986, a nationwide survey of about 10,000 state workers found that only about 30 percent considered the workers' council helpful.[32] Had the council played a more prominent role in the firm, it could have prevented decisions unfavorable to workers from being made or would have lent more legitimacy to the firm's decisions. As the council has no influence on the tenure or promotion of the manager, its supervisory function lacks a power base. In fact, a number of obstacles hinder the workers' council from being effective. First, the selection of council representatives may be controlled by top leaders within a firm. In some SOEs the council is an "elite congress" composed of cadres from different levels. Second, ordinary council representatives often lack knowledge of the firm's operations at higher levels and are unable to make sensible suggestions or criticisms.

Third, the threat of punishment by management is an important reason for the lack of confidence on the part of representatives. From the workers' perspective, participating in the affairs of the firm would not only consume time, but also give the manager the impression that they were preoccupied with "irrelevant" tasks. This may lead to punishment, such as a bonus reduction, or worse, layoff. They may even be regarded as troublemakers. In contrast, obedient workers usually receive better treatment from leaders at various levels. Some workers lose their jobs because of active participation on the workers' council. For example, a factory worker who often made suggestions to management was elected to the workers' council. When the factory began layoffs, a number of leaders, without *ex ante* discussion, decided that this person should be among the first to be laid off, though he was a capable worker. The worker was so angry that he appealed to the labor arbitration department of the city, but in vain.[33] Indeed, many workers are aware of the fact that a considerable number of supervisory organizations in SOEs—including the Party committee, the discipline committee, the trade union, the inspection department, and the auditing department—fail to discipline SOE leaders. How can workers make a difference? Worse still, the measures aimed to speed up the reform of SOEs made by the central government in 1999 further weakened the status of the workers' council, giving workers the right to assess the performance of their leaders but no power to remove them.[34]

Workers' councils prevented large-scale layoffs in some post-communist countries like Poland because SOE directors' plans for layoffs needed their approval.[35] This is not the case in China. Reform plans such as bankruptcy, merger, privatization, and layoffs are commonly carried out without the approval of the workers' council. Yet, despite its weak position, workers in China still look to the council to protect their interests. The reform period has seen a number of attempts by workers to prevent undesirable reform measures on grounds that the reform plan has not been approved by the workers' council.[36] But local governments may claim that SOEs belong to the state, so workers are not the legal owners and their approval is unnecessary. Thus, more often than not, workers' action fails.[37]

Workers' *ex ante* resistance

The weak organizations in Chinese SOEs allow management to assume much authority over workers, and the situation is likely to continue as reform proceeds. A profound implication of management power is that workers' collective action remains difficult due to the persistence of the structural barrier, namely, workers' dependence on the firm. This has shaped workers' behavior since reform began in the 1980s. Workers' participation in the 1989 Tiananmen incident pointed to the strong influence of enterprise authority. While factory leaders' permission or support encouraged worker participation in some firms, repressive enterprise authority curbed participation.[38] The credible threat of punishment remains. A city trade union in Shaanxi province came to this conclusion after investigating scores of public firms in the late 1990s:

> Most production workers would at most complain about their sufferings when their interests were encroached on by the management. If asked to take the lead to appeal to the authorities concerned, most were very likely to refuse. Some said that they had never taken the lead, nor did they plan to. More people believed that if action reaped success, it would be enjoyed by all; but if it failed, only those who took the initiative would be punished. For this reason, it was best to be like everyone else. Although there might be a few workers who wanted to organize their colleagues to appeal to higher-level authorities, they worried that their action would be regarded as "organizing riots," which is a crime. The prevailing attitude thus was "as everyone else wants to avoid offending the leaders, why should I take the initiative?"[39]

To some extent, the government creates this unfavorable situation for workers. Because of political risks, the government is unlikely to allow the formation of an independent trade union. As long as the government depends on the management for the performance of SOEs, it is reluctant to reduce management power. As a result, workers remain in a weak position in relation to management.[40] In a survey of both blue- and white-collar workers in the machinery-manufacturing industry in 1996, about 80 percent indicated that they were not "masters of their firms" or not "masters" with true power.[41] A similar situation has also occurred in post-communist Russia. "The disintegration of the administrative-command system of economic management and the process of de-statization and privatization removed the administrative constraints on management from above so that every enterprise director became a little Tsar in his own kingdom."[42] Consequently, "today even the most modest assertion of the workers' rights and interests makes the protester liable to disciplinary action and dismissal, with much of the legal protection enjoyed by workers under the old regime having been removed."[43]

The power of management thus has significant implications for worker resistance in China. A more effective way to protect one's interests is to prevent unfavorable decisions from being made and carried out. But as a result of workers' weak position, *ex ante* preventive action is less possible. The following example reported by my interviewees shows how dependence on the firm has undermined worker resistance to reform measures that endanger their vital interests, regardless of the number of prospective victims. It also reveals some of the conditions for worker resistance. In 1985, the manager of a state factory with more than five thousand workers triumphed in a power struggle with the Party secretary, forced the latter to transfer, and took the post of Party secretary from 1985 to 1995. He made a series of bad decisions that led to increased losses for the factory. In 1995, he decided to sell almost two-thirds of the factory's land to a real estate company without notifying the workers' council. He announced the sale at a meeting attended by factory cadres. Most factory cadres opposed the decision because loss of the factory land could mean the end of the enterprise and the jobs of thousands of workers. But none of them was bold or powerful enough to prevent the sale. A department manager recalled, "The manager responsibility system means that the manager decides all. No one has the courage to oppose him." This was even more true for average workers. Therefore, no action was taken and one-third of the land was sold.

Things changed when the factory manager was transferred and the former Party secretary returned as manager. This new manager opposed the sale either because he wanted to show opposition to his old rival or because he did not think it was a good deal. When the real-estate company failed to pay on time, the new manager deliberately and subtly made his position known. Encouraged, workers began to build a wall to protect the remaining land. Six of them organized a group voluntarily to watch the wall during the night, in case the real-estate company came to pull down the wall and factory houses. One night, around 12 o'clock, over 50 people hired by the real-estate company arrived at the factory with a bulldozer to pull down the wall and factory houses. When the workers on duty found those intruders, they rang a bell and workers living nearby rushed to the factory. Some workers argued with the people from the real-estate company and a fight broke out. The people hired by the real-estate company were well prepared—they brought sticks with them—and the factory workers were at first in a defensive position. One worker suffered a serious head injury and was sent to a hospital immediately. When more workers arrived, the people from the real estate company became afraid and ran away.

The workers decided to attack the real-estate company and hold a demonstration in the morning. When the local government learned of the news, it commanded the hospital to save the life of the injured worker at all expense and dispatched police to block the factory. To calm the workers, the government declared that the factory could keep the remaining land and the real-estate company had to back down. The workers took action and succeeded because with the support of the factory manager, they did not think that there was a great risk involved. As one worker recalled, "We all wanted to preserve our factory. But if the factory leader wanted to sell the land, nobody would dare openly oppose it. As the new manager opposed the deal, we had nothing to fear."

Management and workers' *ex post* resistance

Concentration of power in the hands of management not only prevents or discourages workers' collective action *ex ante*, but also presents an obstacle to collective action *ex post*. Workers' dependence on the firm is based on the fact that the firm is able to provide jobs and other benefits. In theory, layoffs bring an end to the provision of many welfare benefits, thereby rendering the threat of undesirable job assignments, discriminatory benefit distribution, and demotion meaningless to laid-off workers. Actions taken against management would carry less risk and should therefore increase.[44] But this is only part of the story. If the firm remains in operation, management controls the resources that workers need, and despite layoffs, most laid-off workers are unwilling to sever labor relations with their firms (see Chapter 2).

However, firms do not need laid-off workers, and the latter possess little leverage over firms. They are in a situation similar to that of workers in a market economy that is doing poorly.

> Defensive strikes or riots sometimes erupted during depressions, but they usually had little effect. Not only did employers find it easier to resist strikes when trade was slow and there was less to be lost by halting production, but with jobs scarce, workers were forced to undersell each other in the scramble for employment.[45]

Given its power, the management in Chinese SOEs can curtail worker resistance or shorten its life span. A department manager reported how he dealt with belligerent workers:

> When the names of the 71 workers to be laid off in the department were made known, almost all of them came to argue with me, trying to persuade me to reverse the decision. One of them presented a document from the local government which regulated that we did not have the right to fire workers. I said the directive was too old to be applicable. Moreover, the decision for the layoffs was not made by me since I was newly appointed. If any of them could not accept this arrangement, he or she should approach factory leaders. Finally, I warned them that if they did not accept the decision and continued arguing with me, they would not be given the option of returning to the factory when it improved its performance in the future. Gradually, most workers realized that they would not be able to change the decision and had to seek other solutions on their own. But there were a few exceptions. Four people were particularly aggressive as they had difficulty finding new jobs. Their common claim was that "I will go to your home for food, and I will send my parents to your home because I cannot provide them food." A forty-nine-year-old worker was so agitated that he wanted to beat me up. He tore my shirt and called me an idiot in public. I was so angry that I gave the general manager a phone call and said, "I quit my management job now." Then I turned to the worker, "I am no longer

a cadre now. As a worker, I have the same right to beat you up." I told him to settle the issue with a fight at the top of the building.

When we got there, the worker was no longer that aggressive. At first he argued with me and then tried to persuade me by giving reasons that his family suffered economic problems. But I did not speak and kept smoking. While he talked for half a day, I finished a pack of cigarettes. Finally, I warned him that I would not be a leader once outside the factory. If he dared to go to my home, I would not bear any responsibility if he was beaten to death. I also told the accountant to stop paying the worker his salary until he apologized to me and bought me a new shirt. That guy gave up finally and did what I asked. After all, he needed me, not the other way around. But I also felt sorry for these laid-off workers. This worker's wife and I were classmates.[46]

The power of management also enables it to reject workers' demands to maintain the credibility of its reform measures. The experience of a woman lathe operator reported by my interviewees serves as an example. In the late 1980s, this worker lost three fingers from her left hand while working. At that time the company was competing for the title of "Model Work Unit" and promised that if she kept quiet about the incident, the company would provide her with a livelihood for the rest of her life. This worker agreed. But in 1995, when the factory began to lose money, this woman, like the rest of the 400 workers, was sent home. Carrying the promise of the company on a crumpled piece of paper, she approached company leaders and reasoned with them. But the company leaders refused to give her another job. Despite this woman's many efforts, including approaching various government departments, the company denied her request because the leaders were worried that if they gave her a job, others would make similar requests citing various "special" reasons. Although some people in the general office of the company were very sympathetic to this worker, they could do little for her. As a cadre admitted, "Each time she presented the crumpled piece of paper of the company's promise, we really felt very sorry for her. But we could do nothing except give her some money out of our own pockets."

Hence, in some cases, although there are a significant number of laid-off workers, many are discouraged from taking action. As a worker admitted, "I did not approach enterprise leaders because I did not think that they would accept my demands. There were so many laid-off workers in our enterprise, and the leaders had no reason to accept my request and not that of others." In some firms, layoffs were carried out gradually not merely to adjust to production needs but also to reduce the risk of resistance in the future. As the department manager who laid off 71 workers reported, after the layoffs in his department, the factory began to lay off workers in other departments. Although the layoff rate reached one-third of the factory, collective action against factory authority was rare. In his words, "workers have become more accustomed to it now."

The powerful position of management makes it possible to adopt a strategy of divide-and-reform. Layoffs are widespread, but they are not a problem for all workers within an enterprise. Sequential and proportion-based layoffs often produce fragmentation, which, as discussed in Chapter 4, is a hurdle to collective action.[47] Cooperation between those laid off and those still employed is difficult not only because the two groups do not share interests but also because the participation of a non-laid-off worker carries high risks. As a manager stated:

> Those who are not laid off would at most talk to the management personnel on behalf of a particular person who may be a relative or close friend. But even this does not happen often. Workers understand that the decisions made by the higher-level manager are less likely to be reversed because of their individual opinion. They are less likely to push too much because it is not in their interest to offend the leaders in the enterprise. It is easy for the manager to deal with these people. When pushed too hard, we can simply say, "If you do not want him to leave, he can stay, but you must leave." In my workshop, we have laid off more than 40 people, none of those who remained talked to me about their colleagues. Indeed, workers are easier to manage these days.[48]

When collective resistance is difficult, laid-off workers may resort to individual efforts. In order not to be laid off, some workers follow enterprise leaders around all the time until their requests are accepted, others resort to threats, and still others turn to those who have connections with enterprise leaders for help. For example, a manager reported that when they intended to reshuffle the personnel of his company, a worker tried to keep his position by asking at least 15 cadres in and outside the company to talk to the manager on his behalf, which made it impossible for him to refuse.[49] Those without such resources might appeal to sympathy. For example, some people took their children to the homes of enterprise leaders to profess their difficulties and had their children kneel before the leaders until their requests were granted.[50]

Constraints and management tactics

Although the management of Chinese SOEs is in a much stronger position than are the workers, it faces informal and formal constraints. These constraints, though limited, may create opportunities for worker resistance and make it difficult for management to ignore their concerns. Consequently, management has to be tactful by employing appropriate measures to reduce resistance to reform.

Institutional arrangements and constraints

As most managers in SOEs are appointed by the government or its departments, the most significant constraint on managers is from higher-level authorities. Unconstrained and incompetent managers are not what the government needs. The Chinese government has removed unqualified SOE managers with the participation of workers or their representatives. Between 1997 and 1998, the Chinese government conducted a nationwide inspection of leadership in 115,100 SOEs.[51] As a result, 44,000 leadership groups (*lingdao banzi*) were restructured, and 31,000 of the 86,000 cadres were demoted or removed from their posts.[52] Similar to peasants' reports of village cadres' behavior during inspections by higher-level officials during the Maoist period,[53] workers' opinions receive attention and can matter in the above-mentioned inspections, although they are not conducted frequently.

Another constraint on managers arises from the power structure within SOEs. During the 1990s, SOE leadership often consisted of a general manager, a Party secretary, a number of deputy managers, a general accountant, a general engineer, and the chairperson of the trade union. Sometimes the general manager also functioned as Party secretary. In larger firms, the selection of leaders were not controlled by the general manager. If other leaders like the Party secretary or deputy managers had good connections with higher-level officials, the general manager was not in a position to remove them from their posts. A split or power struggle in the leadership might have provided opportunities for workers to take action. This was especially true when leaders were arrogant and unsympathetic to workers. For example, the dismissal of a corrupt manager of a city factory caught the attention of the provincial government in Anhui province. The manager was removed because he had been unsympathetic to workers and had personal conflicts with the Party secretary. This tyrannical manager had assumed absolute power in the factory and appointed his loyal followers to important posts. He even claimed, "If I want to fix a person, three minutes would be enough." But one day, after a public confrontation with the Party secretary, more than 20 young workers, who could no longer tolerate the manager's arrogance and corruption, went into his office, forced him to turn over the key of the factory car, and drove him out of the factory.[54] Hence, enterprise leaders have to think twice before carrying out arbitrary reforms when they realize that opponents within the firm may mobilize workers to take action.

Other informal constraints

Formal constraints on managers are relatively few as evidenced by their rampant corruption. But there are some informal constraints that more or less compel managers to attend to the needs of workers. First, some managers still believe that it is their responsibility to provide jobs and welfare benefits to workers. They think that their priority is to guarantee that their workers "have something to eat" (*you fan zhi*).[55] Second, despite the reform of SOEs, patron–client relations or personal connections persist. Some of my interviewees reported that their workshop director withheld information on the rate of wastage from the top manager. The factory regulated that if the rate of wastage exceeded a certain level, workers would not receive their salaries. By lying, the workshop director helped workers receive their salaries. As a department manager admitted in an interview, "In most cases, the policy on layoffs is determined by top leaders. If they tell us to lay off two to eight workers, I believe that no lower-level managers would lay off more than two."

Third, enterprise leaders face potential resistance or even retaliation. Individual threats to or attacks on the managers of SOEs have never stopped. A nationwide survey in 1995 revealed that almost 50 percent of SOE managers were once threatened or injured by their workers, and over 28 percent had been threatened or injured at least three times.[56] In Hubei province, for instance, three SOE managers were killed by workers in the first half of 2001, after the adoption of reform measures like layoffs.[57] There is a phenomenon of "tough workers" in SOEs, who have a reputation for aggressively protecting their interests and resorting to violence. In most cases, enterprise leaders do not lay off such workers unless the whole workshop or enterprise is closed. Yet, the number of tough workers is usually very small. In a factory of about 700–800 people, there might be four or five, according to some interviewees. A manager interviewed thus gave reasons for his unwillingness to lay off workers:

> It is not easy for people to find jobs. If you lay off a person, you may force him into a dire economic plight. After all, I am not a capitalist. Laying off workers may invite resistance. Sometimes we encounter a dilemma as we are afraid of laying off tough and belligerent workers but are unwilling to lay off those honest ones.

These constraints have also been reflected in the labor reform discussed in the next section.

Optimal combination of labor

Despite the huge number of redundant workers in Chinese SOEs, serious efforts to streamline the workforce did not begin until the late 1980s. When making reform plans for the central government in 1985, some people proposed that the government reduce the number of state workers by a third. This suggestion was rejected by the then premier Zhao Ziyang, because he was worried about the social instability that might arise from worker resistance. At that time he was positioning himself for promotion to General Party Secretary.[58] Hence, reform was postponed until the late 1980s, but still it failed. In the late 1980s, the government implemented a policy called "Optimal Combination of Labor" to reduce the number of redundant workers in SOEs.[59] This measure not only was strongly opposed by workers but was also rejected by some managers. In one city, for example, the industrial bureau held a meeting attended by managers to discuss the progress of this reform. Three managers cried at the meeting, and another eight were willing to resign rather than continue implementing the reform. One manager said:

> If you lay off a person, you actually deprive him of his source of livelihood. Our factory was established in the 1970s, and many of us joined the factory at the same time. Now, they all have families to support. Who can I lay off?[60]

The government had the same concerns. In some localities, almost all firms that adopted this policy were required to "do whatever they could to assign a job to each worker."[61]

Expectations of the normative role of the firm and the government and the lack of acceptable alternatives resulted in strong worker resistance. Anticipating the resistance, some firms adopted a "3 percent" policy under which they would lay off at most 3 percent of redundant workers to limit the number of troublemakers. But this policy turned out to be a mistake. As the number of workers targeted for layoffs was rather limited, most workers took individual action, including threats and physical attacks, to deal with managers.

In Beijing, 1,600 SOEs implemented the Optimal Combination of Labor policy, which led to the layoffs of over 10,000 workers. Many workers made anonymous calls threatening factory leaders, wrote them threatening letters, cursed them, and even beat or tried to kill them. Some managers installed secret alarm systems in their offices or homes, others armed themselves with batons, and still others hired bodyguards. Many managers asked the public security organizations for help. The Beijing Public Security Bureau dispatched the names of managers who needed help to its branches, ordering them to protect these managers. Although it is difficult to assess the effect of these threats on policy making, the outcome was that almost all 10,000 workers were reallocated jobs in the end.[62] Similar events occurred in many other localities. The Ministry of Public Security had to issue a directive requiring the public security organizations at all levels to cooperate with security departments of SOEs to ensure the safety of managers.[63] "For the sake of the safety, the government once had to allow major leaders of enterprises to bring pistols or electric butts along for self defense."[64] As a manager recalled during an interview:

> At that time, the society could not accept this idea, and workers usually could not find good jobs after being laid off. The resistance was tremendous. Many workers simply did not believe that the enterprise could do this to them. Our factory re-allocated almost all the laid-off workers, and some of them even got jobs better than their previous ones. In one of our departments, a woman was so incompetent that she was even not up to the work of a gatekeeper. But she had three children to feed (apparently she violated the family planning policy), and we simply could not lay her off. Other workers even threatened to commit suicide. Another woman brought two bottles of insecticide to the office and told the department manager that if she were laid off, she would drink one bottle of the insecticide and leave the other for the manager. What could you do with such people?

By the end of 1988, over 36,570 SOEs with about 3.35 million workers adopted the Optimal Combination of Labor, and 847,000 workers were laid off. The policy of "reallocating workers within enterprises is the major approach, supplemented by self-employment and social help" was adopted. Under this policy, about 79 percent of laid-off workers were assigned new jobs by their firms. Due to the costly internal rehiring, many SOEs did not carry out this reform. On average, the number of SOEs that adopted it only accounted for 14 percent of the total number of enterprises in their respective sectors.[65]

Criteria for layoffs

Because of both informal and formal constraints, management has tried to adopt appropriate measures to reduce resistance when carrying out layoffs in the recent reform. An important method is to choose less controversial or "open and fair" criteria for layoffs in order to dispel workers' motivation for resistance.[66] Commonly used criteria include age, performance, and production needs. To be sure, the effectiveness of using fair criteria should not be overstated, not only because those who fail to meet the criteria may still resist but also because it is not easy to find fair criteria that are acceptable to all.

Among the 724 people I surveyed, about 48 percent reported that layoffs in their firms were based on age, the most frequently used method indicated in the survey.[67] Usually, the firm sets different age criteria for men and women, and different firms may use different standards. For example, the cutoff age might be 50 for men, and 45 for women, or 45 for men and 40 for women.[68] Management believes the age criterion to be less controversial. One department manager commented:

> Although layoffs have become common nowadays, it does not necessarily mean that they are easy. This is indeed a most difficult problem faced by managers. As it is now difficult to find jobs, very few people want to be laid off. The criterion used in large-scale layoffs must be objective; otherwise it will give workers a good reason for disputes with the manager. For this reason, we usually use age as the guiding principle and may make limited modifications to attend to the special needs of both the enterprise and some workers. Although this criterion may not remove all the obstacles in the process, it is the best way we have. Once the criterion is used for the first time, people tend to become accustomed to it later.[69]

As the criterion of age usually forces more qualified workers such as technicians to leave, some SOEs base layoffs on performance. Because worker performance in the production line can be measured and recorded, those who perform poorly are the first to be laid off. Still other SOEs may lay off younger workers and retain older ones based on the rationale that young people are more likely to find new jobs.[70]

Compared with the criteria mentioned above, a rotated layoff is a much more effective way to reduce resistance. Due to the shortage of orders, some enterprises lay off workers in rotation. For example, in one factory, as reported by an interviewee, workers came to work every other month, receiving full salary when they worked and 75 percent of their salary when they did not. As the interests of each worker were accommodated, no one stirred up trouble for management. In a county of Hunan province, 23 enterprises adopted this system by 1999.[71] But this method can be adopted only in those firms whose workers are almost equally qualified in terms of their skills and technical knowledge. This is the most important reason for the limited application of this method.

Still other firms use multiple criteria in layoffs, such as early retirement, illness-based retirement or leave, and layoffs with and without labor relations maintained. Intended or not, the adoption of such measures helps to defuse collective action because laid-off workers are affected differently in terms of the amount of subsidies they receive from the firm. Those who receive more compensation may not have the same demands as those who receive less. The use of multiple criteria also reflects the management's intention to accommodate the needs of workers in a selective way, with preferential treatment granted to certain groups, like senior workers.[72]

It should also be pointed out that not all managers employ open and fair criteria. Cadres are often not targeted for layoffs unless the whole enterprise is failing, the whole workshop is closed, or if they offend the leaders. Among the 724 people surveyed, about 6.8 percent were enterprise cadres, most of whom were managers at the production group level. Cadres are less likely to be laid off not only because they have connections with higher-level enterprise leaders, but also because they are more able to organize resistance.[73]

Personal connections or family background is another important and implicit, but sometimes explicit, criterion for layoffs. For example, a company required a department to lay off one of its five employees, including the department head, two young men, a young woman, and a middle-aged woman close to the age of early retirement. Although the young woman was the only one with a college education, she was laid off. The reason given was that the department believed that the two young men could take on difficult work. The middle-aged woman was the wife of a deputy manager in the company and was protected from retrenchment. Hence, the young woman was the only choice left for the department manager.[74] In other cases, some managers use layoffs as a means of punishment or retaliation, and others use them to secure loyal networks and reinforce their power base.[75]

Indeed, layoffs based on personal connections often fuel the discontent of laid-off workers. A survey by a provincial youth league found that almost 20 percent of laid-off workers reported that they were laid off not because they were incapable but because they did not have good personal connections with their leaders.[76] This is especially true when the layoff is small and there is no single criterion implemented across departments. Then, decisions are made at the discretion of lower-level managers. One laid-off worker voiced his resentment:

> There is nothing wrong with layoffs; otherwise the contribution-based distribution of benefits can hardly be achieved. But the question is who should be laid off. In today's society, who can ignore personal connections and power? If one does not have such connections or power, she should not expect to secure her job and will have to look for alternative employment as soon as possible. As to approaching the authorities for an explanation of the criteria for layoffs, it amounts to lighting a candle for the blind—an absolute waste. There is no doubt that one will receive nothing from taking such action.[77]

Relations-based layoffs can be a form of the patron–client relationship between managers and supporters or followers. The implications of the persistence of this relationship are multifold. First, as in the pre-reform period, the patron–client network "provides a structural barrier to concerted worker resistance" in SOEs.[78] Second, this system discourages group solidarity. There are two dimensions of labor relations within a firm: workers versus management (i.e., us versus them) and the individual worker versus the group (i.e., me versus us). As noted in Chapter 4, the divergence or fragmentation of interests influences individuals' attitudes toward collective action. The patron–client relationship is an effective way to serve the individual worker's interests, precluding the necessity of collective action. Hence, although workers share the same identity, they may not share the same situation. In other words, strategic choices benefit some individuals but undermine the "catnet" of a group.

Management as a helpless patron

In November 2000, the Oil Bureau of Daqing in Heilongjiang province arranged for 50,000 workers to receive severance packages based on the number of years served. On average, each laid-off worker received about over 78,000 yuan, an exceptionally generous compensation for laid-off workers in China today, which was accepted by the workers.[79] A year later, workers found that those who stayed were earning much more. They complained that the severance pay was not as good as originally thought, "The managers are getting huge packages and we are getting nothing." On March 1, 2002 the Bureau announced it would stop paying heating bills and insurance premiums for those who had received severance packages, and workers protested. They surrounded the Bureau and demanded that company executives renegotiate their early retirement packages to include some benefits that current employees enjoyed. After weeks of protests, the company rescinded a large increase in fees that severed workers had to pay to keep their medical and old-age insurance.[80]

Workers in Daqing protested not for minimum but for maximum severance pay because they believed that the Oil Bureau and the company had the financial resources to accommodate their demands. This is not common among laid-off workers in that they often face a helpless management. As a worker reported, "In 1998, we were told to go home and were paid 180 yuan per month as the factory ceased production. A few months later, the subsidy was stopped and we went to the factory but could not even find the manager."[81] In those circumstances, laid-off workers have two options. First, they turn to the government for help. According to my survey of 724 laid-off workers, almost 80 percent of collective action was targeted at the local government. Other things being equal, the choice of target is significantly associated with the layoff rate in a firm. The larger the layoff rate, the more likely that workers will target the government.[82] Approaching the government is not unique to Chinese workers. In the late 1980s, Soviet miners targeted the government for the same reason. As Filtzer writes, "Only by going outside...and dealing directly with the government could the miners hope for any success."[83]

Second, workers commonly become self-dependent because the target is not helpful regardless of whether any action is taken. As a woman worker of a tree farm recalled:

> By 1994, I had no work to do and received 70 percent of my salary. My husband sometimes had temporary work. We managed to make ends meet. By 1995, the tree farm could no longer operate because most usable trees had

been cut down. The farm could not support the over 1,000 workers, and we were sent home to wait for reallocation and paid 60 percent of our salary. But even this amount was not paid for a year, and we barely had enough money for food. We approached the leaders of the farm and each was paid 200 yuan, an amount hardly enough for the Spring Festival. Those who had waited at home for reallocation realized that they could not depend on the farm and had to be self-dependent. After the Spring Festival, each sought help from relatives and friends and went to the large cities like Harbin and Shenyang to look for work.[84]

If action is directed at leaders in such firms, it is usually short-lived. A reemployed worker reported his experience in an interview. After his factory repeatedly ceased production, their subsidies were often delayed. Workers often approached the factory authority for overdue subsidies and even jobs. But things soon changed. In June 1997, some workers, including the interviewee, went to the factory for the subsidy. The factory was quiet, and only a few workers were there, taking care of the machines. When they learned that a deputy manager decided to leave to run a private business, they realized that the factory was winding up. The manager was going to leave not because he had better opportunities in a private business but because the factory could not survive. Too many laid-off workers were engaged in private businesses, and most fared poorly because of intense competition. The factory was on the verge of bankruptcy for quite a long time, and the manager could have left earlier had he had a better opportunity. Some workers then approached the government for help, but others, including the interviewee, did not. They thought that although the government might provide some temporary help (*jiu ji*), it could not alleviate their poverty (*bu jiu qiong*). They became self-reliant.

Similarly, a deputy shop-floor manager in a failing company reported her story of reemployment after fruitless appeals to her factory manager. After the 1995 Spring Festival, it was rumored that her factory would go bankrupt. A work group then came to the factory to check the assets and concluded that its debts had surpassed the value of its assets. More than 500 workers were uncertain about the future. Those who usually violated labor discipline by coming to the factory late and leaving it early began to follow rules strictly. But no matter how workers performed, the factory was declared bankrupt. Workers were paid 60 percent of their salaries for six months and 120-yuan unemployment insurance after that. At that time, this cadre was 36 years old. She recalled:

> At that time, my skill was perfect. My husband could not accept my being laid off. He said I was a middle-level cadre and should not be as easily laid off as the average worker. He told me to ask the manager for a job. I did go to the manager, but the sorrowful-looking manager said, "What is the point of distinguishing between workers and cadres now? The factory is gone. You and I are common people. You ask me to give you a job, who helps me?" I really felt sorry for the manager. In other profitable enterprises, managers drive

imported cars; in our factory that had never made any profit, the manager could only use a broken Shanghai-made car. He had been forced to hide himself from workers who always asked him to reimburse medical expenses. He actually had not led a peaceful life for a single day. It might be better not to be a manager in such a factory. I thought it through and became self-reliant.[85]

Managers and workers in such SOEs may feel betrayed and abandoned by the government. SOEs differ not only in their initial resource endowment allocated by the government but also in the policy support they receive. It is not surprising that some fare better than others upon entering the market economy. Hence, dissatisfaction with the state on the part of workers and managers is not difficult to understand. Some enterprise leaders permitted or even encouraged workers to protest against the government. For example, when faced with workers who resented that the factory had not taken care of them, a factory leader replied, "The state has not taken care of our factory, and the factory is unable to take the responsibility for you. If you have the courage, you should approach the city government for a solution."[86]

For this reason, management and workers find themselves facing the same situation, which may smooth over the process of reform. Some laid-off workers explained why they remained silent when their interests were ignored:

> Because the enterprise is in a difficult phase of reform now, we can understand the situation faced by leaders. We should work together with them rather than fight against them merely for our immediate interests. As long as the enterprise survives, it may perform better in the future, and everything will be fine. I believe we will be compensated for our current sacrifice by then.[87]

Therefore, expected future benefits are often crucial to consensus building. For example, in Heilongjiang province in 1998, the Acheng Sugar Factory, which was established in 1905, declared bankruptcy, and its 4,490 workers witnessed the closure of their factory. Another nearby sugar factory, called Peace Sugar Factory, was also plagued by losses—its debt–asset ratio was as high as 146 percent. When Acheng went bankrupt, the Peace Factory organized its cadres and worker representatives to visit Acheng. The miserable situation faced by the Acheng workers shocked these visitors deeply. In order to promote efficiency, the Peace Factory decided to lay off 1,000 of its 3,500 workers. Unexpectedly, the layoffs went smoothly. As a vice manager stated, "Laid-off workers realize that if they are still bound together with those who stay, the outcome is that nobody would survive in the end." In other words, all of them would face the same fate as their counterparts in Acheng.[88] Hence, common interest makes consensus building and reform possible in such firms.

Conclusion

As the collective action of laid-off workers is often goal oriented and has a clear target, the power of and the constraints on the target factor into their cost–benefit calculations and affect their confidence in taking action. Within the firm, workers face two types of target: a powerful management and a helpless management. Collective action directed at powerful management is costly when workers still depend on the enterprise for subsidies. Due to the reform of SOEs in China, management dominates enterprise affairs and holds decision-making power with respect to all important issues. It thereby has the autonomy to reduce and prevent worker resistance through various measures. First, management may mete out credible punishment to those who foment resistance. In those firms that are able to provide subsidies to laid-off workers, continued labor relations create a structural barrier to action. Second, management may adopt measures that fragment workers by creating differences in their interests, and thus reduce the scale of collective action or even prevent it. Specifically, various criteria adopted by the management in layoffs effectively divide and rule workers by making cooperation among potential laid-off workers and that between laid-off workers and those still employed less possible.

The case of Chinese laid-off workers also suggests that individual behavior is shaped by the feasibility of the choices confronting them.[89] Sometimes collective action is less likely not because the management is too powerful but because it is helpless. A firm barely surviving is unable to provide help regardless of whether or not laid-off workers take action. Therefore, if management can convince workers that it is not in a position to solve their problems, workers either remain silent or direct their action at the government. When targeting the government, as detailed in the Chapter 6, Chinese workers face many hurdles, because government policies impose different costs on those who participate in collective action.

6 The government and the prevention of worker resistance

Chinese laid-off workers direct their action not only at their firms but also at the government, usually at the local level. Like their counterparts in other transitional economies, Chinese workers target the government because the government is directly involved in reforms or is believed to be able to address their problems.[1] Facing worker resistance, the Chinese government is not passive and has adopted several measures that have significantly abated resistance from workers, thereby making it possible to carry out reform while maintaining social stability. From 1995 to 1999, the number of industrial SOEs decreased by more than 48 percent,[2] which has inevitably increased layoffs and worker resistance. Yet, by the early 2000s, the Chinese government showed "scant signs of flinching from its programme of industrial reform."[3] Reform measures like layoffs, privatization, and closure have been further extended to large SOEs. From the early 2000s, local governments began to stop establishing RSCs and required laid-off workers to terminate labor relations with their firms and to enter the labor market directly, although the many problems with workers' welfare and reemployment as detailed in Chapter 2 remain.[4]

While state capacity has been fundamental to continued economic reform, it does not amount to repression as far as the Chinese government's policies toward laid-off workers are concerned. The government reduces or prevents resistance largely by employing multiple measures to build up its credibility of withdrawing its economic commitment to most SOEs and their workers, although repressive measures have also been adopted to deal with worker leaders. Specifically, the government has tried to dispel workers' motivation for resistance by building consensus with them or blaming workers for their problems, selectively punished organizers, and exercised patience when confronted by laid-off workers. By examining the interaction between the government and workers, this chapter shows that government strategies increase workers' perceived costs of action and undermine their confidence, thereby making the continuation of reform possible.

Targeting the government

During the reform period, workers target the government for a number of reasons. First, as discussed earlier, because of the lack of an adequate welfare system and the inability of some firms to provide help, unpaid or underpaid laid-off workers have to approach the government if they take action. Second, the government, especially at the local level, is directly involved in reforms, including bankruptcy and privatization, that result in layoffs. As the government owns SOEs, its approval is the precondition for bankruptcy, which makes it a natural target of workers' action.[5] Moreover, a bankrupt firm ceases to exist or loses its ability to solve problems, and workers can direct action only at the government. Similarly, local governments play an important role in privatization by making policies or reform plans for firms.[6] Two forms of privatization have affected workers most severely: (1) selling the firm to an individual or individuals (or to foreigners) and (2) selling it to the employees (i.e., the employee share-holding system). If the firm is sold to one or a few persons, many have to leave. The share-holding system may not be in the interests of workers either. Many workers simply lack confidence in their failing firms and have no incentive to invest. Some local governments require workers to buy shares in order to keep their jobs. A 1988 survey of 640 SOEs in four provinces suggested that almost 63 percent had forced workers to buy shares. Among these firms, about 25 percent admitted that it was the decision of their local governments.[7]

Third, management–labor conflicts cause workers to target the government. Widespread corruption of firm leaders is blatant and takes many forms: using public property for personal purposes, spending public funds for personal consumption, embezzling public property, receiving kickbacks for selling or buying materials and equipment at distorted prices, making self-serving policies, and others.[8] Indeed, in the 1990s, SOE managers were commonly described as "rich monks (i.e., the enterprise leader) in the poor temple (i.e., the failing enterprise)" or "rich monks in the rich temple."[9] In 1998, 27,700 people were investigated for embezzlement and bribery. SOE leaders accounted for about 50 percent.[10] Reports of how corrupt managers pursue personal interests at the expense of firms abound in the Chinese media. What angers workers is that corruption has been a major cause of the poor performance of SOEs.[11] As discussed in Chapter 5, about 90 percent of SOE managers are appointed by the government. Workers have to target the government in order to have despotic and corrupt managers removed or punished. Hence, workers' economic demands often coincide with political demands to punish corrupt managers.[12] In Liaoning province, for example, between January and May of 1998, among 1,170 collective appeals to the governments, with more than 50 participants for each appeal, half were made by workers of public firms. In each case, there were complaints about the misconduct or corruption of firm leaders.[13] In some cases, laid-off workers voiced their resentment of corrupt cadres explicitly. For example, some laid-off workers used the slogan "Laid-off workers do not need to worry; cadres have whatever we need at their homes."[14]

Belief and reaction of the government

Workers' collective action directed at the government is not new in China. There have been conflicts between the state and labor ever since the founding of socialist

China. Yet most of the conflicts have been about economic issues, and political confrontations have been relatively rare, although with some notable exceptions like the Tiananmen incident in 1989.[15] It is clear to all that the Party has vital interests to protect and will not tolerate any action that aims to or is perceived to threaten its authority. Hence, government response to collective action is based on its interpretation of the intention of the participants. It may tolerate economic demands but not political ones. In discussing the 1956 Hungarian repression, Ekiert reports the same finding: "For the Kadar regime, as long as the major principles of state socialism were in danger, terrorist policies were seen as legitimate means used to accomplish the greater end—that is, the preservation of the party-state."[16] China's government policies towards workers' strikes in the 1950s compared to its policies towards workers in the 1989 Tiananmen incident demonstrate how its response is shaped by its perception of workers' intentions and the degree of threat thereof.

In March 1957, the Chinese central government admitted:

> Over the past six months, the strikes of workers and students, the demonstrations of other people, and other similar incidents have increased markedly. In the whole country, there have been strikes of both large and small scale, with the participation of more than 10,000 workers and over 10,000 students. This phenomenon should receive serious attention.[17]

The central government attributed the unrest to the bureaucratic style of some leaders of state firms and permitted protests for the following reasons:

> (1) their behavior has not violated the Constitution; and (2) prohibition will not solve the problem; and (3) as to those demonstrations that lack legitimate grounds or even involve illegal activities, they are not desirable, but they can also be a good thing. The reason is that the Party can use such events to educate cadres and help them overcome bureaucratism...thereby militating the conflicts with the people. If there are any instigators among the masses, this method can also help identify and isolate these "bad elements"...But the masses must be warned against engaging in any illegal activities.[18]

The central government also instructed local Party committees to send some or all Party members to participate in demonstrations in order to control the leaders and to educate the people, preventing them from being misled by "bad elements." "Only when seriously destructive or illegal activities occur can we send armies or the police to surround the masses or use violence."[19] The government was tolerant because most strikes at that time were economic in nature and were not perceived as political threats.[20]

In contrast, the government's understanding of workers' intentions in the 1989 Tiananmen incident was completely different and its response more dramatic. The government believed that those demonstrators, including the students, intended to overthrow its authority.[21] From the government's point of view, the claim that the crackdown was "completely unnecessary and unjustified" is inaccurate.[22] The government was especially disturbed by the growing involvement of workers, because workers could be more powerful than students once mobilized. Given this concern, the government arrested workers before taking action against students.[23]

Capacity, constraints, and government policies

Government response is not only dictated by its beliefs but also by its capacity. In authoritarian regimes, state capacity has two important components: (1) solidarity among the elite in terms of consensus on reform measures; and (2) the strength of its power base. Solidarity among the elite is crucial to the survival of an authoritarian regime.[24] The transitional experiences of former socialist countries suggest that a split among the elite is one of the most important causes of the collapse of socialist systems.[25] The government's power base depends on financial resources and control over the armed forces and the media. As an authoritarian regime relies less on the people's will than on its repressive capacity for survival, the government retains firm control over the armed forces.[26] Control over the media is also critical in that it prevents free communication among individuals in society. When there is unrest, firm control over the media prevents the dissemination of information which may encourage a cascade of demonstrations by other opposition forces in other localities.[27]

In the reform period, the Chinese government retains strong state capacity. Central leaders' attitudes towards the reform of SOEs have been relatively unanimous. Indeed, it was the government's goal to stop large- and medium-sized SOEs from continuing to lose money within three years up to the year 2000.[28] Equally important, the Party retains firm control over the armed forces in China, as evidenced by the crackdown of the student movement in 1989 and the repression of the Falungong in 1999 and the early 2000s. Finally, despite economic reforms, the government still exercises strong control over the media.[29] The media has followed government regulations that "news media should focus more on positive propaganda. Stricter check should be imposed on 'sensitive' reports. To avoid causing instability, government departments should be cautious when issuing news."[30]

Capacity, however, is relative to the political influence of social groups.[31] Although Chinese citizens have been unable to organize into interest groups as citizens in democracies have, their occupational status approximately reflects their political influence.[32] A study by the Party Committee of Beijing municipality suggests that the political influence of Chinese citizens, in descending order, is from cadres, intellectuals, workers, to peasants.[33] Government polices toward a social group can thus be affected by its political influence. This was reflected in government policies towards streamlined bureaucrats, laid-off workers, and peasants searching for jobs in urban areas.

Chinese workers have long complained of the discriminating policies of the government: "Now, intellectuals can enjoy favorable policies, so do old cadres, but workers are excluded. Government agencies do not dare to offend cadres and intellectuals when making policies, but they are not afraid of workers."[34] An important political reform of the Chinese government in the 1990s was the streamlining of the bureaucracy. In 1998, more than 47 percent of the bureaucrats were streamlined in the central government. But the government took on the entire responsibility of reallocating these people except for those who were willing to be self-employed.[35]

Despite workers' limited political influence compared to that of bureaucrats, the government can hardly ignore such a large number of laid-off workers who either have difficulty finding jobs or fail to receive subsidies. As elsewhere, a natural choice would be to provide alternatives. For example, in the United States, during the Great Depression, "they (protests) were declining largely as a result of the Roosevelt Administration's more liberal relief machinery, which diverted local groups from disruptive tactics and absorbed local leaders in bureaucratic roles."[36] In China, in addition to the many measures discussed in Chapter 2, Chinese local governments have adopted some policies at the expense of peasants searching for jobs in urban areas.[37] For example, in 1997, the government of Beijing municipality increased the types of work that were prohibited to nonlocal labor from 15 to 35.[38] Similarly, in 1998, the Wuhan government decided to lay off peasant-turned-workers in order to create jobs for laid-off workers. It decreed that 24 types of businesses could not use nonlocal labor, mainly peasants, and that such people should be laid off if they had been hired.[39] Despite these efforts, it is beyond the ability of the government to provide laid-off workers with sufficient help, as illustrated in previous chapters.

While full accommodation is not practical, neither can the government simply repress workers. First, the demands of most laid-off workers are economic in nature, and the government is reluctant to repress such nonpolitical demands for the sake of legitimacy.[40] Legitimacy is important in that its absence not only causes resentment among the people but also demoralizes or "weakens the loyalty of the social control agents," making it difficult for the regime to survive a crisis.[41] Chinese laid-off workers often explicitly raise economic demands to dispel governments' suspicion of political motives.[42] Some demonstrating workers used slogans such as "Do not oppose the Party," "Do not raise riots," "Need jobs," and "Need food."[43] These slogans focus entirely on economic issues and are likely to garner the sympathy of other people. Others sang the Party's song "No Communist Party, No New China." Still others wore simple uniforms to prevent outsiders from participating.[44] Although laid-off workers sometimes demand punishment of corrupt managers, this noneconomic demand is legitimate, because anticorruption is a goal of the government and it has offered rewards to citizens who report corrupt cadres.[45]

Second, repression is not always effective. Arguably, "the general effect of sustained repression is not to build up tensions to the point of a great explosion, but to reduce the overall level of collective action."[46] But even anticipated repression may fail to deter protests when potential participants are ignorant of the true risks or define risks differently.[47] In addition, repression, in the long run, tends to create more militant and better organized opponents, and ineffective repression sows the seeds for future unrest. For example, the experience of Polish workers suggests "how the deadly conflict with the party stimulated and shaped the Polish workers' creation of the idea of an independent self-governing trade union."[48] A Chinese police official acknowledged, "If we lose the support of the masses, even if these measures do hold things down for a while, they will rebound and do even more damage."[49]

In contrast, non-repressive measures can be effective. For instance, after the 1956 crackdown in Hungary, the government sought to establish political "re-equilibrium" between the state and society. Reform measures were implemented to consistently raise the standard of living, which was "the best protection from the reoccurrence of political tensions and conflicts."[50] Hence, authoritarian regimes may employ multiple measures to deal with discontented citizens. The Chinese government has tried to silence laid-off workers by dispelling their motivation for resistance, undermining their confidence in action, and increasing their cost of taking action.

Dispelling the motivation for resistance

Although individuals' motivation for resistance alone is not sufficient for them to take action, diluting such motivations is an effective way of reducing or preventing resistance. One measure adopted by the Chinese government to reduce worker resistance is to build consensus with them. In reform, consensus building between reformers and those negatively affected may reduce the resistance of the latter. But whether the two parties will reach a consensus depends on whether reformers can convince the latter that its sacrifice will contribute to a better future. Current research has found that consensus between the state and citizens in post-communist countries has helped facilitate the transition to a market economy. As Ekiert finds, "In all three countries (Hungary, Czechoslovakia, and Poland), political and economic reforms were introduced more rapidly, and there was more of a consensus, both among the elites and the population, regarding transition to a market economy and a liberal democracy."[51] Consensus is also possible when both parties understand the difficulties in addressing common problems. As a Chinese provincial governor admitted:

> Based on my experience in governance work, if we face problems, we do not need to be afraid of them; but we should not hide or evade them either. It is better to let the masses know our difficulties, and they will understand. The more you hide problems and difficulties, the more people distrust you, not to mention support.[52]

However, it is not always easy to reach a consensus. The Chinese government has repeatedly pointed out that "layoffs have made some workers encounter temporary difficulties. At the basic level, the reform will promote economic development and is in accordance with the long-term interests of the working class."[53] But if their basic and immediate interests are not guaranteed, few laid-off workers believe that their long-term ones will be. According to my survey, only about 20 percent believed that reform measures like layoffs are necessary and acceptable. Similarly, a survey of over 500 laid-off workers in Shanghai showed that only about 26 percent reported that they understood the necessity of layoffs.[54]

In addition, as discussed in Chapter 5, workers were discontented because they lost jobs while corrupt managers remained unaffected. Consensus is difficult to reach at the societal level because of widespread corruption of government officials and Party cadres. Workers often complain that while they pay the costs of reform, many others strip the state of its wealth:

> Hundreds of workers work hard simply to support a corrupt manager, and thousands of people work hard to support a few officials. When the manager gets rich and the officials pay to get a promotion, workers are laid off. What kind of reform is this?[55]

As discussed in Chapter 5, consensus building is more likely when enterprise leaders are "clean" or sympathetic and try to improve the performance of their enterprises. It becomes difficult when practical subsistence problems faced by laid-off workers cannot be remedied.

Blame avoidance

Another method that the Chinese government has used to undermine resistance is blame avoidance. Successful blame avoidance is believed to silence the people and reinforce the legitimacy of the government.[56] In China, the central government has tried to avoid being blamed for layoffs. In defense of the central government, a vice premier argued in 1998 that "it reverses the cause and effect to claim that the increased number of laid-off workers is due to the central government's policy" because "there had been a large number of laid-off workers before the central government issued its policy to handle this issue."[57] Indeed, both the central and local governments have gone beyond blame avoidance, and have blamed laid-off workers for their unemployment. A commonly used phrase by officials and the state-controlled media in discussing reemployment in the 1990s was that laid-off workers needed to "change their reemployment mentality." Laid-off workers were blamed for "one type of waiting (waiting for allocation), two types of dependence (on family members or relatives and on enterprises for assistance), three fears (competition in the labor market, discrimination in the market, lack of welfare insurance), and four demands (good treatment on the job, high salary, employer near one's home, and an easy job)."[58]

Two types of evidence have been widely used in the mass media to prove that laid-off workers need to change their "mentality." The first is reports on many cases in which laid-off workers refuse to take jobs in private sectors introduced by the government or its agencies. For example, one district of Beijing municipality had 42 public toilets that charged for service. In 1999, the hygiene bureau of this district decided to invite tenders for the management of 30 of the 42 public toilets in order to provide jobs for laid-off workers. But not a single laid-off worker participated in the bidding. Only one of the 30 winners of the bidding was a young native of Beijing; the others were immigrants.[59] The other type of evidence focuses on how laid-off workers have succeeded with or without government support. The government elected Model Self-Employed Stars and had them deliver reports of success to other workers, in order to convince the latter that they could be financially independent. Apparently, the government intended to make laid-off workers commit an "attribution error"—to attribute one's problem to his or her personal failures rather than to the social or political system.[60]

These efforts, however, have met with limited success, because people may not attribute their miserable circumstances to themselves or may take collective action regardless of blame attribution. In a survey of 874 workers in 1999, only 5.5 percent reported that laid-off workers or the unemployed should be held responsible for their own subsistence and reemployment.[61] Indeed, the government's blaming has caused more discontent than it has dispelled in China. One reason is that official propaganda ignores regional differences. Employment opportunities vary significantly across regions, and less developed and small cities or counties often have more difficulties creating jobs. For example, between 1991 and 1995, the urban poverty-stricken population in China was between 11 million and 14.5 million. But the distribution of these people was skewed toward counties or small cities. In Liaoning province in the late 1990s, the poverty rate was 1.5 percent in cities with a population of more than one million, about 10.5 percent in cities with a population between half a million and one million, and almost 63 percent in cities with a population of less than half a million. Workers from money-losing enterprises constituted the largest number of those people, and the most important reason for their poverty was the lack of reemployment opportunities.[62]

A more important reason for the ineffectiveness of blame avoidance is that official propaganda lacks credibility. As some laid-off workers complain, "The media is biased against laid-off workers. In their report, we laid-off workers are older, lack skills, and have low education with backward reemployment mentality. We do not have a single merit."[63] Journalists themselves admit the bias:

> To a large extent, our reporting of reemployment of laid-off workers is based on leaders' opinion. When higher-level authorities take new measures to address unemployment, journalists would collect numbers and report some successful examples. In our reports, the situation is always good as we ignore the remaining fundamental problems. The lack of serious investigation is common. When reporting reemployment, many journalists would go to the places where the work has achieved some progress and talk to the leaders in charge of the work. After listening to the briefing, they would talk to a few laid-off workers recommended by the leaders. Their reports are based on such information.[64]

What is reported is thus selective and unconvincing, and some successful examples that have been published are fake.[65] Laid-off workers also point out that the propaganda downplays the obstacles to reemployment. As a laid-off woman complained, televisions and newspapers often suggested that laid-off workers need to change their employment mentality and should not be selective in their job search. "But no matter how I change my mentality, I cannot find a job. Last year a department store recruited salespersons. The regulation that applicants must be below 35 years old was sufficient to disqualify me, not to mention other requirements such as the ability of speaking standard mandarin and a height of at least 1.6 meters."[66] An official of the ACFTU who participated in a nationwide survey of laid-off workers also admitted that "the problem with unemployment is by no means the employment mentality of laid-off workers."[67] Given the many practical hurdles to reemployment, some laid-off workers claim that the government should change "its mentality of propaganda."[68] Hence, while some workers might have blamed themselves and remained silent,[69] others did not.[70]

Selective punishment and the risk of action

As non-repressive measures may not silence laid-off workers or confine their action to the boundary of the state, repressive methods are sometimes necessary. The justification for the use of repression usually goes beyond a particular event. As Lovas and Anderson indicate, "because terrorism is not merely the unbridled exercise of violence with certain special features—it is also the *memory* and the *threat*, even the implied threat, that under certain circumstances it could return."[71] Yet, as elsewhere, the Chinese government usually imposes "exemplary punishment" on organizers instead of average participants.[72] As organizers are crucial to collective action, imposing punishment on such people is an effective way of abating collective action.

Organizers and collective action

Joseph Schumpeter points out that "collectives act almost exclusively by accepting leadership—this is the dominant mechanism of practically any collective action."[73] Samuel Popkin likewise suggests that "the importance of the leader as a political entrepreneur—someone willing to invest his own time and resources to coordinate the inputs of others in order to produce collective action or collective goods—should not be underestimated."[74] Organizers of Chinese laid-off workers are not political entrepreneurs in that they neither provide selective incentives or coercion nor have career aspirations. But they do play several important roles in making collective action possible.[75]

One important role of organizers in the collective action of Chinese laid-off workers is to disseminate information. Individuals participate in collective action only when they know others will do the same.[76] Communication and coordination are particularly important for Chinese laid-off workers. After workers are laid off, they no longer have regular contact with one another. In China, most SOEs and urban collective enterprises are located in cities rather than in small industrial towns (except for enterprises like mines), and workers tend to scatter after being laid off. A case reported by one of my interviewees indicates the difficulties and possibility of collective action of dispersed workers.

In the 1980s, a roller chain factory had more than 400 workers. In order to promote the status of the factory, the manager recruited 300 more workers to expand its size. Under the planned economy, hiring more workers did not burden the factory because workers' salaries were guaranteed by the state. The factory also took over some farmland in nearby villages and had to recruit peasants from the villages, as required by the state land-use policy. Over the years, the factory was unable to provide housing for its workers because it was not profitable enough. Only a few cadres were assigned housing by the industrial bureau, whereas most others lived in private houses or housing provided by the work units of family members.

In 1993, the factory stopped production because of a shortage of capital, and workers had to stay home. For the first eight months, the factory tried to pay workers 70 percent of their salary by selling the remaining inventory. When everything was sold, workers stopped receiving payments. Initially, workers took individual or small-scale collective action but little was achieved. When some people finally decided to mobilize workers to appeal to the government, two types of participants constituted the majority: peasants-turned-workers and workers who had telephones, including workers who lived close to those with telephones. As peasants-turned-workers lived in the same or nearby villages, it was easier to disseminate information among them than among workers dispersed throughout the city. Hence, some workers informed those who had telephones and asked them to contact other workers. As a result, only about 100 of the 700 former employees showed up, even though most of them had not found jobs. At that time, it was still uncommon for state workers to secure jobs on their own. The lack of communication was an important reason for the lack of participation of laid-off workers, as they admitted that "nobody told us."[77]

This example suggests that getting information to laid-off workers can be facilitated either by the microenvironment, like neighborhoods (or small communities like villages), or by organizers, or both. Other things being equal, mobilization is easier for laid-off workers who live near each other, so housing provided by SOEs may positively affect the probability of collective action and its scale. According to my survey, among the 138 unpaid laid-off workers, compared with those who did not live in housing provided by their firms, those who did were 50 percent more likely to participate in collective action, holding other things constant.[78]

The example given in the previous paragraphs also shows that coordination of dispersed workers is possible when coordinators or organizers disseminate information by directly contacting as many individuals as possible. In other cases, organizers solve the coordination problem not by going door to door but by creating a focal point. For example, in 1997, a silk factory in the city of Mianyang in Sichuan province was declared bankrupt and the workers' limited subsidies were embezzled by its corrupt manager. On July 6, a worker, reportedly a college student recently assigned to the factory, posted a notice in the factory urging all workers to come to the factory to meet with a vice mayor at 8 o'clock the next morning to discuss their subsistence problem. Many workers came the next day but did not see the vice mayor. The gathering escalated into a large-scale collective action, and workers took to the streets and blocked the traffic. They were soon joined by laid-off workers from other factories. Reportedly, tens of thousands of people participated. This was one of the largest demonstrations in China in the 1990s.[79]

Organizers of Chinese laid-off workers are important because they bear more risks than ordinary participants owing to the government's repressive policies against organizers. The presence of organizers thus not only inspires the confidence of participants but also reduces the risk they face. As some laid-off workers in Beijing claimed, "Now there is no person who is willing to organize demonstrations; if anyone took the lead, I would surely participate."[80] Hence, when organizers appear, collective action is likely. In Nanchong of Sichuan province in March 1996, workers of the city's largest silk factory (called Jialihua), took their manager hostage and paraded him through town, demanding back pay. The unrest began with a few workers of the factory, a state firm that once supported over 10,000 people, including its workers' dependents. The firm's poor performance forced it to lay off workers and reduce the salaries of those who stayed. But the factory leaders were not affected although they were blamed by workers for driving the factory to despair.

In March 1996, the general manager of the factory planned to go to Thailand with his wife on an official inspection tour at the company's expense. A few workers waited at the factory for the manager to arrive. When he showed up, they loaded him onto the back of a flatbed truck. They forced him into the painful and demeaning "airplane position"—bent at the waist, arms extended straight out to the sides. The workers marched 10 kilometers through the rain to the downtown and paraded him through the streets. Meanwhile, more and more workers from this factory and other enterprises heard the news and joined the march. The total number of participants grew to over 20,000. The day-long parade ended at the city government building, with workers blocking the compound. Worker leaders took turns delivering speeches. The rally ended peacefully after the government promised to pay the owed salaries. As expected, four leaders were detained.[81] In this case, a few leaders made large-scale collective action possible by starting the process at unknown risk.

Finally, because organizers are often cadres who have experience dealing with the government, they are able to articulate workers' demands. In the pre-reform period, Chinese citizens in urban areas often pursued personal and collective goals through their work units rather than by going directly to the government.[82] Many of them have not had experience dealing with bureaucrats and must undertake a learning process when approaching the government through unconventional means. Hence, laid-off workers need representatives who can negotiate with the government and articulate their concerns and demands. Organizers often take on this responsibility, making them essential for the success of collective action. As an interviewee admitted:

> If the action is likely to succeed and solve our problem, I will definitely join. But for such action to succeed, it should be effectively organized and there should be some people who are able to articulate our interests and negotiate with the government. I participated in an appeal to the city government once and stopped after that because it was not effectively organized. If you take action, you should do your best to make it succeed.

It is also for this reason that laid-off workers realize the necessity of protecting their leaders. In the protests in Liaoyang in 2002, when a worker leader was detained, workers protested for his release "because if our representative cannot speak for us, what else is there to talk about?"[83]

Punishing organizers

The Chinese government fully realizes the importance of organizers in collective action. A research report by Party organs in Sichuan province in 1998 admits that "over 95 percent of the large-scale collective events involve the organization of some people. They seem to have a labor division, planning, and organizing."[84] Given their importance, government policy toward organizers has been repressive. The old Chinese saying that "The first bird that comes out of the nest is the first to get shot" remains true today. Political events since the founding of the PRC have repeatedly borne out government determination to punish organizers of dissent. Therefore, although demonstrations and assemblies are legal according to the constitution, those who organize such activities can be charged with violating an article of the Criminal Law—"The crime of organizing people and breaking the public order." As an interviewee put it, "The Constitution says you have the freedom to hold a demonstration, but the Constitution does not say you will still have freedom *after* the demonstration." In other words, people, in most cases the organizers, may be punished *ex post*.

The public security department's policies regarding organizers are harsh. "To isolate and punish the minority and to win over, divide, and educate the majority—this is a strategy of taking advantage of the split, winning over the majority, opposing the minority, and dividing and defeating them."[85] Similarly, the secretary of a provincial Political and Legal Commission states the rules in dealing with participants in collective action:

> There should be a clear distinction between crimes and noncrimes, between the few organizers or instigators and the masses in collective events, and between the serious law-violating behavior of a few people and the less serious law-violating behavior of most other participants.[86]

The 1989 Tiananmen incident sent a credible signal that the government would not tolerate any attempt that threatens its authority, nor would it tolerate the organizers of such activities. A more recent example is the punishment of the leaders of the Falungong. In 1999, the government arrested a number of leaders of this sect across the country. The four leaders in its Beijing headquarters were the first to be apprehended and were sentenced to 18, 16, 12, and 7 years in prison, respectively.[87]

In the reform period, both peasant and worker organizers were arrested and sent to jail for organizing activities.[88] In 1995, for example, dozens of workers forced their way into the compound of a city government, demanding payment of overdue salaries and the punishment of their manager. After receiving no response from the government, these workers blocked a bridge, stopping thousands of vehicles along the road. Upon receiving this news, the mayor received the protestors and sent two investigation groups, led by the supervision bureau and the public security bureau to the factory. During the investigation, the supervision bureau found evidence of corruption of the manager and arrested him. In the meantime, the public security bureau arrested two worker organizers who were claimed to have problematic histories.[89]

Government repression of organizers is an effective deterrent. In the 1989 Tiananmen incident, student participants exercised caution:

> Those who walk in the front row of the demonstration and get caught are not the most important leaders. They are young people in their first or second year. They are 17 or 18. For them, it's not so bad. But those in their third or fourth year are more careful.[90]

Some people see the lack of assertive leaders who dared to command the ranks as an important reason for the less effective student movement. "The newly formed student organizations still have no presidents, only committees that are so large that they are ungainly and many of the most talented students are afraid to take an official position in an organization that is branded illegal."[91]

In an interview, a laid-off worker also reported how the fear of punishment resulted in anonymous or leaderless mobilization. She did not know who organized their action. Someone telephoned her and said, "It was said that they [other workers] will go to the government tomorrow, will you go?" The next day, about 200 people from her factory gathered in front of the government office. As they waited, some bystanders suggested that they bring in workers from other factories to join them. But some replied, "Who is willing to take the risk?" After about an hour, a government official came out and said that the government was willing to negotiate with their representatives. But workers replied, "We do not have representatives, and we came here on our own." The official said it was impossible for the government to talk with so many people. The workers then elected 10 representatives, thinking that if the government was likely to punish one or two representatives, it was less likely to punish 10. Chen also finds that the collective action of Chinese laid-off workers tends to be "leaderless" because of the risks involved.[92]

Selective punishment and social stability in China

This policy of selective punishment has a number of important implications for political stability in China. First, it abates collective action by inhibiting the emergence of organizers.[93] Some labor activists have admitted, "We only work as consultants, because organizing is too sensitive... We research the workers' situation, find out what ways work best. We only help workers who request help. If they don't request help it's best to keep a distance from them."[94] Second, it encourages peaceful collective actions, when they occur. Piven and Cloward find that organized action tends to be less effective than unorganized action: "In large part, organizers tended to work against disruption because, in their search for resources to maintain their organizations, they were driven inexorably to elites, and to the tangible and symbolic supports that elites could provide."[95] In China, organized action tends not to be destructive because of the fear of punishment of organizers. It is clear to laid-off workers that government response depends not only on what they say but also on what they do. Hence, violence is seldom used because, as elsewhere, it "merely hastens and insures its failure because its actions increase the hostility around it and invite the legitimate action of authorities against it."[96] Some of my interviewees claimed that they only held "civil demonstrations" (*wenming youxing*). In most cases, laid-off workers adopt moderate modes. If collective action spins out of control, it usually results from unexpected escalation of appeals or catalytic events that provoke strong emotions.

Third, selective punishment helps reduce the scale of resistance. A salient characteristic of the collective action of laid-off workers is that it is based on individual firms, which limits the scale. While cases of cross-firm action are mentioned in Chapter 3, they are not typical. According to my survey, among those 172 people who once participated in collective action, none reported that their action involved other firms, except when laid-off workers from different firms happened to approach the government at the same time. One reason for the rarity of cross-firm action is that the demands of workers of different firms are different or that workers believe they are different.[97] More important, few people are willing to organize cross-firms action. Some workers think that acting with laid-off workers from other enterprises may lower their chances for success because it would raise the government's suspicion.[98] This creates a dilemma. If laid-off workers organize large-scale action, it puts the organizer at great risk; if they engage in small-scale action, it often fails to put enough pressure on the government. As some protesters in Liaoning province said, "If we go in dribs and drabs, nobody pays attention to us. We need all the laid-off workers to go to the government at the same time."[99]

Finally, by preventing the emergence of organizers, the government prevents the establishment of organized networks that could challenge the regime, because such networks must be sustained by devoted leaders. Although the Chinese constitution allows the formation of independent associations, this right is denied in practice. This policy precludes the formation of political alternatives to the Communist Party.[100] That political dissent can hardly take root in China testifies to both the determination and power of the state to prevent such organizations.[101]

Government patience and the cost of sustained action

While the government is less tolerant of organized and destructive action, workers may take peaceful and leaderless action. The government has to convince laid-off workers to become self-reliant in order to continue with reforms. Even peaceful actions may cause chaos in society if they become widespread. As "concessions may whet the appetite of opposition groups and, thus, may become the occasion for expressing more radical demands,"[102] the government must make credible its withdrawal of economic commitment. To this end, a policy of "taking care of your own children" has been adopted in a number of localities, including Shanghai, whose government is well known for its reemployment programs.[103] Under this policy, the government does not take responsibility for workers. Instead, the firm, as long as it exists and regardless of the difficulties it faces, has to "take care of its children" (i.e., the workers). The government may also refuse to make concessions to laid-off workers by engaging in a peaceful standoff. In doing so, it neither represses nor takes care of participants. When government policies gain credibility, laid-off workers will not take action or sustain their struggle.

This strategy is exemplified by a bankruptcy case in Chongqing. In 1992, the city government decided to declare bankrupt the Chongqing Knitting Factory of 3,000 workers. That was the largest bankruptcy case in the country at that time. After workers received news of the bankruptcy, their representatives wrote a long letter, entitled "The Appeal of the Three Thousand Workers," to the city Party, government, and legal organs concerned. In the letter, they pointed out that bankruptcy was a wrong decision and that:

> workers, especially those retired, complain bitterly, and they blame the bureaucrats for their plight and are eager to appeal to upper-level authorities. They have met many times to discuss the measures to check factory leaders, and such complaints have increased dramatically these days. It is very likely that they will take action.[104]

The workers did take action. A government official who came to the factory was detained for over 20 hours, and hundreds of workers took to the streets and blocked traffic for four days. They chanted slogans such as "Chairman Mao, we miss you very much," "We need jobs, we need food, we want to survive," and "Withdraw the bankruptcy application."[105] When a local newspaper reported that bankruptcy would be meaningless if the government continued to reallocate workers, more than 200 workers, mostly women, came out in the extremely hot weather and forced the factory manager and the Party secretary to withdraw the bankruptcy application. The city government, however, did not back down. The mayor made his rationale crystal clear:

> Premised on social stability, we should continue with the reform. The issue of "letting enterprises die" has to be settled sooner or later. Of course, we can help them survive, but as time goes on, we will pay higher costs and cannot

truly ensure the stability. At present, what we can do is to reduce the influence of the bankruptcy as much as possible. The workers of the Knitting Factory asked the government to pay its debts. Even if the government has the ability to clear its debts, can the government pay the debts for all the enterprises in the city? If the Knitting Factory is set up as an example, it would be difficult for us to handle such issues in the future. For this reason, I am for the bankruptcy, and the court should accept it.[106]

After the Chongqing government refused to bail out the factory, other textile factories in the city realized that the government was determined to withdraw its financial commitment. Those with connections or skills tried to leave the textile sector. After November 1992, the number of workers who attended the two driving schools in the city increased every day (they planned to learn how to drive so that they might have the option of becoming taxi or truck drivers if they were laid off). A director of a textile factory said, "The reality is such, and I cannot change it. I have decided to accept the offer of a managerial position in Guangdong province." Some older workers retired early, others maintained membership in their enterprises and found jobs elsewhere, and still others simply resigned.[107]

Peaceful confrontation as a war of attrition

Sometimes, the strategy of peaceful confrontation without concessions amounts to a war of attrition in which laid-off workers first back down because they are under pressure to make ends meet. This produces a profound impact on laid-off workers' confidence in the efficacy of collective action. Individuals tend to take a course of action "that will satisfy more of his desire rather than less, and which has the greater chance of being successfully executed."[108] If workers believe that the government will not make concessions, they will not think that taking action is worthwhile.[109] As a worker reported:

The first time when dozens of us went to the government for back pay, an official first asked us the name of our factory. He then called our factory leaders to take us back. The manager persuaded us to leave and promised that the enterprise would try to pay us. We agreed. But it turned out that once again, the factory could not get any money. The next time we went to the government for help, nobody was willing to come out to talk with us. After almost two hours, an official came out and said that the government would try to help the enterprise to obtain loans to pay us. And we were told to go home. Again, we did not receive any notice for days. The third time when we went there, another official talked with us perfunctorily. We all understood that there was no hope. After that, few of us went to the government any longer. Nowadays, it is common that some people gather in front of the government office, waiting for hours without any outcome.

Similarly, in a reported case, a woman became self-employed after she had sought help from the government several times but in vain. This woman, Li, was laid off although she was once a city model worker in northeast China. When she was laid off, she had two children in school and her husband received only a 90-yuan salary each month because his firm performed poorly. She first approached the city's Women's Association and hoped that it would negotiate with the leaders of her company to allow her to return to work. But the efforts of the Women's Association failed. Li then went to the Bureau of Civil Affairs, hoping that the bureau could provide some help. A cadre in the bureau met with her. Li told him about her family life in great detail, and the cadre was sympathetic to her plight. But before Li finished her story, he shook his head and sighed, "Now the whole city and the whole province are plagued by this problem. We really do not have any solution... Nowadays there are too many people like you, don't you see this notebook?" He took out a very thick notebook containing the names of the laid-off people who had visited the bureau and said, "Look at this, it is beyond our ability to help these many people."

Li was frustrated to tears. She could not believe that as a city model worker, she was left unsupported. The next day, she went to the city government and happened to meet some laid-off workers picketing for jobs in front of the government office and waiting to hear from the government. Li joined them and sat in the plaza. But they did not see any official after waiting for hours. During that time, another woman, Zhang, happened to pass by. Zhang and Li were acquaintances. When Zhang saw Li in the sit-in, she went by to greet her. Knowing Li was laid off, she said, "What are you doing here? I came here several times a few months ago when I was laid off. It was useless. Do you not see so many laid-off workers? Who should be assigned a job? I thought it through later and decided not to look for anyone for help. I have to depend on myself, and I learned how to fix bikes." Li was convinced and later became self-employed. Not long after that, she was elected a city model worker again, this time as Model Self-Employed Laid-Off Worker.[110]

The government's lack of response also prevents workers from engaging in lengthy appeals. In one example, a steel factory of about 2,800 workers could no longer operate due to poor performance (it even failed to pay its electric bills). As a last solution, part of the factory was contracted to a foreign businessman who hired less than one-third of the employees. However, the rent was a meager sum, and many laid-off workers and retirees received nothing. They took action to demand subsidies. The factory was many miles away from the city government, and workers had to take a ride to get to the city. One day in the summer of 1999, more than 200 workers went to the city and blocked the office compound of the city government. They stood there for hours but no official came to talk to them. The workers then walked to the city Party Committee, and still no cadres came. The weather was very hot, and workers were tired, thirsty, and hungry. Their demonstration lasted for only two days and did not succeed. It was said that when the workers' demonstration was reported to the city government, the mayor said, "As long as they are not tired of the sun, they can carry on for as long as they wish."[111] Similarly, in Shenyang, the capital city of Liaoning province, about 30 percent of the workers of the state and collective sectors were laid off by the late 1990s,[112] but there was not much unrest launched by laid-off workers.[113] As Kiernen also finds, "In Shenyang today workers appear indifferent to such actions because they know that marches and protests will not change their fate. For this reason, relative peace and quiet has now returned to the streets of the city. But an increase in other social problems is still proof of the crisis in the city: suicide, crimes, divorce and prostitution are on the rise."[114]

As the government's withdrawal of support to loss-making SOEs gains credibility, it produces a discouraging effect. Fewer people now believe that the government will provide jobs for them. For example, a survey conducted in August 1997 found that about 79 percent of the laid-off workers hoped that the government would provide jobs. By November of 1998, only 9.5 percent of laid-off workers surveyed held the same hope, whereas about 72 percent replied that they would try to find jobs by improving their skills.[115] This is perhaps the most important reason that most workers focused on layoff compensation or subsidies instead of job allocation, as discussed in Chapter 3. While the media promotes the idea that this is due to a change of "reemployment mentality," laid-off workers know that it is simply the more practical choice. A worker described his realization that the government had withdrawn its commitment to workers in an interview:

> I had worked in a state enterprise for more than twenty-five years before I was laid off. At first I thought that layoffs only meant a temporary leave. Once the factory performed better, I could return. But the factory never performed better. When I realized that I had no chance of returning to the enterprise, I expected that the government would provide help. As we were workers of a state factory and had made contributions in the past, it was unlikely that the government would abandon us. Even for the sake of social stability, the government should allocate jobs to us. But as time passed, while I was not allocated a job, more and more people were laid off. In the meantime, my life became difficult because the subsidies were so limited and payment was sometimes suspended. It was then that I realized that we could not depend on the government for reemployment. Times are different, as is the government.

Disillusionment with the government makes laid-off workers realize that "one cannot simply spend the rest of his time approaching the government every few months for a living."[116] They have to be self-reliant. Hence, despite the lack of job security and welfare benefits, most laid-off workers take on jobs in the private sector or become self-employed, as discussed in Chapter 2.

Conclusion

The reform of the state economy in China makes confrontation between the state and workers inevitable. Without the enterprise as a buffer, the government has been targeted either because it is directly involved in the reform process or because it is expected to assume responsibilities for workers. While it is in the interest of the government to attend to the needs of laid-off workers, it is often beyond its ability to do so. Given that the government has no legitimate reason to suppress the nonpolitical demands of laid-off workers, the use of force is not a justifiable way to tackle resistance, even though it remains a credible means. The ways in which the government deals with laid-off workers demonstrate that an authoritarian regime does not necessarily utilize repression to achieve its goals. In fact, the Chinese government relies more on non-repressive measures.

The government has adopted a number of different measures to weaken laid-off workers' motivation for resistance, increase the costs of action, and undermine their confidence. Specifically, the government tries to build consensus with workers and convince laid-off workers that they should blame themselves for their problems. Another key method is to impose punishment on organizers of collective action. This method is effective because organizers are often crucial to the occurrence of collective action. By preventing the emergence of leaders, the government determines the occurrence, nature, and scale of worker resistance. The government also engages in wars of attrition with laid-off workers. In so doing, it puts direct economic pressure on laid-off workers because the longer they sustain their action, the longer they go without income. This measure has produced a discouraging effect and works to the advantage of the government. However, the existence of difficulties does not imply that collective action is impossible or that the government never makes concessions. As will be discussed in Chapter 7, workers are still able to take action and force the government to accommodate their interests, often depending on the types of their demands and their ability to mobilize.

7 The collective action of Chinese laid-off workers

Chapter 6 illustrates that massive layoffs in China have prompted the government to adopt a variety of policies to mitigate worker resistance. While these measures have helped the government continue with economic reforms, they do not imply that the reform process has been smooth. As indicated in Chapter 3, numerous incidents of worker resistance have occurred since the 1990s and have stumbled the pace of reforms.[1] The occurrence and success of worker resistance point to the limitations of the government's preventive measures or to the power of workers. What needs to be explained, given the many hurdles discussed in earlier chapters, are reasons for the occurrence and the success of laid-off workers' collective action, as well as the implications of worker resistance for the economic transition in China.

This book has argued that workers' collective action is a result of dual interactions: one among workers and the other between workers and the target of their action. My thesis on the interaction among workers posits that collective action is more possible when a sufficient number of workers face the same undesirable situation and have difficulty finding alternatives. My study on the interaction between workers and the target suggests that workers will have more confidence in taking action when they believe that the target cannot afford to ignore their demands. This chapter demonstrates that collective action occurs when Chinese local governments face constraints in dealing with workers whose demands are nonpolitical and whose actions are peaceful. These conditions preclude the government from using repression at will and provide opportunities for workers to exploit, although they do not automatically lead to success. On the other hand, having sufficient participants is more possible when reform measures affect many workers simultaneously. Collective action is also facilitated by worker leaders and a micro-level environment conducive to communication and consensus building among prospective participants. While worker resistance may achieve success in some cases, it is unlikely to threaten the reforms because the ways in which the reforms are carried out, together with government policies, are not conducive to large-scale resistance.

Constraints on the government

As discussed in Chapter 6, laid-off workers often direct their action at the local government in China. In doing so, workers need to put sufficient pressure on the government in order to succeed, and this is possible only when the government faces significant constraints. In an authoritarian regime like China, local officials are accountable to their supervisors rather than to the public. Given the administrative hierarchy, constraints on officials only come from higher-level authorities. Hence, one method that workers can use is to have their voice heard by high-level officials in order to have their problems addressed. If their claims and demands are legitimate, higher-level governments may need to respond either symbolically or substantially in order to maintain legitimacy or to prevent the escalation of conflict. Pressure from higher-level authorities is thus a significant constraint on local officials that creates political space for collective action in China.

Local governments and political space in China

In China, local governments are responsible for social stability as well as social and economic development. While failure in either task is undesirable, failure to maintain social stability can be more damaging than economic failure to an official's career.[2] This is because many factors that affect economic development are beyond the control of the local government, whereas social instability is usually related to its efforts or policies. Political considerations may, therefore, have priority over economic motives. For example, before 1989, a state-owned bike factory in Hebei province was closed due to poor performance. Workers were sent home and paid 150 yuan per month. Yet, after the Tiananmen incident, the local government asked the workers to return to the factory daily for political education and to clean up the factory, which doubled the factory's monthly expenses.[3]

Individual and collective action can be indicators of local officials' failure to fulfill their administrative responsibilities or maintain local stability. Chinese citizens may expect local governments to solve their problems before action escalates to social unrest. Such an expectation of government response is based on the space made available in the political system. As early as the 1950s, the central government required local governments at the county level and above to establish complaints bureaus (*xinfangju*) to handle people's letters and appeals.[4] Higher-level officials pay attention to citizens' appeals for symbolic and instrumental reasons. Some officials say:

> By listening to people's complaints and solving their problems, the government will not only dispel their discontent but also strengthen its relations with the people. The government can thus create an image of serving the people wholeheartedly and obtain information on the policy implementation at the grassroots level and the performance of cadres. This is a method whereby the masses check cadres.[5]

The complaints system, therefore, not only contributes to the legitimacy of the regime by making citizens' political participation possible but also provides information on local governments to higher-level authorities. The system can also exert pressure on local officials through the administrative hierarchy. According to officials working in complaints bureaus:

> If the local government ignores the decisions issued by complaints bureaus, we will refer the case to their higher-level leaders. If the issue remains ignored, we will report it to even higher-level authorities. If that is still insufficient, we will report the case to the central complaints bureau (which is a joint organization of the Central Party committee and the State Council) and ask them to put the case high on the agenda. The central complaints bureau can assign points to local cadres, based on the number of appeals from the locality, the number of cases the locality has resolved, and the outcomes of the settlement. If too many points are deducted, the career of local officials may be affected.[6]

The complaints system regularly selects model cadres who are often credited with helping citizens and maintaining social stability.[7] This constraint on local officials imposed from above shapes people's perceptions of the government in the sense that "cadres have their own bosses, and they cannot always do what they want to do to us."[8] Also, because of the ineffectiveness of the legal system,[9] citizens prefer to appeal to higher-level authorities or leaders. For example, in the late 1980s, top leaders, like Jiang Zemin and Li Peng, received about 1,500 letters per week. Sometimes, high-level officials do read and hand over letters of complaint to lower-level governments, requiring them to solve the problems and report back with the result.[10]

More significant, the complaints system allows collective appeals, as long as the number of participants is no more than five and the action is peaceful.[11] This makes possible more dramatic "boundary-spanning" action,[12] such as blocking traffic or government offices, because dramatic action often escalates from collective appeals. As the five-person limit is frequently violated, the boundary between collective appeals and more aggressive forms of action is often blurred.[13] Indeed, people tend to believe that "big trouble for the government, big possibility of having one's problem addressed; small trouble, small possibility; and no trouble, no possibility."[14] They can make big trouble by taking action that involves a large number of participants, by creating large-scale peaceful or nonviolent chaos, or by appealing directly to higher-level authorities. Some researchers observed how peasants exerted pressure on their local government:

> Appeals targeting the township Party committee and the township government usually involved many peasants and the scale was large. Most groups had more than 100 people, and some had seven to eight hundred or even more than a thousand... Most of these peasants threatened the government by claiming to appeal to higher-level authorities. Some of them collected money from peasant households for the trip to make appeals to higher-level authorities.[15]

Hence, while some collective actions in China are legal or "in the shadow of law,"[16] others are "outside the shadow of law" but "in the shadow of reasonableness" (*he qing*). For example, in the four versions of the constitution of socialist China, the one enacted in 1954 does not grant the right to hold strikes, the 1975 and 1978 versions do permit strikes, but the 1982 version removes that right once again. Despite the 1954 constitution, numerous strikes were held in the mid-1950s. Rather than suppressing the workers, the government blamed its agents for their bureaucratic work style.[17] Likewise, workers and college students held strikes periodically in the 1980s. According to an incomplete count of 15 provinces, in the first half of 1993, the number of strikes totaled 180. The longest one lasted 40 days, and the largest one involved more than 4,500 people.[18] Strikes have increasingly become a means by which peasants-turned-workers fight against management.[19] If dramatic action like a strike is possible, other modes of action, such as blockades of government offices and traffic (which can be an escalation from collective appeals), should not be surprising.

As collective appeals and other forms of collective action pose a threat to stability, local officials have a strong incentive to prevent them, especially those actions directed at higher-level authorities. It has become a rule that conflicts occurring within a locality should not be taken to higher-level governments. Local governments have adopted four principles for handling appeals: no appeals to the central government, no recurring appeals, no collective appeals, and no unsettled old cases. For example, after 1994, the provincial government in Henan province adopted a so-called one-vote-veto system and a responsibility-locating system, in which government officials are punished for the occurrence of collective appeals, regardless of their other achievements.[20] A similar system was adopted in some counties in Beijing municipality.[21] Other local governments regulate that if collective appeals to higher-level authorities occur because of the incompetence or ignorance of the departments concerned, those departments must take back the protestors within a regulated period of time. They should give a satisfactory reply to the people within a week and report the solution to the city government. "If the people of a work unit make more than two appeals to higher-level authorities within a year, the leaders of the work unit must report to the government the reasons for the events and proposed solutions."[22] Reportedly, this policy has significantly reduced appeals to higher-level authorities.[23]

Constraints and concessions

To achieve the goals set by higher-level governments, local officials may use repression to silence the discontented. Yet, resorting to repression without just cause can be risky. For example, a city Party secretary of Henan province was removed from his post and expelled from the Party mainly because, between 1993 and 1997, he ordered the public security department to withhold more than 200 complaint letters, to search for the letter writers, and to punish them.[24] In another example, in 2000, a group of Muslims in a county in Shandong province appealed and then protested against a self-proclaimed Muslim restaurant that served pork to its customers. The local government put down the demonstration, killing six of the protestors. The officials involved were punished.[25] The constraint imposed on local governments not to punish people at will implies that concessions are needed. Some local governments have adopted a system called "visiting the people" (*xiafang*). "To maintain the political stability in society, efforts should be made at the grassroots level in order to remove the sources of instability."[26] With this method, the government actively seeks to solve the problems creating discontent, thereby preempting collective action.

The constraint to make concessions significantly increases the chances for successful action. For example, some laid-off workers from a county factory approached the provincial government to appeal for the punishment of their manager, whose corruption caused the factory to stop production and lay off workers. Just after they arrived at the provincial government, people sent by the county magistrate also arrived. The county officials asked the workers to leave and promised to investigate the case. These workers agreed, and the corrupt manager was duly punished.[27] Another laid-off worker reported a similar case:

> It was just before the 1995 Spring Festival. We had not received a penny from the factory for six months. Some retired people and couple workers (husbands and wives working in the same factory) could no longer stand. They organized themselves and gathered in front of the county government, demanding lay-off subsidies for the Festival. At that time, the mayor [i.e., the immediate boss of the county government] happened to be inspecting our county. He immediately allocated some funds to pay each worker a three-month salary for the Festival... The city mayor was so angry that right then and there he wanted to auction the car of the county magistrate to obtain the money to pay workers. In the end, only when our factory manager promised to sell his car was the county magistrate's spared.[28]

The example also shows that the timing of action can increase the odds of success. Local governments tend to suffer the most pressure on important occasions, such as National Day, because social stability is often the top priority of the government at these times.

> Group-based action often takes place during periods of important meetings such as the people's congress, the political consultative conference, the Party representatives' conference, and the government's work conference. It also occurs on important occasions or memorial dates of important events. The timing is thus politicized in order to increase social influence and to put more pressure on the Party committee or the government.[29]

For example, a city complaints bureau in Shaanxi province fell on hard times in 1993 when the central and provincial governments were holding important meetings. In one month, about 30 people from a county went to the city government to protest. They blocked the office compound and traffic four times within eight days and threatened to organize a group of 100 people to take their complaints to the central government. At the same time, 3,000 workers of a munitions factory who had not been paid for eight months held a demonstration, chanting "We want to survive and we want to eat." In addition, workers from another company and some peasants also held demonstrations. The head of the city complaints bureau remained at the office for five consecutive days to handle the appeals, although his wife was at that time hospitalized. Together with his staff, they attended to the protestors' demands and proposed remedies to appropriate authorities. While the problems of protestors were solved, the head of the complaints bureau was so overworked that he passed out.[30]

Hence, despite the authoritarian system in China, an effective means for citizens to address their problems is not to bypass but to approach the government. According to a survey of over 1,460 people in four provinces, about 53 percent replied that they would approach the government when their interests were ignored, whereas about 30 percent replied that they would use legal channels.[31] For example, in Shanghai in 1998, 80 percent of the 106 cases of collective labor disputes could be settled through arbitration or lawsuits, but only 21 percent were resolved this way. About 38 percent were settled at the grassroots level under the guidance of higher-level authorities, and 31 percent were resolved directly by higher-level authorities. According to the people in the arbitration department, the most important reason for settlement through government intervention was the belief among workers: "Raising the issue to higher authorities will make it more likely to be resolved and resolved in a way that brings more benefits to them." It was also true that solutions obtained with the intervention of higher authorities brought more benefits than those obtained through legal channels.[32]

Since the late 1990s, the central government has frequently convened meetings to address the issue of laid-off workers and has repeatedly required local governments to guarantee payment of layoff subsidies and worker pensions.[33] This provides a legitimate basis for workers' collective action. Yet, it must be pointed out that while collective action in China may not be risky, it does not necessarily lead to success. Both workers and peasants have experienced significant failures.[34] In a notorious case, due to the corruption of the manager, a factory of 600 workers suffered severe losses, leaving workers in dire straits. The workers appealed for retribution to nine Party and government organs at the city and county levels numerous times but without success.[35] There can be many reasons for such failures, including a lack of resources available to high-level authorities. A government official admitted in an interview that officials sometimes hide from citizens seeking help because some problems are beyond their ability to solve. Laid-off workers are more likely to succeed when their needs are easier to accommodate. This also explains why most laid-off workers focus on subsistence subsidies instead of jobs in their action. Equally important, the success of workers' collective action often depends on their ability to mobilize participants and exert pressure on the government. Hence, another crucial issue is how workers can mobilize themselves to exploit the political space.

Mobilization and collective action

Laid off workers' collective action is possible when there are enough participants who can coordinate themselves. A significant mechanism for mobilization is coordinators or leaders. These people are especially essential to Chinese workers' collective action because they perform multiple functions in the absence of independent trade unions, as discussed in Chapter 6. On the other hand, whether or not enough participants can be mobilized often depends on the way layoffs are carried out. Other things being equal, those who are simultaneously laid off are more easily organized into action than those who are sequentially laid off. The following section explains why and how self-made leaders emerge to lead workers' collective action and the conditions under which there can be sufficient participants.

Emergence of organizers

The emergence of leaders of rebellious collective action is a serious challenge to pure rational choice theory, which highlights the importance of material benefits. Some authors suggest that individuals will not assume the role of political leader if they do not receive additional benefit from the action.[36] But because there is no guarantee that they will benefit more than others, others point to the importance of nonmaterial interests. "A leader might derive some pleasure (utility) simply from being the head of the administrative apparatus required to make collections and supply collective goods."[37] Chong holds that "what is typically required is a core of highly dedicated, extremely moral—some might say extremely 'irrational'—individuals who are willing to assume leadership roles and to constitute in effect the critical mass that instigates the growth of collective action."[38] In the case of Chinese laid-off workers, moral considerations can be one, but not the only, reason for the emergence of leaders.

Both organizations and individuals can be organizers of collective action. In market economies, worker protests are usually organized by trade unions. For obvious reasons, trade unions in China are not allowed to organize activities independent of state control, and organizers must be workers. Leaders of Chinese workers' collective action differ from a typical political entrepreneur in that they may not be able to provide selective incentives or make sanctions, and collective action is usually based on laid-off workers' voluntary participation. Perry and Li's study of Chinese workers in the Cultural Revolution suggests that the "unusually forceful personalities" and personal ambitions of some individuals drove them to become rebellion leaders.[39] But laid-off workers have no personal ambitions beyond their struggle for economic benefits such as back salaries. In fact, being an organizer in China does not bring more benefits; instead, it puts one at high risk for punishment through the government's repression.

Based on my fieldwork and reported cases, initiators or organizers of the collective action of laid-off workers include current enterprise leaders, previous enterprise cadres, retired workers, soldiers-turned-workers, non-cadre Party members, and ordinary workers (Table 7.1). Most of these people are the elite among workers who wield more influence than the rank and file.[40] Many of them have experience dealing with the management or the government, because they are or were cadres, and can articulate the demands of laid-off workers. They are

Table 7.1 Backgrounds of organizers in Chinese workers' collective action ($N = 41$)

Background	Number	Frequency (%)
Previous enterprise leaders	12 (4 retired people)	29.2
Party-member workers	9 (4 retired people)	22
Current enterprise leaders	7	17
Military veterans	4	9.8
Others	9	22
Total	41	100

Source: Author's collection.

willing to lead often because of their personal stake in the action, community pressure, a sense of justice, or a combination of the three.

Self-interest

Some people become initiators or organizers to satisfy personal goals. Collective action serves as a means to an end that is beyond the reach of individual action. In this circumstance, the leaders' motives may or may not be the same as those of other participants. As Table 7.1 shows, many organizers are former or current enterprise cadres. The reform of SOEs in China has not only affected the average worker but has also hurt the interests of some cadres. Hence, some of them assume the role of organizer to protect their economic benefits, just like other participants. In 1995, for example, a county ship factory was on the verge of closure, and the industry bureau decided to lay off some of its workers. One 58-year-old worker presumed that he was unlikely to be laid off because he was close to retirement. Yet, it turned out that he was among those to go. He was so disturbed that he decided: "You lay me off, I will appeal to the government; you make me have no work to do, and I will give you something to do." He had been a middle-level cadre in the factory, had 40 years of work experience, and enjoyed some prestige among the workers. He became the organizer after he conferred with other laid-off workers. By leading about 200 people to appeal to the factory, the industrial bureau, and the government, this person did indeed give factory management "much to do." The leaders of the industrial bureau, the labor bureau, and the factory repeatedly met with this organizer to resolve the workers' demands. The factory leaders also asked factory cadres and Party members to donate relief money to the laid-off workers. Once some concessions were made, this organizer decided that collective appeals were no longer needed.[41]

In other cases, organizers may not have the same motivations as the rest of the participants, but they do share the same desire to take action against enterprise leaders. Power struggles and personal conflicts are not rare in SOEs in China. Some cadres, especially those removed from their posts, may mobilize workers who have been hurt economically to fight against the enterprise authority. In some cases, cadres filed false accusations against enterprise leaders and encouraged workers to participate with promises of promotions or Party membership.[42] Thus, it should not be surprising that in some firms, current or former cadres tend to be more active participants in collective action. A study of a loss-making textile factory with 6,000 workers and a failing company with 20,000 workers found that 30 percent of former leaders at the enterprise level and 50 percent of former cadres at the middle level (below enterprise manager) or above participated in collective action at least once, whereas only 15 percent of the rank and file did the same.[43] In addition, the influence these cadres can exert may make them more confident to take action, compared with the rank and file.

Community pressure

A second reason why some people become organizers is because of community pressure. Individuals are embedded in social networks and value their relationships. People who obtain a certain degree of popularity or status tend to conform to the expectations of others.[44] As Chong suggests, "There may be substantial community pressure on such individuals to lend their prestige and the leadership skills associated with their current roles to the new political enterprise, especially if it is perceived that collective action is impossible without the active involvement of these pivotal individuals."[45] The stress on nonmaterial benefits should not be entirely attributed to altruism. "An altruist person cares about how someone else feels, whereas a person motivated by popularity or esteem cares about how someone else feels about *him* (or *her*)."[46] Yet it is true that a combination of community pressure and altruism or a sense of justice makes it more likely that some individuals will assume the role of organizer.

In the case of Chinese laid-off workers, current and former cadres, as well as those Party-member workers who are involved in collective action, may feel community pressure to lead because laid-off workers usually have high expectations of them. Leadership is often a capacity that is transferable from one realm to another. "People regarded as leaders in one context... will hurt their status and credibility if they do not uphold their reputations in other situations which call for them to marshal their resources."[47] This may help explain why cadres tend to become the natural organizers of the collective action among laid-off workers. Sometimes, when laid-off workers elect representatives to deal with the government, cadres are very likely to be selected. As one interviewee reported:

> There were about fifty of us. We first went to the industrial bureau and talked with the officials about our subsidies. But one official who was a director of the general office in the bureau told us that the number of laid-off workers like us was too large in the whole industrial sector, and the industrial bureau was trying to get help from the government. But he was not sure whether they would succeed. What he said meant nothing to us. After we went out, we stood in front of the office, discussing what to do next. When someone suggested that we could go to the government, almost all of us looked at a previous shop-floor manager who was the highest ranking cadre among us

at that moment. This person thought for a while and said, "Let's go." He led us to the complaints bureau and selected three other people among us and they talked with the official there on our behalf.

Still other people become leaders because of their sense of justice. But these people also weigh community pressure against the possible costs or risks. They take the role of organizer often because they believe that *peaceful* action presents little risk. Ensuring that collective action remains peaceful, however, may be beyond their control. Hence, they lead because they fail to anticipate the risks *ex ante* and will often refuse to lead when the risk becomes obvious. In the workers' protests in Liaoyang of Liaoning province in 2002, a few leaders, driven by their sense of justice, secretly planned protests. Out of caution, three leaders drafted an emergency plan listing several other workers who would take over if police detained the three of them. After the protest began, the police did arrest all three leaders. A fourth activist was supposed to take the lead. Hundreds of workers gathered outside this worker's apartment building, waiting for him to come out and to tell them what to do, but he never showed up. He was scared: "You have to understand, I came under intense pressure from above [i.e., the government] after they [i.e., the other leaders] were arrested. I was told I would be sent to prison if I dared do anything similar." After he abandoned the workers, the labor movement began to disintegrate. The protests to free the detained leaders attracted fewer and fewer people, and soon they stopped altogether. Meanwhile, police were making their way down a list of more than 50 worker leaders, visiting one after another. Fearful of arrest, unsure of whom to trust, the organizers split up and went into hiding.[48]

Sufficient participants

While leaders are often crucial for collective action, it will be effective only when there are sufficient numbers of participants who can make "big trouble." As some interviewees said, "We often say that the more people the more power (*ren duo liliang da*); for the leaders, the more participants, the bigger the trouble (*ren dou mafan da*)." My survey also finds that, other things being equal, more participants are more likely to achieve success.[49] This is also important for motivating the participation of workers because they believe that individual contribution is important. "If more people approach the leaders, they can put more pressure on them. If only a few people approach the leaders, the latter can easily turn their backs on you and tell you to leave."[50]

The issue, then, is when are there sufficient participants and thus large-scale collective action. Usually, large-scale action is possible when the interests of a larger number of people are threatened at the same time, because most, if not all, of them face losses. If this is true, the mode in which workers are laid off may affect the possibility of action in the sense that, other things being equal (e.g., they are unpaid or under-compensated), simultaneous layoffs are more likely to lead to action than are sequential layoffs. First, in simultaneous layoffs, fragmentation of interests is less serious and consensus building is easier because a larger number of people are affected and motivated. In addition, the short time span in which layoffs occur limits the number of people who are able to find other jobs. When workers are laid off simultaneously, it often means that the firm is bankrupt, closing, or stopping production. Because of budget constraints, these firms may also fail to pay their laid-off workers, and their action, if it exists, will be directed at the government. In contrast, workers who are laid off sequentially often receive subsidies because their firms are still in operation. This is especially true for laid-off workers from large SOEs with more financial resources (see Chapter 2). In addition, collective action in such firms is difficult also because the management still has power over laid-off workers.

Second, simultaneous layoffs also affect cadres, who may then become organizers. In contrast, sequential layoffs prevent the emergence of leaders. For one, sequential layoffs often do not affect cadres unless the whole firm is failing or most people are retrenched. For another, those cadres who are sequentially laid off may lack the incentive to become organizers. As discussed in Chapter 4, compared with average laid-off workers, laid-off cadres are much more likely to find jobs through personal connections or greater abilities, or both. A survey of 1,000 laid-off workers conducted by the ACFTU in 1997 also suggested that while about 18.5 percent of laid-off workers were able to find jobs, the reemployment rates for laid-off technicians and cadres were 22 percent and 33.3 percent, respectively.[51] This implies that in sequential layoffs, some employees, including cadres, who are laid off earlier may find jobs before others are laid off.

The lack of organizers or leaders can be a significant obstacle to the collective action of sequentially laid-off workers. It is common for some firms to lay off workers sequentially and pay them in the initial period. But as the financial situation of the firms worsens, payments may be discontinued. As workers who are sequentially laid off lack opportunities for regular interactions, leaders are necessary to organize them to take action. In addition, sequential layoffs may be based on individual reasons, like poor performance, and people may blame themselves. Self-blaming workers need to be motivated or mobilized to participate. Thus, workers' collective action depends not only on how many are laid off, but also on who is laid off and how.

Scenarios for collective action

The discussion in the previous section suggests that, other things being equal (e.g., the unavailability of subsidies), the emergence or absence of organizers and the existence or lack of sufficient participants significantly affect the likelihood of collective action. Table 7.2 indicates the possibility of collective action by unpaid or undercompensated laid-off workers. Collective action is most likely when unpaid workers are laid off simultaneously and organizers are present, and least likely when workers are laid off sequentially and organizers are absent. When communication among prospective participants is possible, workers may also take spontaneous action but often with the mobilization of behind-the-scenes organizers. Profitable firms or those that make marginal losses are more likely to employ

Table 7.2 Situations in which unpaid or under-compensated laid-off workers take action

	Simultaneous layoffs	Sequential layoffs
Presence of organizers	Most likely	Likely
Absence of organizers	Possible	Least likely

sequential layoffs, and since their laid-off workers are often paid, the workers lack the incentive to act. Simultaneous layoffs often occur in firms undergoing ownership reforms, such as bankruptcy or privatization.[52] A halt in production and the suspension of salaries have the same effect as a simultaneous layoff.

The following section illustrates how different situations give rise to workers' collective action. Some protests are planned and executed by organizers, and others are spontaneous. In either case, communication among prospective participants is essential. Existing research on collective action suggests that "consistent, strong, and replicable findings are that substantial increases in the levels of cooperation are achieved when individuals are allowed to communicate face to face."[53] Communication facilitates collective action by exchanging mutual commitment, increasing trust, creating and reinforcing norms, developing group identity, and promoting the confidence of participants.[54]

Simultaneous layoffs, leaders, and collective action

Thus far, large-scale collective action by laid-off workers in China tends to result from the implementation of reform measures such as bankruptcy, which involves the simultaneous layoff of a large number of workers who receive very limited or no compensation. In such cases, many laid-off workers, including able people like cadres who may become leaders, find themselves in a common and undesirable situation.[55] For instance, in February 2000, in a town called Yangjiazhangzhi in Liaoning province, over 20,000 miners, joined by thousands of family members, smashed windows, blocked traffic, burned cars, and fought with armed police for days. Order was restored after the government sent the army and police to the town. As expected, a few worker leaders were arrested. The unrest began with the bankruptcy of the mine. Workers were offered a lump sum severance pay on the basis of 560 yuan for every year served. After the payments were made, there would be no additional unemployment subsidies. A worker who had worked for 20 years at the mine would receive compensation that would hardly support his family for more than two years. In addition, workers were asked to pay pension contributions from this amount. It was clear to all that the amount was far too little. Underpaid compensation was a direct motivation for action. Equally important, as the economy of the town depended on the mine, there was little chance of finding other jobs locally. The simultaneous layoff of such a large number of people put most workers in the situation of having no alternatives. The emergence of leaders, who were also victims of the reform measure, also made collective action possible.[56]

One of my interviewees also reported how bankruptcy led to collective action in his factory of about 500 workers. In 1998, the factory declared bankruptcy, and workers were given lump sum compensation. But the factory had not paid retirement insurance for its workers for three years. Workers and cadres alike worried that if the factory did not make up for this, they would not receive their pensions. After workers received the news of bankruptcy, they were upset. Several hundred workers gathered in the factory to discuss this issue, and it was not difficult for them to take further action. When they gathered around a few middle-level cadres of the factory, the leaders suggested taking their grievance to the city government. The workers had no reason to disagree and went to block the government compound. The city government resolved the issue by forcing a firm that owed money to this factory to pay the insurance claims.[57]

In other cases, although a firm may not lay off all of its workers, collective action is still possible if the number of laid-off workers is sufficiently large and if cadres are affected. In 1998, a factory of about 700 workers adopted an employee shareholder ownership plan based on a proposal approved by the city government. According to the plan, each worker was required to invest at least 5,000 yuan in company shares in order to keep his or her jobs. Those who refused would be laid off or fired. Given the poor performance of the factory, a number of workers worried that they would never recover their initial investment of 5000 yuan, a large amount of money for most workers. Over one hundred workers, including some workshop managers, refused to buy shares and were laid off without pay. Four cadres assumed leadership roles and led workers to appeal to the government. They divided the workers into three groups and asked them to block the government office compound in three shifts from morning to evening every day until their goal was achieved. The worker leaders made it clear to the government that they would not leave until the problem was solved. In the end, the government told the factory not to force its workers to buy shares.[58] In this case, the emergence of leaders and the cooperation of participants put workers in a stronger position to negotiate with the government.[59]

Sequential layoffs, leaders, and collective action

Compared with simultaneous layoffs, as noted above, sequential layoffs are less likely to produce leaders who can organize and mobilize collective action. Yet once leaders emerge, collective action is possible. In a case reported by an interviewee, a factory of 400 workers merged with another firm under the guidance of the city government. About 95 percent of the workers were laid off sequentially because of the deteriorating situation in the firm that merged. In the end, laid-off workers were not paid and retirees lost their pensions. Some workers appealed to the industrial bureau and local government, but little was achieved because their action was too small to pressure the government to negotiate. The lack of large-scale action was not only due to some laid-off workers' ability to secure temporary jobs but, more important, due to a lack of mobilization. Things changed when a retired worker, who was once a soldier and had fought against the KMT (Kuomintang) in China's civil war, assumed leadership. He complained, "Damn it, I fought against the KMT (*kang guo qiang*) and ate rice bran (*chi guo kang*). But now I cannot even get my pension."

A number of workers followed this leader to block the office building of the company and went to the industrial bureau. The leaders of the industrial bureau moved their offices to avoid meeting these troublemakers. As a last resort, the retired worker led about 50 people to block the office compound of the local government. Although he was not a charismatic leader, he spoke to the workers and succeeded in mobilizing them to take their protest to the local government for a few days. The government finally conceded to their demands, but it adopted a divide-and-rule strategy. While it promised to pay retired workers their pensions, it told non-retired workers to approach their firm for a solution. The retirees, including the leader, stopped the collective action after they achieved their goal—to obtain their pensions. The split between retired workers and non-retired workers brought an end to the collective action.

Spontaneous collective action

Not all collective actions involve explicit or identifiable organizers; some collective actions need less mobilization by leaders and can be seen as spontaneous, although behind-the-scenes mobilization or consensus building is often indispensable. For example, in 1998, a failing ship transportation company with about 900 workers could no longer pay subsidies or pensions to its workers and retirees. By January 1999, workers had not received their salaries for six months. With the Spring Festival approaching, workers felt the pressure to have some money for the most important Chinese festival of the year. The company was large by standards of the city in terms of the number of workers and its business scale. It had built houses on a piece of its land for hundreds of workers. This made it easy for them to discuss shared problems and to build consensus. Retired workers were especially resentful of losing their pensions. Some proposed that they appeal to the government, and many others, including non-retirees, agreed. They took a leaderless action (i.e., without explicit organizers). As discussed earlier, the government is more willing to make concessions on important occasions, such as the Spring Festival or National Day. Timing increased the odds of success, and the government paid those workers two-months' salary or pension for the festival.[60]

Spontaneous collective action is also possible among temporary communities. In 1999, a city government decided to restrict the number of pedicabs by imposing annual inspections. The pedicab drivers, many of whom were laid-off workers, all understood that an annual inspection meant more fees, which would reduce their hard-earned income. When drivers met one another on the streets, they discussed the issue, voiced their discontent, and reached a consensus that they should ask the government to repeal its decision. One worker recalled the process: "We did not have an organizer, but the more we talked, the more we agreed with each other. When many of us (pedicab drivers) rallied together, some suggested approaching the government. Everyone seemed to agree, and we did that." Dozens of drivers drove their pedicabs to block the office compound of the government, stopping traffic in neighboring areas. Meanwhile, they also agreed that they would not charge customers on that day in order to obtain the support of the people. Although it is difficult to assess whether the second measure had any impact on the government, the collective action turned out to be a great success. Because the pedicabs had effectively blocked traffic, the local government responded very quickly. In addition to revoking annual inspections, it abolished several other fees previously levied on pedicab drivers.

Spontaneous action is more likely when catalytic or tragic events provide dramatic evidence that people's vital interests are being ignored. Such events provoke intense emotional reactions that can mobilize great numbers of people.[61] In a county in Zhejiang province, a factory with about 100 workers started incurring losses in 1994. But the corrupt manager did not stop embezzling funds from the factory for his personal benefit. By December 1998, workers had not received salaries for 18 months, and were making a living as retailers, tricycle drivers, ironsmiths, and the like. Yet, significant collective action to punish this corrupt manager was not taken until a retired worker committed suicide. This worker had not received his 200-yuan monthly pension for a year and had felt hopeless. He drowned himself in a river after writing a letter, and his body was discovered five days later. This tragic event immediately provoked the workers to demand that the government investigate the corrupt manager. The government accepted the case and arrested the manager after it gathered evidence. Similarly, in a factory in the southwest, workers had not been paid for years. A retired worker committed suicide by jumping out of a window of a building. Shocked, hundreds of retired workers held a demonstration, carrying the body of that worker.[62] In such cases, prospective participants often have strong consensus about action, and collective action can be discussed into existence. What is needed is for someone to articulate the proposal. Such actions are also less risky because the target is often in a morally weak position.

Scale of resistance and reform

The importance of leaders and the modes of layoffs analyzed earlier also help in assessing the impact of massive layoffs on social stability in China. Usually, social stability is more likely to be threatened by large-scale action that can be taken by workers from several firms or workers of one large firm. For reasons discussed in Chapter 6, cross-firm action is risky. If cross-firm action is less possible, large-scale action can only be taken by large firms with many workers. While there have been large-scale actions taken by workers of large SOEs, the government's reform policy reduces such actions.

We can use motivation and mobilization to examine the possibility of large-scale collective action. If holding motivation at a constant, laid-off workers from large SOEs are better able to mobilize on three accounts. First, when many laid-off workers from large SOEs are laid off, there is a greater likelihood of having sufficient participants and organizers. Second, laid-off workers from large SOEs tend to be less scattered, at least compared with laid-off workers from small SOEs. According to my survey of 724 laid-off workers, about 25 percent lived in houses assigned or sold to them by their firms. Others either lived in private houses or in housing provided by the work units of their family members. Large firms are more likely to assign housing to their employees. For example, only 16 percent of those working in firms with fewer than 300 people were assigned housing, as opposed to 66.7 percent of those working in firms with 5,000 or more employees (Table 7.3).[63] Chinese SOEs often build housing for workers on their own land or on land they have bought, in which case their workers live in close communities. In contrast, the lack of a housing provision on the part of small SOEs indicates that their laid-off workers are scattered and, after layoffs, face more difficulties in mobilization, as discussed in Chapter 6.[64]

Finally, workers from large SOEs may be more confident than their counterparts in small firms in taking action, because large-scale action is more likely to attract the attention of the government. Local governments in China have grown accustomed to small-scale peaceful action. Some laid-off workers, therefore, have begun to take more dramatic action, such as blocking highways, railways, or bridges. But for this mode of action to succeed and to be low in risk, a small number of participants is not sufficient. As elsewhere, "If very few people are haranguing in the streets, they may be ignored or merely told to move along. If moderate numbers are milling about and seemingly potentially dangerous, they may be suppressed with full force. But if very large numbers are organized and even marching, there may be little that the state can do short of bringing draconian force to bear, and it may choose not to do that or it may be unable to do that."[65] One survey of 26 contentious collective actions by laid-off workers, such as traffic or office-compound blockades, suggests that all of them had more than 200 participants, and 88 percent (or 23) had more than 500 participants.[66] Such scale of action, however, is often beyond the reach of laid-off workers from small SOEs.

In China, the administrative rank of the owner of the SOE not only indicates the scale of the SOE in terms of its assets but also in terms of its number of

Table 7.3 Laid-off workers' welfare provision ($N = 724$)

SOEs by the number of employees	LOWs assigned housing (%)	Unpaid LOWs (%)[a]	LOWs in each group (%)
<300	15.9	23.6	28.7
301–500	20.4	20.9	27.1
501–1,000	25.8	19.5	17.7
1,001–3,000	32.2	14.9	12.0
3,001–5,000	39.7	11.5	10.8
>5,000	66.7	7.4	3.7
Average/Total	25.3	17.7	100.0

Source: Author's survey, 1999.

Notes
a Including those who were paid for less than three months. LOWs: Laid-off workers.

employees. The higher the administrative rank of the owner, the more likely the firm has more workers. Hence, SOEs under higher levels of government tend to have more employees. By 1995, the average number of employees of SOEs under the central, provincial, city, and county governments were 2,290, 871, 600, and 224, respectively.[67] This implies that firms under higher-level authorities are more able to take large-scale action, other things being equal.

While the above comparisons are made by holding motivation constant, motivation is not constant in reality. Laid-off workers from large SOEs often lack the motivation for action because their needs are more likely to be accommodated. The reform policy of "retaining large SOEs and letting go of small ones" in the 1990s caused a disproportional number of small SOEs to be privatized, closed, or declared bankrupt. From 1995 to 1998, the number of industrial SOEs decreased by more than 44 percent. While the number of both large and medium firms increased by about 14 percent, small-sized industrial SOEs decreased by more than 53 percent.[68] As a result, laid-off workers from large SOEs comprised a very small percentage of the total (Table 7.3). In 1998, for example, laid-off workers from firms under the central government accounted for only about 9 percent of the total.[69]

Equally important, large SOEs are more likely to provide subsidies or compensation to their laid-off workers, whereas small SOEs are less able to make profits or receive financial support. In 1997, about 32 percent of laid-off workers from small industrial SOEs failed to receive subsistence subsidies, compared to 8 percent of laid-off workers from SOEs under the central government.[70] Hence, although laid-off workers from SOEs under the central government accounted for more than 13.5 percent of the total number of laid-off workers, they accounted for less than 5 percent of the total number of unpaid laid-off workers.[71] This pattern is also reflected in my survey (Table 7.3). Precisely because large SOEs have more financial resources, they are more likely to conduct sequential rather than simultaneous layoffs, which, as discussed earlier, are not conducive to collective action.

The mode of reform favoring larger SOEs, together with government policies toward organizers, has significantly reduced the frequency of large-scale action, often making worker resistance individual-firm based, small-scaled, non-contentious, and short-lived. This is an important reason why massive layoffs in China have not posed a serious challenge to the social and political stability of China. This, however, by no means suggests that the resistance of laid-off workers does not have an impact on the government. Laid-off workers achieve two forms of success through collective action. One, they receive concrete concessions like back pay. Less direct but not insignificant, numerous and persistent collective acts produce an aggregate impact on high-level authorities that makes policy changes possible.

Piven and Cloward point out that the power of the poor lies in their ability to create institutional disruptions that threaten social or economic operations.[72] Chinese laid-off workers are not in a position to create economic disruptions; what they can do, at most, is to create peaceful chaos for local governments.

The power of Chinese laid-off workers thus lies in the fact that the impact of resistance goes beyond a single individual or collective action. In other words, constant pressure applied through many small-scale actions makes the government see the potential effect of a flood of resistance. James Scott describes the resistance of the weak: "[T]he aggregation of thousands upon thousands of such 'petty' acts of resistance has dramatic economic and political effects."[73] It is in this sense that the weak have power, though they may not realize that each of their acts contributes to the aggregate impact. In China, the resistance of laid-off workers has not only slowed some reform measures like privatization,[74] it has also pushed the Chinese government to take layoffs seriously and to make great efforts to guarantee the payment of lay-off subsidies and pensions.[75]

As the reform proceeds, the Chinese government faces even more pressure, because it now has to deal with large SOEs. By the end of 1998, the ratio of loss-making large and medium SOEs (i.e., 55 percent) was, for the first time, higher than that of small ones (i.e., 47 percent).[76] From 1998, the government began to target about 6,600 large and medium SOEs for reform. The government adopted three reform measures: (1) providing loans to SOEs with subsidized interests for technological innovations, (2) mergers and bankruptcy, and (3) turning SOE debt into bank shares.[77] Despite these measures, the reform proved difficult. By 2000, the government closed or declared bankrupt about 1,000 large and medium SOEs, but those firms whose worker numbers exceeded 10,000 only accounted for 2 to 3 percent of the total.[78]

In 2001, Premier Zhu Rongji admitted that industrial reform had to be pursued in a way that would maintain social order: "Of course, we have to be on the safe side and slow down a little some of our major reforms according to the current conditions... if you want to reform and ask two-thirds of the (workers) to go, where will you tell them to go?"[79] In 2001, the Supreme Court ordered provincial courts not to proceed with bankruptcy of SOEs with assets in excess of 50 million yuan, unless they had received prior approval from the Supreme Court. Centralization of decision-making with respect to SOE bankruptcies signaled that "crucial industrial reforms are being slowed down as Beijing concentrates on warding off social unrest."[80] In 2002, the central government decided that 2,900 large- and medium-sized SOEs would be declared bankrupt within four years, affecting 57 million employees. The government planned to allocate 290 billion yuan for implementing the reform.[81]

Yet, while worker resistance has slowed the reform of large SOEs, it would be difficult for workers to stop the reforms altogether. To be sure, there have been a few significantly large labor protests in the three provinces in the northeast (i.e., Heilongjiang, Jilin, and Liaoning) in the early 2000s, especially in Liaoning province, which has the most large- and medium-sized SOEs in China.[82] However, these cases point to the difficulties of, rather than to a general tendency for, labor unrest in China. First, only a few provinces in China have a great concentration of large SOEs. Second, few cities have experienced repeated large-scale labor unrest. Although the protests in Liaoyang and Daqing lasted for an unprecedented period of time, government policies toward organizers sent a strong signal that organizing large-scale collective action would not be tolerated. The coexistence of a large pool of connected participants and fearless leaders is not always available. In addition, the ineffective resistance of workers laid off earlier may exert a discouraging effect on those to be laid off in the future.

Conclusion

This chapter explains why collective action occurs and sometimes succeeds under an authoritarian regime. It finds that worker resistance is neither a way of releasing frustration or anger nor a risk-ridden move. Rather, it occurs in a context in which there exists a chance of success and where risk is limited. The conditions for collective action arise from the continuities and changes within the communist regime. Local governments in China face constraints that serve as opportunities for worker resistance. The constraints are a result of the high-level government's prohibition against the use of force at will by local governments. Hence, opportunities for resistance are unlike those arising from changes occurring within the political system, as stressed in the literature on social movements.[83] The implication of these opportunities is that the cost of participation is not prohibitive, and a certain degree of mobilization is possible. This political space creates opportunity for action. It also provides flexibility in the political system and reduces or prevents backlash, which might otherwise occur in an entirely repressive system. In a broader sense, the channels for political participation strengthen the "degree of government" of the Chinese state by reducing the gap between the channels of participation and the mobilized discontented masses.[84]

This chapter also examined the role of organizers and how they emerge. The reasons for assuming a leadership role include having a personal stake in the action, community pressure, and a sense of justice. What may prevent or facilitate worker resistance is also the way workers are laid off. Other things being equal, those who are simultaneously laid off are more likely to act, compared with those who are laid off sequentially. Despite the numerous instances of worker resistance, the state usually finds such actions tolerable because they are often small in scale and pose no threat to political stability and to the continuation of reform in China.

8 Conclusion

This study explores laid-off workers' varied responses to retrenchment by demonstrating the difficulties and possibilities of collective action under an authoritarian regime. Rather than focusing entirely either on worker resistance or on their silence, my study adopts a dual-interaction approach to explain variations in workers' responses to reforms in terms of their collective action. It sees collective resistance, and its absence thereof, of Chinese workers as the result of two types of interactions. One is interaction between laid-off workers and the reformer and the other is the interaction among the workers themselves. This approach contributes to an understanding of collective action by showing how action against the government is possible under an authoritarian regime. It suggests that solidarity and coordination mechanisms of workers are preconditions for action, and that, without them, the capacity of workers to act is undermined. On the other hand, collective action and its outcome are influenced by the power of and constraints on the targets of their action, that is, the government and the management. While such constraints may create opportunities for collective resistance, the target has the power to adopt various measures to weaken resistance. Its policies determine the nature, mode, and scale of resistance, thereby producing noninstitutionalized politics by shaping people's incentive and ability to act. The following summarizes the rationale behind Chinese workers' resistance and its implications for better understanding the collective action of the deprived, government reform strategies, and the relations between political institutions and economic transitions.

Shared interests and the potential of collective action

When collective action depends on individuals' voluntary participation, the scale of action, to a great extent, is determined by the number of people with shared interests or a focal issue (or issues). A focal issue can serve as a coordination mechanism. In other words, the goal *per se* may be the most important motivation for participation. For instance, many people, including workers, participated in the Tiananmen incident in China in 1989 because the issues raised by the students held broad appeal. High inflation and the demand for anticorruption measures were focal issues for most of the participants, which made it possible for students to receive widespread support.[1]

Conclusion   121

In the recent spate of layoffs, at the firm level, a lack of a focal point implies that within an enterprise, fully employed workers and laid-off workers tend not to cooperate because they do not have shared interests, at least in the short run. Coordination of workers is further weakened by the lack of independent trade unions or workers' councils, coupled with powerful management. Unlike trade unions in some democratic systems,[2] Chinese trade unions are not in a position to coordinate worker resistance by providing selective incentives or sanctions. Hence, workers' participation is interest driven. It is those who have not received subsistence subsidies and lack alternatives that are more likely to take action. In contrast, those who have alternatives do not see collective action as a means to their end and cannot be forced to participate. In fact, for these laid-off workers, participation would increase their opportunity cost in the sense that they are under pressure to make ends meet for their families.

Worker resistance in other countries has also pointed to the importance of focal issues and the "catnet" of participants. In the former Soviet Union in the late 1980s and early 1990s, common economic concerns, together with the relaxation of political control, made strikes possible.[3] In Poland, workers, who were instrumental in bringing an end to the socialist regime, were often affected by the government's economic policies simultaneously. In the 1970s and 1980s, price increases were the focal issue of workers' protests across the country, which laid the foundation for Solidarity.[4] More important, in their struggle to achieve a common economic goal, Polish workers strengthened their organizational ability. Large-scale strikes held in the early 1970s and 1976 gave Polish workers much-needed experience in dealing with the government and in organizing workers across factories and regions. Hence, by 1980,

> All the structural components that would allow the workers to create Solidarity in 1980 had thus been conceived, tested, and internalized by workers in the coastal areas in 1970. The first two organizational tools—the sit-down strike and the interfactory strike committee—had been forged. The central ideological step had also been taken: the articulation of the demand for independent unions. A new frame for worker struggle now existed on the Baltic Coast.[5]

Common suffering was the catalyst for the rise of Solidarity in 1980. This movement began with the government's attempt to introduce a limited price increase in order to prevent a crash of the market, especially in the food market. The price increase affected the living standard of many workers, which provided a direct motivation for nationwide protests. As in the 1970s, when workers learned the news of price increases, they conducted strikes and resumed work only after they received a wage increase. The success of the "early risers" encouraged many more workers to strike and thereby triggered the wave of strikes across the whole country, which changed the course of the Polish labor movement.[6]

In China, broadly speaking, the gradual or partial mode of reform in SOEs is a significant reason for its relatively smooth process. The Chinese government has not faced insurmountable problems because state employees are affected by reform measures differently. Employees in sectors that are not affected are less likely to join the struggle of those who suffer the full impact of unprecedented reform measures. As some laid-off workers reported, "In today's China, some people want to have something to eat, whereas others want to have something good to eat."[7] At the societal level in contemporary China, social groups often have distinct demands rather than shared interests. Focal points are lacking, other than the issue of corruption. Stratification among Chinese citizens suggests that some people have benefited more from reform than have others. The struggle for concrete economic benefits by one group can hardly appeal to others. As Perry and Selden point out, "[T]he laments of laid-off workers do not readily resonate with the outcries of over-taxed farmers or the complaints of critical intellectuals, or the protests of minority nationalities or women."[8] Research on dramatic social change like revolution has found that "[r]evolutions are not made; they come."[9] When structural crises happen and simultaneously affect a significant number of people, including powerful social groups, collective action against a declining state is possible because powerful groups have the ability to take action. It is in this circumstance that revolutionary action is difficult to suppress.[10]

Coordination and collective action

A focal issue only points to the *potential* or *possible scale* of collective action rather than its inevitability because of the difficulties involved in organizing participants. This study finds that three factors significantly affect Chinese workers' ability to mobilize themselves: the presence of organizers, the micro-level environment in which individuals interact, and the modes of layoffs. While studies of collective action highlight the importance of leaders, little empirical effort has been expended to examine why and how leaders, who do not benefit more from the action and often bear more risk, emerge. This study suggests that self-interest may be an important reason why some people become leaders, as collective action serves as an irreplaceable means to achieve their personal goals. Moreover, community pressure and a sense of justice may also motivate some individuals to take up leadership roles. However, the Chinese government is not tolerant of organizers and may employ strategies to discourage their emergence, making collective action difficult.

A second factor that affects Chinese workers' mobilization is the micro-environment in which workers operate. As laid-off workers often lack the opportunity for regular interaction after layoffs, those who live in close proximity are more able to overcome the problem of coordination. Therefore, laid-off workers who are scattered after layoffs would encounter more difficulties in organizing collective resistance unless leaders emerge. Due to the individual-enterprise-based welfare system in China, workers' access to public housing depends on the financial resources of individual enterprises. Usually, larger SOEs are more likely to provide housing for workers, making it easier for their laid-off workers to mobilize than workers from small SOEs.

Another factor that affects Chinese workers' mobilization is the way layoffs are carried out. The problem for workers is not only the number of workers laid off, but also the manner and target of layoffs. In China, workers are laid off either simultaneously or sequentially. As discussed in Chapter 7, other things being equal, workers who are laid off sequentially are less likely to take action than are those who are simultaneously laid off. First, simultaneous layoffs are more conducive to mobilization because people tend to receive the news of the layoff at the same time and may know of one another's willingness to participate more easily. Workers who are laid off sequentially lack the opportunity for regular interaction, and sharing information becomes more difficult without organizers. Second, sequential layoffs often affect a limited number of people within a firm, and the scale of resistance is thus smaller. In addition, workers laid off in this way are often paid unemployment compensation at least initially and have a weaker incentive to take action. Some may find jobs before others are laid off. Third, simultaneous layoffs are more likely to affect cadres, who can organize collective action. Finally, in sequential layoffs, firms may adopt seemingly objective criteria and workers may blame themselves for being laid off.

The relationship between the mode of layoffs and collective action also helps us to understand why militant Polish workers became silent in the post-communist period when a significant number of them were laid off. In post-communist Poland, because of the fear of workers' strong resistance arising from job loss, the government had begun the process of privatization slowly. Yet, when the "shock therapy" was set into motion, those once militant workers did not take action as expected. In the early 1990s, the Polish government managed to provide generous compensation to workers to encourage them to accept early retirement. This measure gradually became a financial burden for the government, but the reform continued. By late 1993, the unemployment rate reached an unprecedented level of 25 percent or higher, and laid-off workers accounted for a significant portion of the unemployed.[11] Still, these workers did not stage contentious protests. An underlying cause for inaction can be traced to the mode of layoffs.

In the late 1980s, the Polish government legislated elaborate restrictions on massive layoffs, making them "highly unattractive." SOE directors who wanted to undertake mass layoffs were obligated to obtain the consent of the workers' council. Cumbersome procedures made the practice onerous. Once the proposal for layoff was approved by the council, a director had to provide at least 45 days notice to all affected workers. Workers who were laid off in this manner were entitled to up to three months of severance pay plus up to six months of supplemental compensation. In contrast, workers who were laid off individually received nothing. Because of these restrictions, large-scale layoffs were not a common choice for Polish SOE directors, and workers were usually laid off on an individual basis.

This policy significantly reduced workers' collective resistance by preventing the emergence of large and concentrated groups of angry laid-off workers. As Kramer points out:

> To the extent that the unemployment pool included workers who were laid off, the large majority were dismissed for individual reasons, often for disciplinary infractions. This pattern was by no means fortuitous. From the

outset, the Polish government deliberately imposed cumbersome restrictions on mass layoffs and gave workers' council a major role in the process. These concessions may have been economically detrimental in the short term, but they proved to be a lasting political asset.[12]

The cases of China and Poland both suggest that the mode of layoffs significantly impacts coordination efforts and the scale of collective action. This policy is especially important in preventing workers from large firms from taking contentious action because it fragments their interests. This being the case, large-scale resistance is only possible with the mobilization efforts of organizers or leaders. The mode of layoffs may thus bear on the continuation of the reforms.

Government and reform policies

Workers' ability to take action is determined not only by their solidarity and mobilization, but also by their interaction with the government. This study has argued that the Chinese government's reform measures have reduced the possibility of worker resistance. In reform, those affected may resist in a number of ways, including creating social, economic, or political disruptions.[13] This is why reform is an undertaking replete with uncertainties and risks.[14] In China, laid-off workers are no longer able to create economic disruptions because they no longer retain economic resources. Given this constraint, the power of laid-off workers lies in whether they are able to create peaceful chaos through nonviolent protests targeting the local government. But the government's policy of "retaining the large and letting go of the small" (RLS) has significantly reduced the scale of disruptions because the policy affected mostly small SOEs rather than large ones at least in the 1990s. This policy has both economic and political rationales. Economically, larger SOEs pay more taxes and provide more jobs. In 1997, Zhu Rongji, then a vice premier, pointed out:

> The profits and taxes of the 1,000 large and medium SOEs to which we give special support account for 85 percent of the total profits and taxes generated by all enterprises in the country. This not only indicates the economies of scale but also points to the dominant status of the state economy. The way to improve the performance of SOEs is "retaining the large and letting go of the small." If we can promote the efficiency of these 1,000 SOEs, our country will be hopeful. "Letting go of small SOEs" may take different forms... as long as they can operate, small SOEs will have a chance to develop and the burdens of the state will be alleviated.[15]

What is more relevant here is the political rationale behind the policy of RLS. The reform of large SOEs has proved difficult not only in China but also in other transitional economies like Russia.[16] But because of the government's policy of RLS, as discussed in Chapter 2, most laid-off workers are from small and medium SOEs. Although some workers from large SOEs have also been laid off, they are less likely to take action. Laid-off workers from large SOEs are often paid when they are laid off, as large SOEs often have more resources. Precisely because large SOEs often have more financial resources, they tend to conduct sequential layoffs instead of wholesale closure or privatization. While workers from small SOEs may have more incentive to take action, the lack of organization makes action difficult. Equally important, action is often less disruptive because of their smaller scale. This is why large-scale collective acts have been relatively infrequent, although some did occur in some areas like Liaoning province.

At the firm level, collective resistance arising from reform can be reduced if the firm does not lay off those employees who have more power. In some countries, strikes over large-scale layoffs may not be due to the loss of jobs *per se* but because layoffs endanger a powerful organization—the trade union. As Golden suggests, "industrial action over job loss occurs most often not where job loss itself is most frequent...but instead where institutional protections for union representatives on the shopfloor are weakest."[17] Hence, laying off too many shopfloor union representatives would threaten the union as an organization. The union's ability to mobilize its people makes industrial action more probable. Without independent unions, Chinese workers' resistance can be organized only by the workers themselves. Hence, one way to reduce resistance is to avoid laying off those capable of organizing resistance. Cadres have more power than average employees and are thus less likely to be laid off. By the same token, holding other factors constant, if cadres are among those to be laid off, collective action is more likely because they have the ability to mobilize and organize workers.

Flexibility of the Chinese political system

It is beyond doubt that the reform of SOEs has led to incessant resistance from workers. However, such action may not be an indicator of the inability of the government to maintain social and political stability in China. Huntington has long pointed out that social order may be endangered when the gap between the channels of participation and mobilization increases.[18] Hence, a political system that is able to preempt disputes without causing serious damage to the system can be seen as being highly flexible. The findings of this study suggest that an authoritarian regime can be flexible.

In explaining the absence of a positive relationship between discontent and aggressive political participation in the United States, Muller and Jukam attribute the inadequate impact of discontent to the democratic system. "In a democratic political system, electoral institutions provide opportunities for citizens to bring about peaceful political change. Discontent with specific performance is thus unlikely, by itself, to afford a strong incentive for participation in civil disobedience or violence."[19] Resentful Chinese workers are situated in a political setting that does not provide such opportunities. Yet this does not mean that the lack of resistance is due to repression by the government, although selective imposition of punishment on leaders is sometimes enforced. Indeed, one can argue that the

Chinese government's policies in dealing with disgruntled people are not much different from what is done in some democratic regimes.

In democracies, because of the pressure arising from the electoral system, politicians have to be careful when carrying out reform in order to retain the support of their constituents. Paul Pierson points out that politicians may minimize political resistance by using obfuscation, division, and compensation in dismantling a welfare state.

> They may seek to manipulate information flows to decrease public awareness of their actions or of the negative consequences of them. Alternatively, they may endeavor to divide their potential opponents. Finally, retrenchment advocates may offer 'side payments' to compensate some of those adversely affected by proposed changes.[20]

What has been used in democratic systems like the United States and Britain has also been used by the Chinese government in the reform of SOEs. While studies of regime responses to popular resistance have paid more attention to repression and concession, my study suggests that a wide range of strategies fall between these two responses. Non-repressive measures have been the most important mode of response from the Chinese government. Consensus building, blame avoidance, peaceful confrontation without concessions, and selective concessions combine to reduce resistance. These measures prevent worker resistance by shaping their incentives or by imposing different types of costs on participants. It is beyond dispute that the Chinese government retains strong capacity in carrying out its reform programs, but strong capacity does not always mean repression. This study has found that the government's punishment of workers is highly selective. It has also employed non-repressive measures because of its concern for legitimacy as well as other formal and informal constraints. Hence, although the political system in China is sometimes repressive, it also leaves room for citizens to pursue their interests through a number of channels, including collective action.[21]

Political space in China

The Chinese political system is characterized by hierarchical power structures, in which lower-level officials or party cadres are held accountable to higher-level authorities rather than the public. Chinese officials are thus only constrained by higher-level officials. The problem is whether higher-level authorities are willing to put constraints on lower-level officials, thereby pressuring them to attend to the needs of the people. Authoritarian governments have reasons to discipline lower-level agents. First, even authoritarian regimes need legitimacy because an entirely repressive regime invites backlash. Second, a government entirely dependent on repression will incur high costs because it needs to exert constant pressure on society. Hence governments in communist systems tend to provide benefits to the people in exchange for compliance.[22] Third, abusive and undisciplined agents tend to create more tension between state and society and may make higher-level authorities doubt their usefulness.

In addition to the legal system (although riddled with problems) and a huge number of arbitration organizations, the Chinese government's willingness to allow people to pursue their interests is also reflected in the adoption of the appeals system. From the central to the county government, there is a complaints bureau on every level. Former socialist countries also had appeals systems,[23] but the system in China is highly institutionalized. The appeals system serves both symbolic and instrumental purposes for the Chinese government. Symbolically, it enhances its legitimacy. Instrumentally, it provides information to higher-level authorities and becomes a way of disciplining lower-level officials. Between 1996 and 1998, the central complaint bureau submitted thousands of pieces of information and cases to the central government. Within these three years, a third of the total number of pieces of information or suggestions received by the central government came from the central complaints bureau.[24] This is also the case at the local level. In Henan province, for example, by 1998, there were more than 3,000 complaints organizations at the county level or above. They received about 681,860 appeals and letters and reported 12,000 pieces of information to different levels of Party committees and governments.[25] While many factors limit the effectiveness of the appeals system, it does impose constraints on local officials.

The central authority's willingness to attend to citizens interests for the sake of legitimacy or social stability has also been reflected in the fact that the central government has time and again punished local officials. In the 1990s and early 2000s, the central Party and government organs issued directives that held major local leaders responsible for the occurrence of events that may threaten social stability. In the early 2000s, the central government investigated a series of disastrous incidents and punished local officials regarded as ignoring citizens' interests. Those cases include the repression of Muslims in Shandong in 2000 that caused six deaths, the bombing of a primary school in Jiangxi in 2001 that killed 42 students, the bombing of a residential building in Shijiazhuang of Hebei in 2001 that claimed 108 lives, and a fire in Luoyang of Henan in 2001 that caused 309 deaths.[26]

Placing constraints on local officials adds flexibility to the political system in an authoritarian regime and helps maintain social stability. As the local government does not have the right to use violence at will, the Chinese people, including laid-off workers, are able to take action that may be illegal as long as it falls "within the shadow of reasonableness." As elsewhere, this leads to under-enforcement of the law. "Lawbreaking, which is implicit in several forms of protest, tends to be tolerated by the police. Law enforcement is usually considered as less important than peacekeeping."[27] Exceptions do exist. But even in those cases, the central government tends not to take the side of local agents. In Jiangxi province in 2001, for example, a county government, under the pretext of arresting criminals, opened fire on a group of peasants and killed two of them. Despite the local government's attempt to justify the killings, the central government took the case seriously and investigated the officials involved. Some high-ranking local officials subsequently resigned.[28] Therefore, existence of the principal–agent relation between different levels of governments serves more or less the interests of the people when the higher-level authority finds that it is in its best interest to accommodate the needs of the people.

This study finds that in the reform of SOEs, workers have achieved success in their action in two ways. First, resistance has wrested specific concessions from local governments, such as overdue salaries and subsistence subsidies. Second, the continual and numerous actions of laid-off workers have yielded a cumulative effect on the central and high-level governments, and have prompted them to pay more attention to the issue of layoffs. In addition to urging local governments to establish RSCs, the central government has also allocated financial resources to subsidize local governments in their efforts to handle the issues of laid-off workers.

Yet, the central government and its local agents share the same goal—to prevent collective action that may threaten the authority of the regime. This unified goal determines the nature of people's resistance and sets limits on the mode of action. Both local and central governments will not allow large-scale, organized, or destructive action. Over the years, the Chinese government has built a reputation for blocking such action. In the reform period, this reputation and the measures adopted by the government make it clear to workers that they should not overstep the boundaries. While government tolerance provides opportunities for popular resistance, its intolerance of authority-threatening action effectively limits people's action. It is thus important to highlight the fact that workers' action has been within or hovering near the boundaries set by the state. In many cases, laid-off workers' contentious resistance often starts with collective appeals to the government, which is permitted, and ends in demonstrations or protests, which are tolerated if they are peaceful. Violence is exceptional rather than typical. Therefore, for the government, what is important is not the occurrence of resistance *per se*, but the kind of resistance.

Evolution toward more institutionalized state–society interaction

The Chinese government's tolerance of nonconventional actions by no means implies that the government does not feel the pressure of resistance. The many measures employed by the government suggest that it is fully aware of the seriousness of the issue of laid-off workers. The pressure behind the tolerance may drive the government to build new systems to institutionalize state–society interactions, which will serve the interest of the government in the long run.[29] No state wishes to be engaged in incessant conflicts with its people. If people have to rely on noninstitutional methods to pursue their interests, it will be difficult for the government to remove the roots of social instability. As an official in Liaoning province admitted:

> In recent years, the degree of organization of mass incidents has intensified; the period of inception is quite long, and there are abundant preparations

made... There are even budding tendencies toward the formation of spontaneously organized "trade unions," and "associations" and other unapproved organizations for defending rights."[30]

A government that only listens to its people when they take undesirable action may also lose its legitimacy. More important, there is always the possibility that discontented people will develop organizations or tools beyond the state's expectation or control. In Poland, for example, "Solidarity gradually evolved from spontaneous political mobilization into well-established organizational structures that encompassed a growing number of people and expanded to all areas of social life and all parts of the country."[31]

The state has the incentive to build new institutions because its repressive capacity is not without limitations. The growing number of collective acts of the poor has motivated the government to speed up the establishment of a social welfare program in China. Central government leaders like Premier Zhu Rongji admitted that "a well-established social insurance system is not only an important condition for the reform and development of state enterprises but also a guarantee of social stability."[32] The former Labor Ministry was turned into the Ministry of Labor and Social Security in 1998, and the framework of a new unified welfare system has also been developed. The recognized importance of a welfare system notwithstanding, progress should not be overestimated because of budget constraints. What is important, however, is that the government is determined to move in that direction by requiring enterprises of all types of ownership to pay into the welfare fund for employees.

Continual resistance of the deprived has also become a force prompting the government to adopt new systems to solve social conflict. The government fully understands that repression without the establishment of institutional channels will be self-defeating in the end. One such effort is the establishment of institutions to resolve disputes between the employer or the state and the workers (not necessarily workers who have been laid off). Internal and external arbitration and mediation organizations play an increasingly significant role in resolving management–labor conflicts. The Chinese government has also introduced and promoted collective bargaining in firms to protect workers' interests. According to a sampling survey of 3.43 million employees in 15 provinces by the ACFTU in 1997, about 47 percent reported that their enterprises adopted a collective bargaining system; and over 47 percent of them reported that they had signed a collective labor contract with their firms. It is also true that some workers, although the numbers were limited, believed that their situations had improved after the adoption of the collective contract.[33]

To be sure, the government may be faced with dilemmas when adopting new systems because they may contradict other goals. Yet it will have an incentive once it realizes that it is in its interest to do so. One such example is the adoption of the salary-guarantee system in Shenzhen. There are many foreign firms and a large number of migrant workers in this city. Some foreign businesses left the city without giving advance notice, thereby evading the responsibility of paying their workers. As a last resort, workers often approached the government for help. Such incidents were so frequent that people in the labor department of the city often overworked to settle these issues. In 1997, some scholars proposed to the government that it adopt a salary-guarantee system, under which foreign investors would deposit a certain amount of money to serve as a bond. The local government, however, worried that this would drive investors away and did not agree. But because of the repeated occurrence of such events and workers' continued appeals to the government, it finally decided to adopt this system in 1999.[34]

It often takes time for governments to respond to social demands by creating new institutions, and authoritarian regimes are no exception. Political, economic, social, and cultural factors all influence the establishment of new polices and the pace at which they are implemented. In China, there remains a significant gap between the enactment of policies and their implementation. Many laws that protect peoples' interests are often not strictly enforced, and it remains a gigantic task for the government to strengthen the legal institutions. Indeed, achieving this goal is crucial to future reform as well as to social and political development. Although this is a subject for future research, the findings of this study suggest that once the government realizes the importance of these institutions, it will have the incentive to strengthen them. Popular resistance in China can thus become a force that prompts the government to institutionalize state–society interaction. Regardless of China's authoritarian regime, such institutions will become political assets that render economic transition and political reform possible without social and political disorder.

Appendix
Data collection

In July 1998, I conducted pre-survey fieldwork by interviewing 33 laid-off workers in one city in eastern China. On the basis of the interviews and many Chinese publications, I carried out the survey with pre-tested questions in eight provinces in 1999. The eight provinces were chosen according to their numbers of laid-off workers in 1997 as reported in *The Chinese Labor Statistical Yearbook 1998*. I selected five provinces from the top 10 provinces that had the most laid-off workers, two from the 10 that had fewer, and one from the 10 that had the least (Tibet was excluded because it did not have laid-off workers according to the 1998 yearbook). I chose more provinces that had the most number of laid-off workers for several reasons. When massive layoffs began in China in the second half of the 1990s, the welfare system was far from adequate. According to Chinese publications, those provinces that had the most laid-off workers had more difficulties providing subsistence subsidies or creating jobs for those workers. As this study aims to examine an individual's reaction to deprivation, it is thus reasonable to select provinces with more laid-off workers.

Due to the nature of this study, the localities have to remain anonymous. The five provinces that had the most laid-off workers in 1997 include one from the northeast, one from the east, one from the middle part, one from the south, and one from the west. The two that had a medium number of laid-off workers are respectively in the middle and south of China. The one that had the least laid-off workers is from the south. In each of the five provinces that had the most laid-off workers, I selected two cities and one county; in the rest three provinces, I chose two cities and two counties in order to include more people from these provinces. This procedure yielded 16 cities and 11 counties or 27 localities altogether. For the three localities in each of the five provinces with the most laid-off workers, I chose the capital city of each province because the capital city is usually above the average in terms of its net income per capita. As for the other two localities, I chose one city and one county. For the city, I chose one from four to six cities whose net income per capita was close to the average of the province in 1997. A particular city was finally chosen not only because of its economic development level but also based on the access to interviewees. Given the sensitive nature of this study, a good access to laid-off workers was the most important guarantee of the quality of the data collected. The county was chosen from four to six counties whose income per capita was at the bottom of the province also by taking into account the access to interviewees. For the 12 localities in the other three provinces, I chose the capital city, another city, and two counties in each province. The city was chosen in the same way as in the case of the five provinces in the first group. The two counties were also chosen in the same way except that one was from four to six of the counties with a middle income level and the other from four to six with the lowest income level. Twenty-five trained interviewers conducted interviews in 25 cities and counties, and I conducted 44 interviews in two cities. Each interviewer was asked to interview 30 laid-off workers from different enterprises in a locality. Most interviewers chose interviewees based on their personal connections or used the snow-ball method. This was to ensure the reliability of the data collected. The total number of valid interviews was 724 or 26.8 percent people in each locality on an average.

Survey questions used in this study[1]

Background of laid-off workers

1. Age; gender; education
2. The time when you were laid off
3. The position you held when you were laid off
4. The name of your enterprise from which you were laid off
5. The industry or business type of your enterprise
6. The ownership of your enterprise
7. The number of employees in your enterprise
8. The number of people who were laid off at the time when you were laid off; the enterprise's announced percentage of layoffs
9. Your salary before layoff
10. Do you live in the house provided by your own enterprise (or sold by your enterprise to you)? If not, where do you live?
11. Did your enterprise buy insurance (i.e., retirement, unemployment, medical) for you before your were laid off? Did it buy it for you after the layoff?
12. Do you still keep labor relationship with your enterprise? If yes, how long will you be able to keep it?
13. What criteria for layoffs were adopted in your enterprise?

Deprivation and dissatisfaction

1. After being laid off, did you receive subsistence subsidies? If yes, how much was it? How long have you been receiving it? How much longer will you be able to receive it? Where did you receive it?
2. You felt that there is _____ (a big, some, little, or no) decrease in your income after being laid off.
3. Were you satisfied with your economic and employment status after being laid off? (no, yes, or indifferent)

Confidence and costs in collective action

1. (Based on your experiences before being laid off) After being laid off, did you think it would be useful (i.e., have your problem addressed) if you and your colleagues (e.g., two or more) together presented your grievances or demands to, or write letters to, or take other types of group action directed at the enterprise or the authorities concerned? (useful, may be useful, not useful)
2. (Based on your experience before being laid off) Did you believe that if more people, including yourself, took part in group action, it would be more likely for your problem to be addressed? (yes, no)
3. (Based on your experiences before being laid off) After being laid off, did you think that it would be acceptable to the authorities concerned (i.e., your target) if you and your colleagues undertook group action to have your problems addressed? (yes, no)
4. (Based on your experiences before being laid off) After being laid off, did you think it would be time-consuming if you and your colleagues took group action to have your problem addressed? (yes, no)

Participation in collective action

1. After the layoff, did you and your colleagues (e.g., two or more) approach or write letters to or take other types of action directed at the enterprise authority, government agencies or other departments concerned for help? (yes, no) Please specify the action you and your colleagues took and the target of your action.
2. If you participated in any type of these acts, what kind of help did you seek? (Please specify). Did you receive that help before you took action? (yes, no).Was your action helpful (i.e., bring any benefits for you)? (yes, no)
3. Did you ever take action with employees from other enterprises? (yes, no)
4. Please describe your collective action (organization, process, and scale)

Individual action

1. After being laid off, did you approach or write letters or take other types of action directed at the enterprise authority or government agencies concerned for help as an individual? (yes, no). Please specify the action you took and the target of your action
2. If you have taken any individual action, what kind of help did you seek? (Please specify); Did you receive that help before the action was taken? (yes, no); Was the action helpful? (yes, no)
3. Did you take any individual action before participating in any collective action with your colleagues? (yes, no); If yes, was it helpful? (yes, no)

Alternatives

1. Were you eager to find a job after being laid off? (yes, no)
2. Were you able to find a job after being laid off? (yes, no). How long did it take for you to find a job? What is your salary?
3. Through which channel did you find your job?
4. Was it a temporary or a long-term one (i.e., you believed that you would be able to work for more than 18 months)? Did your employer buy insurance for you? Which sector (i.e., public or private) did you work in?
5. Did you feel that it was difficult to find a job after being laid off (very difficult, difficult, not difficult)? Why was it difficult or why not?
6. Did you receive any help from the RSC? (yes, no). If yes, what kind of help did you receive?
7. After being laid off, how much was your family income? How much was it before the layoff?

Opinions on layoffs

1. Do you think that retrenchment is a necessary and acceptable reform measure? (yes, no); Explain your answers.
2. What were the reasons for your being laid off?

Notes

1 Introduction

1 J. Linz and A. Stepan, *Problems of Democratic Transition and Consolidation: Southern Europe, South America, and Post-Communist Europe*, Baltimore, MD: Johns Hopkins University Press, 1996.
2 D. Ost and S. Crowley, "Introduction: The Surprise of Labor Weakness in Postcommunist Society," in S. Crowley and D. Ost (eds), *Worker after Workers' States: Labor and Politics in Postcommunist Eastern Europe*, Lanham, MD: Rowan & Littlefield Publishing, 2003, pp. 1–12; M. Arandarenko, "Waiting for the Workers: Explaining Labor Quiescence in Serbia," in S. Crowley and D. Ost (eds), *Workers after Workers' State*, 2001, pp. 159–80.
3 Kramer, Mark, "Polish Workers and the Post-Communist Transition, 1989–1993," *Communist and Post-Communist Study*, 1995, vol. 28, no. 1, 71–114.
4 J. R. Blasi, M. Kroumova, and D. Kruse, *Kremlin Capitalism: The Privatization of the Russian Economy*, Ithaca, NY: Cornell University Press, 1997, p. 41.
5 S. Clarke, P. Fairbrother, and V. Borisov, *The Workers' Movement in Russia*, Hants, UK: Edward Elgar Publishing Limited, 1995, p. 410.
6 Zhao Yining, "Wei shehui ruoshi qunti 'xuezhongsongtan' " (Providing Crucial Help to the Deprived in Society), *Liaowang* (Perspective), 2002, no. 15, 11–13.
7 D. Solinger, "Labor Market Reform and the Plight of the Laid-off Proletariat," *The China Quarterly*, 2002, no. 170, 304–26.
8 F. Chen, "Subsistence Crises, Managerial Corruption and Labor Protests in China," *The China Journal* 2000, vol. 44, 41–63; C. K. Lee, "From the Specter of Mao to the Spirit of the Law: Labor Insurgency in China," *Theory and Society*, 2002, vol. 31, no. 2, 189–228; The State Planning Commission, "Shijizhijiao de zhongguo shehui xingshi" (The Social Situation in China at the Turn of the Century), *Jingji gongzuozhe xuexi ziliao* (Studying Materials for Economic Workers), 2000, no. 23, 2–11.
9 The Research Group of the Ministry of Organization, *2000–2001 Zhongguo diaocha baogao: xinxingshi xia renmin neibu maodu yanjiu* (2000–2001 China Investigation Report: A Study of People's Internal Contradictions in the New Era), Beijing: Zhongyang bianyi chubanshe, 2001.
10 C. K. Lee, "Pathways of Labor Insurgency," in Elizabeth Perry and Mark Selden (eds), *Chinese Society: Change, Conflict and Resistance*, London: Routledge, 2000, p. 57.
11 Workers' resistance has slowed the pace of reform. Y. S. Cai, "Relaxing the Constraints from Above: Politics of Privatizing Public Enterprises in China," *Asian Journal of Political Science*, 2002, vol. 10, 94–121.
12 The Document Research Office of Chinese Communist Party Committee, *Shisi da yilai guoyou qiye gaige he fazhan dashi jiyao* (A Record of the Important Events of the Reform of State-Owned Enterprises After the 14th Party Congress), Beijing: Zhongyang wenxian chuabanshe, 1999, p. 211.

13 As will be discussed in the following sections, according to my survey, a greater proportion of laid-off workers have not taken collective action. Also see M. Blecher, "Hegemony and Workers' Politics in China," *The China Quarterly*, 2002, no. 170, 283–303.
14 E. E. Thompson, "The Moral Economy of the English Crowd in the Eighteenth Century," *Past and Present*, 1971, vol. 50, 76–136; J. Scott, *The Moral Economy of the Peasant: Rebellions and Subsistence in Southeast Asia*, New Haven, CT: Yale University Press, 1976.
15 L. Cook, *The Soviet Social Contract and Why it Failed: Welfare Policy and Workers' Politics from Brezhnev to Yeltsin*, Cambridge, MA: Harvard University Press, 1993; J. Ludlam, "Reform and the Redefinition of the Social Contract under Gorbachev," *World Politics*, 1991, vol. 43, no. 2, 284–312.
16 Cook, *The Soviet Social Contract and Why it Failed*, p. 1–2.
17 A. Walder, *Communist Neo-Traditionalism*, Berkeley, CA: University of California Press, 1986.
18 One might question whether the people of a communist system enter into this relationship voluntarily. See M. Kramer, "Introduction: Blue-Collar Workers and the Post-Communist Transition in Poland, Russia, and Ukraine," *Communist and Post-Communist Studies*, 1995, vol. 28, no. 1, 3–12; S. Crowley, *Hot Coal, Cold Steel*, Ann Arbor, MI: The University of Michigan Press, 1997.
19 Thompson, "The Moral Economy of the English Crowd in the Eighteenth Century," 76–136; Scott, *The Moral Economy of the Peasant*, chapter 2.
20 C. F. Sable, *Work and Politics: The Division of Labor in Industry*, Cambridge, MA: Cambridge University Press, 1982.
21 M. P. Posusney, "Irrational Workers: The Moral Economy of Labor Protest In Egypt," *World Politics*, 1993, vol. 46, no. 1, 83–120; J. Kopstein, "Chipping Away at the State: Workers' Resistance and the Demise of East Germany," *World Politics*, 1996, vol. 48, 391–423.
22 Chen, "Subsistence Crises, Managerial Corruption and Labor Protests in China."
23 T. Gurr, *Why Men Rebel*, Princeton, NJ: Princeton University Press, 1970, pp. 12–13.
24 T. Leung, "Labor Fights For Its Rights," *China Perspectives*, 1998, vol. 19, 6–21.
25 C. K. Lee, "The 'Revenge of History': Collective Memories and Labor Protests in Northeastern China," *Ethnography*, 2000, vol. 1, no. 2, 217–37.
26 D. Kahneman and A. Tversky, "Prospect Theory: An Analysis of Decision under Risk," *Econometrica*, 1979, vol. 47, 263–91; A. Tversky and D. Kahneman, "The Framing of Decisions and the Psychology of Choice," *Science*, 1981, vol. 211, 453–58.
27 Chen, "Subsistence Crises, Managerial Corruption and Labor Protests in China."
28 Walder, *Communist Neo-Traditionalism*, p. 249.
29 Crowley, *Hot Coal, Cold Steel*, p. 17.
30 Chen, "Subsistence Crises, Managerial Corruption and Labor Protests in China."
31 Blecher, "Hegemony and Workers' Politics in China."
32 E. Hung and S. Chiu, "The Lost Generation: Life Course Dynamics and Xiagang in China," *Modern China*, 2003, vol. 29, no. 2, 204–36.
33 Laid-off workers were found to blame the state for their problems. The Research Group of the Ministry of Organization, *2000–2001 Zhongguo diaocha baogao: xinxingshi xia renmin neibu maodu yanjiu*, p. 148.
34 Blecher, "Hegemony and Workers' Politics in China."
35 Lee, "The 'Revenge of History'."
36 Song Baoan and Wang Yushan, "Changchun shi xiangang zhigong de wenjuan diaocha" (Questionnaire About Laid-Off Workers in Changchu), in Lu Xin, Lu Xueyi, and Shan Tianlun (eds), *1999 nian: zhongguo shehui fenxi yu yuce* (1999: An Analysis and Prediction of Chinese Society), Beijing: Shehui kexue wenxian chubanshe, 1999, pp. 156–78.

37 H. Kim and P. S. Berman, "The Structure and Dynamics of Movement Participation," *American Sociological Review*, 1997, vol. 62, 70–93.
38 Also see Solinger's study: it also sees the Chinese government and laid-off workers as two parties in interaction and discusses the different reactions of each party. Yet her study has not focused on the impact of government policies or the varied participation of laid-off workers in collective action. D. Dorothy, "The Potential for Urban Unrest: Will the Fencers Stay on the Piste?," in D. Shambaugh (ed.), *Is China Unstable?* Armonk, NY: M. E. Sharpe, 2000, pp. 79–94.
39 D. Chong, *Collective Action and the Civil Rights Movement*, Chicago, IL: University of Chicago Press, 1991.
40 M. Olson, *The Logic of Collective Action*, New York: Schocken, 1965.
41 M. Lichbach, "Rethinking Rationality and Rebellion," *Rationality and Society*, 1994, vol. 6, no. 1, 8–39.
42 Olson, *The Logic of Collective Action*; R. Hardin, *Collective Action*, Baltimore, MD: The Johns Hopkins University Press, 1982; R. Axelrod, *The Evolution of Cooperation*, New York: Basic Books, 1984.
43 B. Klandermans, "Mobilization and Participation: Social–Psychological Expansions of Resource Mobilization Theory," *American Sociological Review*, 1984, vol. 49, 583–600.
44 S. Popkin, "Public Choices and Peasant Organization," in C. R. Russell and N. K. Nickolson (eds), *Public Choice and Rural Development*, Washington, DC: Resources for the Future, 1987, pp. 256–57.
45 S. Lohmann, "The Dynamics of Information Cascades: The Monday Demonstration in Leipzig East Germany, 1989–1991," *World Politics*, 1994, vol. 47, 42–101.
46 Indeed, it has been found that there is no causal relationship between an individual's identity (or her consciousness of a common status) and her participation in collective action. R. Hardin, *One for All: The Logic of Group Conflict*, Princeton, NJ: Princeton University Press, 1995.
47 C. Tilly, *From Mobilization to Revolution*, New York: Random House, 1978, chapter 3.
48 R. J. Oestreigher, *Solidarity and Fragmentation: Working People and Class Consciousness in Detroit 1875–1900*, Urbana, IL: University of Illinois Press, 1986; Sable, *Work and Politics*.
49 E. Perry, *Shanghai on Strike*, Berkeley, CA: University of California Press, 1993, p. 29.
50 Thus, "different workers engage in different politics" in the sense that workers organized on the basis of group characteristics such as skill, ethnicity, gender, and educational level. For this reason, she also suggests that fragmentation across groups may "set boundaries on the development of collective action." Ibid., pp. 30, 339.
51 Lee, "The 'Revenge of History'"; Perry also points out that workers in Shanghai before 1949 did not act for the benefits as a class but for the demands specific to their groups. Perry, *Shanghai on Strike*.
52 For a critique of resource mobilization theory, see D. McAdam, *Political Process and the Development of Black Insurgency 1930–1970*, Chicago, IL: The University of Chicago Press, 1999, chapter 2.
53 Indeed, the theory's emphasis on formal social movements tends to "overestimate and overgeneralize the importance of formal organization for collective mobilization." H. Kitschelt, "Resource Mobilization Theory: A Critique," in D. Rucht (ed.), *Research on Social Movements*, Boulder, CO: Westview Press, 1991, pp. 323–47.
54 X. G. Zhou, "Unorganized Interests and Collective Action in Communist China," *American Sociological Review*, 1993, vol. 58, 54–73; Crowley, *Hot Coal, Cold Steel*.
55 For a discussion on the importance of ecological effects on collective action, also see D. X. Zhao, *The Power of Tiananmen: State–Society Relations and the 1989 Beijing Student Movement*, Chicago, IL: University of Chicago Press, 2001, chapter 8.
56 For a discussion of the importance of organizers for industrial action, also see M. Golden, *Heroic Defeats: The Politics of Job Loss*, New York: Cambridge University Press, 1997.

57 N. Frohlich, A. Oppenheimer, and O. R. Young, *Political Leadership and Collective Goods*, Princeton, NJ: Princeton University Press, 1971; Olson, *The Logic of Collective Action*; Hardin, *Collective Action*.
58 Frohlich et al., *Political Leadership and Collective Goods*; Chong, *Collective Action and Civil Rights Movements*.
59 J. Goldstone and C. Tilly, "Threat (and Opportunity): Popular Action and State Response in the Dynamics of Contentious Action," in R. R. Aminzade, J. Goldstone, D. McAdam, E. Perry, W. H. Sewell, S. Tarrow, and C. Tilley (eds), *Silence and Voice in the Study of Contentious Politics*, New York: Cambridge University Press, 2001, pp. 179–94.
60 Walder, *Communist Neo-Traditionalism*.
61 M. Michael, "State Power, Institutional Change, and the Politics of Privatization in Russia," *World Politics*, 1995, vol. 47, 210–43.
62 Goldstone and Tilly, "Threat (and Opportunity)."
63 Tilly, *From Mobilization to Revolution*; McAdam, *Political Process and the Development of Black Insurgency 1930–1970*; S. Tarrow, *Power in Movement: Social Movements, Collective Action and Politics*, Cambridge, UK: Cambridge University Press, 1994.
64 D. McAdam, "Conceptual Origins, Current Problems, Future Directions," in D. McAdam, J. McCarthy, and M. Zald (eds), *Comparative Perspectives on Social Movements*, New York: Cambridge University Press, 1996, pp. 23–40.
65 Ibid., p. 29.
66 S. Tarrow, "States and Opportunities: The Political Structuring of Social Movements," in D. McAdam, J. McCarthy, and M. Zald (eds), *Comparative Perspectives on Social Movements*, New York: Cambridge University Press, 1996, pp. 41–61.
67 But these protests were usually not held by laid-off workers. G. Ekiert and J. Kubik, *Rebellious Civil Society: Popular Protest and Democratic Consolidation in Poland, 1989–1993*, Ann Arbor, MI: The University of Michigan Press, 1999.
68 W. Connor, *Tattered Banners: Labor, Conflict, and Corporatism in Postcommunist Russia*, Boulder, CO: Westview Press, 1996, p. 152.
69 D. Filtzer, *Soviet Workers and the Collapse of Perestroika: The Soviet Labor Process and Gorbachev's Reforms, 1985–1991*, New York: Cambridge University Press, 1994.
70 L. Cook, "Workers in the Russian Federation: Responses to the Post-Communist Transition, 1983–1993," *Communism and Post-Communism Studies*, 1995, vol. 28, no. 1, 13–42.
71 Zhou, "Unorganized Interests and Collective Action in Communist China." For a discussion of opportunities in the Chinese context, also see T. Wright, *The Perils of Protest: State Repression and Student Activism in China and Taiwan*, Honolulu, HI: University of Hawaii Press, 2001.
72 E. Perry, "Shanghai's Strike Wave of 1957," *The China Quarterly*, 1994, vol. 137, 1–27.
73 Indeed, the political atmosphere at that time was so harsh that nonparticipation might have been seen as a political error. S. G. Wang, *Failure of Charisma: The Cultural Revolution in Wuhan*, New York: Oxford University Press, 1995.
74 E. Perry and X. Li, *Proletarian Power: Shanghai in the Cultural Revolution*, Boulder, CO: Westview Press, 1997, p. 99.
75 A. Walder and X. X. Gong, "Workers in the Tiananmen Protests: The Politics of Beijing Workers' Autonomous Federation," *The Australian Journal of Chinese Affairs*, 1993, vol. 29, 1–29; S. G. Wang, "Deng Xiaoping's Reform and The Chinese Workers' Participation in the Protest Movement of 1989," *Research in Political Economy*, 1992, no. 13, 163–97.
76 M. Oksenberg, L. R. Sullivan, and M. Lambert (eds), *Beijing Spring, 1989: Confrontation and Conflict: The Basic Documents*, Armonk, NY: M.E. Sharpe, 1990; J. Unger (ed.), *The Pro-democracy Protests in China: Reports from the Provinces*, Armonk, NY: M.E. Sharpe, 1991.

77 Zhao, *The Power of Tiananmen*.
78 T. Saich, "The Rise and Fall of the Beijing People's Movement," in J. Unger (ed.), *The Pro-Democracy Protests in China*, Armonk, NY: M.E. Sharpe, 1991, pp. 8–34.
79 McAdam, *Political Process and the Development of Black Insurgency 1930–1970*, p. xi.
80 J. Herbst, "How the Weak Succeed: Tactics, Political Goods, and Institutions in the Struggle over Land in Zimbabwe," in F. D. Colburn (ed.), *Everyday Forms of Peasant Resistance*, Armonk, NY: M.E. Sharpe, 1989, pp. 198–220.
81 The constraint of legitimacy lies in the fact that its absence may threaten a regime's survival in crises. Oberschall, Anthony, "Opportunities and Framing in the Eastern Europe Revolts of 1989," in D. McAdam, J. McCarthy, and M. Zald (eds), *Comparative Perspectives on Social Movements*, New York: Cambridge University Press, 1996, pp. 172–99.
82 Tarrow, *Power in Movement*, p. 3.
83 To some extent, it can be seen as a way of increasing "the degree of government" in China. See S. Huntington, *Political Order in Changing Societies*, New Haven, CT: Yale University Press, 1968.
84 J. Scott, *The Weapons of the Weak: Everyday Forms of Peasants Resistance*, New Haven, CT: Yale University Press, 1985.
85 Fan Qin, "Xiagang shishui—woguo xiagang renyuan jiegou fenxi" (Who Were Laid Off—An Analysis of the Composition of the Laid-Off Workers in Our Country), *Zhongguo guoqing guoli* (The Situation and Strengths of China), 1998, no. 5, 20–22; *Chinese Labor Statistics 1999*, p. 441.

2 The ending of a socialist contract and retrenchment

1 K. Fukui, *Japanese National Railways Privatization Study*, Washington, DC: The World Bank, 1992.
2 Y. Z. Cao, Y. Y. Qiang, and B. R. Weingast, "From Federalism, Chinese Style to Privatization, Chinese Style," *Economics of Transition*, 1999, vol. 7, no. 1, 103–31.
3 It belongs to one type of "relative deprivation" according to Ted Gurr. See T. Gurr, *Why Men Rebel*, Princeton, NJ: Princeton University Press, 1970.
4 D. Solinger, "Labor Market Reform and the Plight of the Laid-off Proletariat," *The China Quarterly*, 2002, no. 170, 304–26.
5 N. R. Lardy, *China's Unfinished Economic Revolution*, Washington, DC: Brookings Institute Press, 1998.
6 Zhang Huiming, *Zhongguo guoyou qiye gaige de luoji* (The Logic of the Reform of State Enterprises in China), Taiyuan: Shanxi jingji chubanshe, 1998, p. 296.
7 *Zhongguo gaige bao* (China Reform News), October 27, 1999.
8 Kong Zhangsheng, "Yanghang kua shengshi fenhang de qianqian houhou" (The Process of the Establishment of Cross-Provinces Branches by the Central Bank), *Dadi* (The Land), 1999, no. 2, 19–21.
9 Wu Jinglian's talk at Stanford University, November 19, 1999.
10 Another micro-level factor is that the government's "soft landing" policy after 1993 also restricted SOEs' access to bank loans. See Hua Ercheng, *Zhongguo jingji de ruan zhuoluo* (The Soft Landing of the Chinese Economy), Beijing: Zhongguo caizheng jingji chubanshe, 1997.
11 In fact, the difficulty faced by small- and medium-sized enterprises in obtaining loans has forced the government to figure out solutions, because these enterprises have played an increasingly important role in solving the unemployment problem in China. *China Daily*, February 24, 1999.
12 *Zhongguo qiye zhenggong xinxi bao* (Information on the Political Work in Chinese Firms), July 28, 1999.
13 For a discussion of government policies and their impact on the performance of SOEs, see E. Steinfield, *Forging Reform in China: The Fate of State-Owned Industry*,

14 The Expert Group of China's Reform and Development, *Xianshi de xuanze* (Realistic Choices), Shanghai: Shanghai yuandong chubanshe, 1997.
15 Li Peeling, "Lao gongye jidi de shiye zhili: hou gongyehua he shichanghua" (Dealing With the Unemployment in the Old Industrial Bases: Post-Industrialization and Marketization), *Shehuixue yanjiu* (Sociological Research), 1998, no. 4, 1–12.
16 Fan Qin, "Xiagang shishui—woguo xiagang renyuan jiegou fenxi" (Who Were Laid Off?—an Analysis of the Composition of Laid-Off Workers in Our Country), *Zhongguo guoqing guoli* (The Situation and Strengths of China), 1998, no. 5, 20–22.
17 The number of laid-off workers and the number of state employees are reported in *Chinese Labor Statistical Yearbook 1998*, pp. 235, 433; The fiscal revenue and loss made by firms of each province are reported in The State Statistical Bureau, *1998 Zhongguo fazhan baogao* (1998 China Development Report), Beijing: Zhongguo tongji chubanshe, 1998, pp. 321, 352.
18 See *Chinese Labor Statistics 1998*, pp. 433–42.
19 The State Statistical Bureau, *Datoushi* (A Comprehensive Perspective), pp. 3–4.
20 Both provinces are among the top five in terms of their population. Another five provinces among the top 10 with the largest number of laid-off workers in 1997 include Hubei, Jiangsu, Sichuan, Shandong, and Guangdong. *Chinese Labor Statistics 1998*, p. 433.
21 The State Economic and Trade Commission and the Document Research Office of the Central Party Committee, *Shisida yilai dang he guoia lingdaoren lun guoyou qiye gaige he fazhan* (Talks by Central Leaders on the Reform of State-Owned Enterprises After the 14th Party Congress), Beijing: Zhongyang wenxian chubanshe, 2000, p. 165.
22 The State Statistical Bureau, *Datoushi*, p. 31.
23 *Chinese Labor Statistics 1999*, pp. 441–42.
24 The All China Federation of Trade Unions, *1997 Zhongguo zhigong zhuangkuang diaocha* (1997 Investigation of Chinese Employees), Beijing: Xiyuan chubanshe, 1999, p. 95; *Chinese Labor Statistics 2000*, p. 409; *Chinese Statistical Yearbook 2000*, p. 126.
25 Yu Bin, "Gaozhu 'santiao baozhangxian' " (To Build "Three Protection Lines"), *Liaowang* (Perspectives), 1999, no. 37, 27–29; Also see S. Dorothy, "Why We Cannot Count the 'Unemployed'," *The China Quarterly*, 2001, no. 167, 671–88.
26 Zhou Enlai admitted that "this measure not only hurts their (returned workers) tendons or bones; it is just like a knife stabbed in their bodies, and there is blood whenever you move the knife." CCTV Channel 1, September 14, 1999.
27 *Jingji ribao* (Economic Daily), February 9, 1998.
28 Wang Haibo and Dong Zhikai, *Xin zhongguo gongye jingji shi (1958–1965)* (The Industrial History of China 1958–1965), Beijing: Jingji guanli chubanshe, 1995.
29 Solinger, "Labor Market Reform and the Plight of the Laid-off Proletariat."
30 According to this policy, four groups of people were covered by the unemployment insurance: workers of bankrupt firms, laid-off workers of those firms to be declared bankrupt and were in the process of reorganization, workers whose labor contracts were terminated, and those who were fired. The policy also entitles workers to unemployment insurance payments for up to 24 months, depending on the number of years of service. Song Xiawu, Zhang Zhongjun, and Zhen Dingquan, *Zhongguo shehui baozhang zhidu jianshe 20 nian* (The 20 Years of the Construction of Social Security in China), Zhengzhou: Zhongzhou guji chubanshe, 1999.
31 *Gongren ribao* (Workers' Daily), March 12, 1998; *Gongren ribao*, April 19, 1993.
32 Cheng, Biwei, *Zhongguo shehui baozhang tixi de gaige yu wanshan* (The Reform and Improvement of China's Social Security System), Beijing: Minzhu yu jianshe chubanshe, 2001, p. 107.

Notes 141

33 Lu Xin, Lu Xueyi, and Shan Tianlun (eds), *2000 nian: zhongguo shehui fenxi yu yuce* (2000: An Analysis and Prediction of Chinese Society), Beijing: Shehui kexue wenxian chubanshe, 2000, p. 260.
34 *Gongren ribao*, August 27, 1998.
35 The State Planning Commission, "Shijizhijiao de zhongguo shehui xingshi" (The Social Situation in China at the Turn of the Century), *Jingji gongzuozhe xuexi ziliao* (Studying Materials for Economic Workers), 2000, no. 23, 2–11.
36 The significant gap between the reported figures and the survey outcomes was due to the different methods of statistical data collection. While the official figures were based on the report of work units, the survey outcome was obtained by interviewing employees. Zhu Qingang, "Chengzhen pinkun renkou de tedian, pinkun de yuanyin he duice" (The Characteristics of and the Reasons for Urban Residents' Poverty and Some Solutions), *Shehuixue yanjiu* (Sociological Research), 1998, no. 1, 62–66.
37 This was after the central party conference on the issue of laid-off workers in May 1998. Lu Xin, Lu Xueyi, and Shan Tianlun (eds), *1999 nian zhongguo shehui xingshi fenxi yu yuce* (1999: An Analysis and Prediction of Chinese Society), Beijing: Shehui kexue wenxian chubanshe, 1999, pp. 244–53.
38 The Joint Research Group, *Qiji shi ruhe chuangzao de* (How Was the Miracle Made?), Shanghai: Fudan daxue chubanshe, 1998, p. 8.
39 Zhang Zhilin and Feng Lei, "Guanyu guoyou qiye xiagang zhigong wenti de kaocha yu sikao" (Observations of and Some Thoughts on Laid-Off Workers of State Enterprises), *Jingji gongzuo zhe xuexi ziliao* (Study Materials for Economic Workers), 1999, no. 9, 34–47.
40 Ibid.
41 Hunan Statistical Bureau, "Guoqi zaijiuye fuwu zhongxin jianli yu yunzuo qingkuang" (The Situation of Establishment and Operation of the Reemployment Service Centers of State Enterprises), *Tongji ziliao* (Statistical Materials), 1999, no. 13, 13–19.
42 Interview, China, 1999, no. 14.
43 *Gongren ribao*, November 19, 1998.
44 *Chinese Labor Statistics 1999*, p. 442.
45 Xiang Huaicheng, *1999, Zhongguo caizheng baogao* (1999 China's Fiscal Report), Bejing: Zhongguo caizheng chubanshe, 1999, p. 140.
46 *Zhongguo laodong baozhangbao*, September 2, 1999.
47 *Gongren ribao*, August 8, 1998.
48 *Chinese Labor Statistics 1999*, p. 443.
49 A survey of 10,000 laid-off workers in 1999 suggested that over 73 percent of them reported that they were most worried about these two issues. *Zhongguo gaige bao* (China Reform News), March 21, 1999.
50 Jia Qinglin, "Dali shisi zaijiuye gongcheng, tuijin shoudu gaige yu fazhan" (Making All Efforts to Promote the Reemployment Work and Promote the Reform and Development of the Capital City), in the Research Office of Beijing Party Committee and Beijing Labor Bureau (ed.), *Zaijiuye gongzuo de yanjiu yu shijian* (A Study of Reemployment and the Practice). Beijing: Jingji guanli chubanshe, 1998, pp. 4–20.
51 This situation is also true in post-communist Russia: "State-paid unemployment benefits are in any case very modest and are weak motivation for workers to cut ties to the plant that may still provide something they cannot get otherwise." W. Cannor, *Tattered Banners: Labor, Conflict, and Corporatism in Postcommunist Russia*, Boulder, CO: Westview Press, 1996, p. 172.
52 Shuai Bin, "Xiagang zhigong zai da menwai paihuai" (Laid-Off Workers Lingered Outside the Door), *Zhongguo gongren* (Chinese Workers), 1999, no. 8, 12–13.
53 Research by the State Labor Science Research Institute of the Ministry of Labor and Social Security found that in the late 1990s, labor recruitment in the state sector only increased by 0.53 percent. *Liaoning ribao* (Liaoning Daily), July 3, 1998.

54 *Gongren ribao*, August 27, 1998.
55 *Gongren ribao*, June 30, 1998.
56 Wang Meng, "Chengshi jumin ruhe kan 'yigai'" (How Urban Citizens Think About the Reform of Medical Care), *Gaige yu kaifang* (Reform and Openness), 1999, no. 8, 13–14.
57 A. Chan, *China's Workers under Assault*, Armonk, NY: M.E. Sharpe, 2001.
58 Accidents in private and foreign enterprises have been widely reported. In two districts in Shenzhen in 1997, for example, the number of accidents was 10,800. *Gongren ribao*, August 18, 1999.
59 A woman reported that during the half year she worked in a company, the only time she was allowed to leave work early was when the company distributed bonuses and welfare subsidies to its employees but not to her. Interview, China, 1998, no. 6.
60 *Gongren ribao*, March 27, 1999. In 1998 among the estimated 6.7 million laid-off workers who entered RSCs, almost half did not sign an agreement with RSCs regarding the termination of their labor relations. See *Gongren ribao*, January 7, 1999. In Tianjin, among 260,000 laid-off workers, only 5,000 (or 1.9 percent) terminated their relations with their previous firms. *Gongren ribao*, April 10, 1998.
61 Interview, China, 1998, no. 12.
62 Interview, China, 1998, no. 3.
63 The Investigation Group of Beijing Economic Commission, "Gongye xitong fuyu renyuan xiagang fenliu shishi zhaijiu ye de xiangzhuang yu jianji" (The Current Situation of Layoffs and the Reemployment of the Redundant Employees in the Industrial Sector and Some Suggestions), in the Research Office of Beijing Party Committee and Beijing Labor Bureau (eds), *Zaijiuye gongzuo de yanjiu yu shijian* (A Study of Reemployment and the Practice), Beijing: Jingji guanli chubanshe, 1998, pp. 21–42.
64 Huang Chenxi and Wang Daben, "Shanghai shi guoyou qiye xiagang renyuan fenliu anzhi de xianzhuang, wenti yu duice" (The Current Situation and Problems of the Reallocation of Laid-Off Workers in State Enterprises in Shanghai and Countermeasures), *Shichang yu renkou fenxi* (Market and Demographic Analysis), 1999, no. 4, 22–25.
65 Xu Jianchuan, Zhou Dingchun, and Zhao Xuwei (eds), *Xiagang zhigong jiben shenghuo baozhang yu zaijiuye gongzuo shouce* (A Handbook on the Basic Allowance for Laid-Off Workers and Reemployment), Beijing: Zhongguo jiancai chubanshe, 1998.
66 Interview, China, 1999, no. 7.
67 Xu, Zhou, and Zhao (eds), *Xiagang zhigong jiben shenghuo baozhang yu zhai jiuye gongzuo shouce*, p. 139.
68 H. Y. Lee, "*Xiagang*, the Chinese Style of Laying off Workers," *Asian Survey*, 2000, vol. 40, no. 6, 914–37.
69 That was the first time a work report by the government failed to pass the People's Congress in Wuhan. Ruan Ying, "Wuhanshi zaijiuye gongcheng baogao weihe yidu bei foujue" (Why the Report on the Reemployment Work of Wuhan was Not Approved), *Minzhu yu fazhi* (Democracy and Law), 1997, no. 12, 16–17.
70 Chen Lu and Yang Lianyun, "Xiagang zhigong zai jiuye nandian wenti de diaocha fenxi yu duice jianyi" (An Analysis of the Difficult Problems in the Reemployment of Laid-Off Workers and Countermeasures), *Qiushi* (Seeking the Truth), 1999, no. 3, 19–22.
71 Interview, China, 1999, no. 24.
72 Zhang Chunlin, "Tiaochu 'lushan' shi zhenmian" (To Gain the Truth), *Xinwen jizhe* (Journalists), 2000, no. 5, 56–57.
73 The Research Group, "Chengzhen qiye xiagang zhigong zaijiuye zhuangkuang diaocha: Kunjing yu chulu" (An Investigation of Laid-Off Workers' Reemployment: Plight and Solutions), *Shehuixue yanjiu* (Sociological Research), 1997, no. 6, 24–34.

74 The City Investigation Team of the State Statistical Bureau, "Xiagang zhigong jiuye qingkuang diaocha" (An investigation of the Reemployment of Laid-Off Workers), *Tongji ziliao* (Statistical Materials), 1998, no. 16, 10–12.
75 Chen Qingtai, Wu Jinglian, and Xie Fuzhan (eds), *Guoqi gaige gongjian 15 ti* (15 Critical Issues in the Reform of State-Owned Enterprises), Beijing: Zhongguo jingji chubanshe, 1999; *China Daily*, August 30, 1999.
76 Solinger, "Labor Market Reform and the Plight of the Laid-off Proletariat."
77 This is also partly due to the lack of comparative advantages of laid-off workers. See Solinger, "Labor Market Reform and the Plight of the Laid-off Proletariat."
78 Chen, Wu, and Xie, *Guoqi gaige gongjian 15 ti (15 Critical Issues in the Reform of SOEs)*.
79 *Chinese Labor Statistics 1999*, pp. 441–42.
80 Hunan Statistical Bureau, "zenyang kandai xiagang yu zaijiuye" (How to Look at Layoffs and Reemployment), *Tongji ziliao* (Statistical Materials), 1998, no. 20, 16–22.
81 *Gongren ribao*, July 23, 1998.
82 Zhu Qingang, "Chengzhen pinkun renkou de tedian, pinkun de yuanyin he duice" (The Characteristics of and the Reasons for Urban Residents' Poverty and Some Solutions), *Shehuixue yanjiu* (Sociological Research), 1998, no. 1, 62–66.
83 Liu Jiesan and Wang Xueli, "Zhigong gongzi wai shouru yu guanli" (Employees' Extra Income and Management), in the Research Group of the State Council (ed.), *Chengzhen jumin shouru chaju yanjiu* (A Study of the Income Gap Among Urban Citizens), Beijing: Zhongguo yanshi chubanshe, 1997, pp. 21–34.
84 It has been suggested that benefits related to housing have been the most important reason for the income gap. See A. R. Klan and C. Riskin, "Income and Inequality in China: Composition, Distribution and Growth of Household Income, 1988–1995," *The China Quarterly*, 1998, no. 154, 221–53.
85 Liu Yong, *Disanci shiye gaofeng: xiangang, shiye, zaijiuye* (The Third Peak of Unemployment: Layoffs, Unemployment, and Reemployment), Beijing: Zhongguo shuji chubanshe, 1998, p. 19.
86 In 1996, while many laid-off workers received nothing from their enterprises, about 58 percent of the laid-off workers received a monthly income of less than 200 yuan, which was barely enough to feed a single person. *Zhonguo Gaige Bao* (China's Reform News), February 11, 1999.
87 Wu Bangguo, 'Qieshi zuohao guoyou qiye xiagang zhigong jiben shenghuo baozhang he zaijiuye gongzuo' (To do a Good Job of Providing Minimum Allowance for Laid-Off Workers and Helping Them Secure Reemployment), *Qiushi* (Seeking the Truth), 1998, no. 13, 2–7.
88 *Gongren ribao*, March 12, 1998.
89 In Hubei province, the number of laid-off workers reached 700,000 in 1998, accounting for 10 percent of the total number of employees in this province. About 60 percent failed to receive the subsidy as regulated; the income per capita of 30 percent of the families was less than 90 yuan per month. Tan Biyuan, Ke Shanfan, and Li Hongshan, "Zhigong guanzhu de ridian, nandian wenti jiqi duice" (The Problems that Workers are Concerned With and Solutions), *Neibu wengao* (Internal Manuscripts), 1998, no. 14, 16–19.
90 *Jinwanbao* (Evening News Today), August 31, 2000.
91 Before the housing reform, employees rented houses from their enterprises by paying a very low rent. As required by the new housing reform measures, however, employees must buy their homes, which may be beyond their financial abilities.
92 The Chinese description of this phenomenon is "*yi ren gongfei, quan jia gongfei*." This welfare system covers the child of a public servant but not other adults of the family. Some public servants may use it to obtain free service for the adults in their families.
93 Zuo Fu, *21 shiji shui geili fanchi* (Who Will Feed You in the 21st Century?), Nanchang: Baihuazhou wenyi chubanshe, 1998, p. 91.

94 Interview, China, 1999, no. 15.
95 Solinger, "Labor Market Reform and the Plight of the Laid-off Proletariat."
96 Reportedly, in Yancheng city of Jiangsu province in 2002, a group of 28 factory workers attempted to commit mass suicide by jumping off a high building to protest against a lack of retrenchment and medical benefits. They were stopped by police. Reported in *The Straits Time*, August 28, 2002. For similar reports, see *Zhongguo jingji shibao* (China Economic Times), March 19, 1996.
97 Zhen Xiang, "Shishi zaijiuye gongcheng" (To Institute a Reemployment System), *Zhongguo gongren* (Chinese Workers), 1996, no. 3, 10–11.
98 The Research Group of Laid-off Workers and Their Employment, "Xiagang zhigong de shenghuo zhuangkuang jiqi shehui zhichi" (The Living condition of Laid-Off Workers and Their Social Support), *Xiaofei jingji* (Economy of Consumption), 1997, no. 1, 48–51.
99 The Joint Research Group, *Qiji shi ruhe chuangzao de* (How Was the Miracle Made?), Shanghai: Fudan daxue chubanshe, 1998.
100 Ma Cheng, *Xiagang zhihou* (After Layoffs), Beijing: Minzhu yu jianshe chubanshe, 1988, p. 129.
101 Reported in *Jingjiyanjiu zilaio* (Materials for Economic Study), 1998, no. 7, p. 40.
102 J. Scott, *The Moral Economy of the Peasant: Rebellions and Subsistence in Southeast Asia*, New Haven, CT: Yale University Press, 1976; C. Sable, *Work and Politics: The Division of Labor in Industry*, Cambridge: Cambridge University Press, 1982. This rationale is also seen as a reason for the popular support of the Nazi movement in Germany. "The resentments that…nourished the Nazi movement were those of the 'little man' angry at the injustice of a social order that threatened or failed to reward the virtues of hard work." See B. Moore, *Injustice: The Social Bases of Obedience and Revolt*, White Plains, NY: M.E. Sharpe, 1978, p. 453.
103 F. Chen, "Industrial Restructuring and Workers' Resistance in China," *Modern China*, 2003, vol. 29, no. 2, 237–58.
104 She became self-dependent later. Yu Xiu, *Zaoyu xiagang* (Facing Retrenchment), Beijing: Zhonghua gongshanglian chubanshe, 1998, p. 143.
105 Jin Ye, *Jieceng de fubai* (Corruption of Social Groups), Zhuhai: Zhuhai chubanshe, 1998, p. 301.

3 Retrenchment and laid-off workers' responses

1 D. Solinger, "Labor Market Reform and the Plight of the Laid-off Proletariat," *The China Quarterly*, 2002, no. 170, 304–26; E. Hung and S. Chiu, "The Lost Generation: Life Course Dynamics and Xiagang in China," *Modern China*, 2003, vol. 29, no. 2, 204–36.
2 See, among others, J. D. McCarthy, and M. N. Zald, "Resource Mobilization and Social Movements: A Partial Theory," *American Journal of Sociology*, 1977, vol. 82, no. 6, 1212–41.
3 E. Muller, H. A. Dietz, and S. E. Finkel, "Discontent and the Expected Utility of Rebellion: A Case of Peru," *American Political Science Review*, 1991, vol. 85, no. 4, 1261–82.
4 Some people argue that this is one of the important shortcomings of resource-mobilization theory. See S. M. Buechler, "Beyond Resource Mobilization? Emerging Trends in Social Movement Theory," *The Sociological Quarterly*, 1993, vol. 34, no. 2, 217–35.
5 M. Drakeford, *Social Movements and Their Supporters*, Hampshire: Macmillan Press, 1997, p. 10.
6 S. E. Finkel and E. N. Muller, "Rational Choice and the Dynamics of Collective Political Action: Evaluating Alternative Models with Panel Data," *American Political Science Review*, 1998, vol. 92, no. 1, 37–49.

7 F. Chen, "Subsistence Crises, Managerial Corruption and Labor Protests in China," *The China Journal*, 2000, vol. 44, 41–63; C. K. Lee, "The 'Revenge of History': Collective Memories and Labor Protests in Northeastern China," *Ethnography*, 2000, vol. 1, no. 2, 217–37.
8 M. Blecher, "Hegemony and Workers' Politics in China," *The China Quarterly*, 2002, no. 170, 283–303.
9 See Chen, "Subsistence Crises, Managerial Corruption and Labor Protests in China"; D. Solinger, "The Potential for Urban Unrest: Will the Fencers Stay on the Piste?," in D. Shambaugh (ed.), *Is China Unstable?*, Armonk, NY: M.E. Sharpe, 2000, pp. 79–94; C. K. Lee, "Pathways of Labor Insurgency," in E. Perry and M. Selden (eds), *Chinese Society: Change, Conflict and Resistance*, London: Routledge, 2000, pp. 41–60; A. Liu, *Mass Politics in the People's Republic: State and Society in Contemporary China*, Boulder, CO: Westview Press, 1996; T. Leung, "Labor Fights For Its Rights," *China Perspectives*, 1998, vol. 19, 6–21.
10 Liao Mingtao and Hua Shanqing, "Jiti laodong zhengyi he tufa shijian de zhuyao tedian he chuli yanjiu" (A Study of the Main Characteristics and Settlement of Collective Labor Disputes and Mass Action), *Shanghai gongyun* (Workers' Movements in Shanghai), 1998, no. 3, 12–14; *Chinese Trade Union Yearbook 1998*, p. 224.
11 In fact, as discussed in Chapters 6 and 7, participants in collective action often far outnumber three. Workers understand that a small number of participants often fail to exert sufficient pressure on the government.
12 Local governments also admit that appeals are the most important mode of collective action among Chinese citizens, including workers. The Ministry of Organization of the CCP Central Committee, *2000–2001 Zhongguo Diaochao baogao* (2000–2001 China Investigation Report), Bejing: Zhongyang bianye chubanshe, 2001, p. 283.
13 While such incidents were widely reported outside of China, some have also been reported by the media in China, though often indirectly. For example, as detailed in Chapter 7, in Yangjiazhangzi of Liaoning province in 2000, over 20,000 workers of a mine joined by several thousands of their family members launched labor protests for many days. See James Kynge, "Chinese miners riot over severance pay," *Financial Times*, April 3, 2000. This event was mentioned in the report by the Ministry of Organization, *2000–2001 China Investigation Report*, pp. 202–03.
14 The National Complaints Bureau, *Zhongguo xinfang xiezhen* (A Record of People's Letters and Visits in China), Beijing: gongren chubanshe, 1998.
15 S. Tarrow, *Power in Movement*, New York: Cambridge University Press, 1994, p. 2.
16 Huang Daosheng, "Ruhe yufang yueji shangfang" (How to Prevent Appeals to Higher-Level Authorities), *Jiangsu jijian* (Jiangsu Discipline Inspection), 1999, no. 10, 17; Local governments are often praised for their success in preventing collective appeals to the central government. See *Henan Yearbook 1999*, p. 62.
17 *Liaoning ribao* (Liaoning Daily), August 13, 1999.
18 The Chinese translation is *wending yadao yiqie*.
19 The Party secretary of Chongqing said: "As to Chongqing, the issue of reemployment has become one that is more urgent than the migration of people due to the Three Gorge Project." The Party secretary of Hunan province also stated that "as a provincial Party secretary, I, more than at any other time, feel that 'where to allocate these people' is the most difficult problem China faces now." *Gongren ribao*, March 10, 1998.
20 Y. S. Cai, "Managed Participation in China," *Political Science Quarterly*, 2004, vol. 119, no. 3, 425–51.
21 The Ministry of Organization, *2000–2001 Zhongguo diaocha baogao*; Others estimated that it increased by more than 27 percent per year in the late 1990s. See Wang Chunguang, "1997–1998: Zhongguo shehui wending de diaocha" (1997–1998: An Investigation of China's Social Stability), in Lu Xin, Lu Xueyi, and Shan Tianlun (eds),

Zhongguo shehui xingshi fenxi yu yuce (1998: An Analysis and Prediction of the China's Social Situation), Beijing: Shehui kexue wenxian chubanshe, 1998, pp. 121–47.
22 Wei Lei, "Jiejue nongmin jiti shangfang de fangfa" (Methods of Solving Peasants' collective appeals to the Government), *Lilun tantao* (Exploration of Theories), 1999, no. 4, 94–98.
23 He Pin and Hu Manhong, "Ouxin lixue wei renmin" (Working Wholeheartedly For the People), *Minzhu yu fazhi* (Democracy and Law), 1999, no. 3, 18–20.
24 For example, in 1998, the State Complaints Bureau received 460,000 letters and appeals made in person from across the country. A third of them were written or made by urban residents, including laid-off workers. *Zhongguo gaigebao* (China Reform News), September 2, 1999.
25 Wang Daming, "Zhengque chuli qunti shijian, quebao wending daju" (Correctly Handling Mass Action and Ensuring Stability), *Qiushi* (Seeking the Truth), 2001, no. 4, 1–3.
26 Wu Chenguang, "Fangbao jingcha: saohei jianbing" (Riot Police: The Vanguard of Crushing Crimes), *Zhongguo xinwen zhoukan* (Chinese Newsweek), 2001, no. 7, 3–6.
27 Reported in *Neibu canyue* (Internal References), 1999, no. 9, 18–19.
28 The talk by the provincial governor, Hong Hu, was reported on the Website of the Jinlin provincial government, http://www.jl.gov.cn/jlzb/zb200109/zb2001-09-01.htm (accessed April 10, 2001).
29 A talk by a Chinese scholar, Stanford University, March 31, 2000.
30 The government may be willing to negotiate with an individual firm but not a group of coordinated firms because cross-firm collective action organized by workers may be seen as a basis for better organized action in the future. Interview, China, 2002, no. 3.
31 Jin Weixin, "Bufen qiye qinfan zhigong quanli shi quntixing shijian zengduo" (The Encroachment of Workers' Interests Led to More Collective Action), *Zhengfa cankao* (References of Political and Legal Affairs), 2002, no. 10, 15–16.
32 The talk by the provincial governor, Hong Hu, was reported on the Website of the Jinlin provincial government, http://www.jl.gov.cn/jlzb/zb200109/zb2001-09-01.htm (accessed April 10, 2001).
33 The government promised to provide half of the back salary and severance pay, help workers secure new jobs, and investigate workers' claims of corruption. The protests declined significantly towards the end of March because of workers' exhaustion, cold weather, fear of government punishment, and partial success. M. Lev, "7,000 Chinese Workers Unite in Daring Protest," *The Chicago Tribune*, March 13, 2002; E. Eckholm, "Where Workers, too, Rust, Bitterness Boils," *The New York Times*, March 20, 2002; J. Pomfret, "With Carrots and Sticks, China Quiets Protesters," *Washington Post*, March 22, 2002.
34 Blecher, 2002, "Hegemony and Workers' Politics in China."
35 Also see Muller, Dietz, and Finkel, "Discontent and the Expected Utility of Rebellion."
36 E. Mueller and T. O. Jukam, "Discontent and Aggressive Political Participation," *British Journal of Political Science*, 1983, vol. 13, 159–79.
37 E. E. Thompson, "The Moral Economy of the English Crowd in the Eighteenth Century," *Past and Present*, 1971, vol. 50, 76–136.
38 A. Walder, *Communist Neo-Traditionalism*, Berkeley, CA: University of California Press, 1986.
39 Muller and Jukam, 1983, "Discontent and Aggressive Political Participation."
40 It is only less than 2 percent.
41 E. Mueller, "The Psychology of Political Protest and Violence," in T. R. Gurr (ed.), *Handbook of Political Conflict*, New York: Free Press, 1980, pp. 69–99.
42 The Research Office of Beijing Party Committee and Beijing Labor Bureau (eds), *Zaijiuye gongzuo de yanjiu yu shijian* (A Study of Reemployment and the Practice), Beijing: Jingji guanli chubanshe, 1998, p. 135.

43 Li Dahong, "Shehui wending: lishun qingxu huajie maodun" (Social Stability: To Resolve the Contradictions), *Liaowang* (Perspectives), 1999, no. 10, 52–53.
44 Therefore, he believed that as long as workers changed their mentality, reemployment would not be a problem, *Jingji ribao* (Economic Daily), March 14, 1998.
45 See D. Ost, and S. Crowley (eds), *Worker after Workers' States: Labor and Politics in Postcommunist Eastern Europe*, Lanham, MD: Rowan & Littlefield Publishing, 2003, especially chapter 8 by M. Arandarenko and chapter 10 by S. Crowley.
46 S. Clarke, P. Fairbrother, and V. Borisov, *The Workers' Movement in Russia*, Hants, UK: Edward Elgar Publishing Limited, 1995, p. 399.
47 G. Ekiert and J. Kubik, "Contentious Politics in New Democracies: East Germany, Hungary, Poland, and Slovakia, 1989–1993," *World Politics*, 1998, vol. 50, 547–81.
48 S. Lohmann, "The Dynamics of Information Cascades: the Monday Demonstration in Leipzig East Germany, 1989–1991," *World Politics*, 1994, vol. 47, 42–101.
49 In some cases, workers may also demand punishment of their corrupt managers. See Chen, "Subsistence Crises, Managerial Corruption and Labor Protests in China."
50 In the case of Chinese laid-off workers, opportunity cost can be viewed as what a laid-off worker would have received from the option (e.g., engaging in money-making activities instead of participating in collective action) she did not choose, had she chosen it.
51 M. Olson, *The Logic of Collective Action*, New York: Schocken, 1965.
52 For a discussion on the ways to overcome the collective action problem, see M. Lichbach, "Rethinking Rationality and Rebellion," *Rationality and Society*, 1994, vol. 6, no. 1, 8–39.
53 D. Chong, *Collective Action and the Civil Rights Movement*, Chicago, IL: University of Chicago Press, 1991.
54 Bonds mean that some workers were required to buy shares from their firms. Some laid-off workers also raised demands such as the punishment of corrupt managers or the choice of a certain form of ownership reform. Those were included in the 16 percent that made up the category of "others."
55 Coefficients of logistic regression can be interpreted using the odds ratio. The odds ratio is the ratio of the probability that an event will occur to the probability that it will not, and it can equal any nonnegative number. Simply put, if the odds ratio equals "1," it means that the change in the independent variable does not affect the odds. This serves as the baseline for comparison. If the odds ratio is greater than "1," it means that the probability is higher that an event will occur than not. If the odds ratio is smaller than "1," it means that the probability that an event will occur is lower than it not occurring. See A. Agresti, *An Introduction to Categorical Data Analysis*, New York: John Wiley & Sons, 1996.
56 $\text{Exp}(-0.3287) = 0.7199$, and $1/(0.7199) = 1.389$.
57 J. Elster, *Making Sense of Marx*, Cambridge, UK: Cambridge University Press, 1985, p. 9.
58 Chong, *Collective Action and Civil Rights Movements*, p. 11.
59 S. Popkin, "Public Choices and Peasant Organization," in C. R. Russell and N. K. Nickolson (eds), *Public Choice and Rural Development*, Washington, DC: Resources for the Future, 1987, pp. 256–57.
60 Finkel and Muller, "Rational Choice and Dynamics of Collective Political Action."
61 Chong, *Collective Action and Social Rights Movements*, p. 4.
62 $\text{Exp}(-1.026) = 0.3584$, and $1/(0.3584) = 2.79$.
63 $\text{Exp}(-0.5237) = 0.5923$, and $1/(0.5923) = 1.69$.
64 This is an analysis based on a logistic regression. The dependent variable is dichotomous: participation or nonparticipation. $N = 672$, coefficient $= 1.207$, standard error $= 0.4026$, odds ratio $= 3.343$.
65 S. Tarrow, *Power in Movement*, New York: Cambridge University Press, 1994, p. 21.

4 Fragmentation and collective action

1. J. Gibson, "Mass Opposition to the Soviet Putsch of August 1991: Collective Action, Rational Choice, and Democratic Values in the Former Soviet Union," *American Political Science Review*, 1997, vol. 91, no. 3, 671–84.
2. M. Olson, *The Logic of Collective Action*, New York: Schocken, 1965.
3. C. Tilly, *From Mobilization to Revolution*, New York: Random House, 1978.
4. C. K. Lee, "The Labor Politics of Market Socialism: Collective Inaction and Class Experiences among State Workers in Guangzhou," *Modern China*, 1998, vol. 24, no. 1, 3–31.
5. This is because it involves coordination. See R. Hardin, *One for All: The Logic of Group Conflict*, Princeton, NJ: Princeton University Press, 1995.
6. H. Gutman, *Work, Culture, and Society in Industrializing America: Essays in American Working-Class and Social History*, New York: Vintage Books, 1976; M. Davis, "Why the US Working Class is Different," *New Left Review*, 1980, vol. 123, 3–44; D. Montgomery, "To Study the People: The American Working Class," *Labor History*, 1980, no. 21, 485–512; S. Aronowitz, *False Promise: The Shaping of American Working Class Consciousness*, New York: McGraw-Hill, 1973; Sombart Werner, *Why is There no Socialism in the United States?* London: Macmillan Press, 1976.
7. R. J. Oestreigher, *Solidarity and Fragmentation: Working People and Class Consciousness in Detroit 1875–1900*, Urbana, IL: University of Illinois Press, 1986, pp. 24–25.
8. C. Sable, *Work and Politics: The Division of Labor in Industry*, New York: Cambridge University Press, 1982, p. 137.
9. B. Moore, *Injustice: The Social Bases of Obedience and Revolt*, White Plains, NY: M.E. Sharpe, 1978, p. 87.
10. Ibid., p. 273.
11. E. Honig, *Sisters and Strangers: Women in Shanghai Cotton Mills, 1919–1949*, Stanford, CA: Stanford University Press, 1986, p. 246.
12. G. Hershatter, *The Workers of Tianjin: 1900–1949*, Stanford, CA: Stanford University Press, 1986, p. 237.
13. Ibid., p. 238.
14. E. Perry, *Shanghai On Strike*, Berkeley, CA: University of California Press, 1993.
15. Oestreigher, *Solidarity and Fragmentation*.
16. H. Braverman, *Labor and Monopoly Capital: The Degradation of Work in the Twentieth Century*, New York: Monthly Review Press, 1974.
17. See, among others, D. Solinger, "The Chinese Work Unit and Transient Labor in the Transition from Socialism," *Modern China*, 1995, vol. 21, no. 2, 155–83; Chapters by D. Solinger, A. Chan, and J. Howell in G. O'Leary (ed.), *Adjusting to Capitalism: Chinese Workers and the State*, Armonk, NY: M.E. Sharpe, 1998; A. Chan, *China's Workers Under Assault*. Armonk, NY: M.E. Sharpe, 2001.
18. Zhan Qinghe and Bai Ningxiang, "Yingdang dui dangqian gongren fei zhengshi zuzhi jinxing yanjiu" (Workers' Informal Organizations Should Be Studied), *Xueshujie* (Academia), 1999, no. 3, 78–83.
19. Also see W. F. Tang and W. Parish, *Chinese Urban Life under Reform: The Changing Social Contract*, New York: Cambridge University Press, 2000, chapter 6.
20. Tilly, *From Mobilization to Revolution*.
21. Tang and Parish, *Chinese Urban Life under Reform*.
22. The ACFTU, *Dangqian woguo gongren jieji zhuangkuang diaocha ziliao huibian* (A Compilation of the Investigation Materials of the Working Class of Our Country in the Contemporary Period), Beijing: Zhonggong zhongyang dangxiao chubanshe, 1983, p. 40.
23. The ACFTU, *Zhongguo zhigong duiwu zhuangkuang diaocha 1986* (An Investigation of Chinese Workers 1986), Beijing: Gongren chubanse, 1987, p. 286.

24 The ACFTU, *1997 Zhongguo zhigong zhuangkuang diaocha* (1997 Investigation of Chinese Employees), Beijing: Xiyuan chubanshe, 1999, p. 1175.
25 Li Peilin, "Lao gongye jidi de shiye zhili: hou gongyehua he shichanghua" (Dealing with Unemployment in the Old Industrial Bases: Post-Industrialization and Marketization), *Shehuixue yanjiu* (Sociological Research), 1998, no. 4, 1–12.
26 A survey conducted in Beijing and Shenzhen in 1998 suggested that among the top 30 socially respected occupations, neither managers nor workers were included. Ye Xingping and Yi Songguo, "Shenzhen shi 100 zhong zhiye de shehui shengwang" (The Social Respect for the 100 Occupations in Shenzhen), *Shehui* (Society), 1998, no. 11, 24–25; This finding confirms the result of another survey conducted in Nanjing in 1996, in which among 50 types of occupations, the jobs of lathe operators and foundry workers were ranked 42nd and 43rd respectively in terms of the degree they were respected in society. See Ye Nanke, "Nanjing shimin dui zhiye shengwang de pingjia" (Citizens' Evaluation of the Social Respect for Occupations in Nanjing), *Shehui* (Society), 1997, no. 1, 8.
27 Zhang Jianhua (ed.), *Zhongguo mianlin de jinyao wenti* (Pressing Problems Faced by China), Beijing: Jingji ribao chubanshe, 1998. Hence, to push their children to study harder so as to secure better employment in the future, some parents took their children to factories to convince them that it was highly undesirable to be workers. Wu Junping and Xu Ying, *Woshishui* (Who Am I?), Huhehaote: Neimenggu renmin chubanshe, 1997, p. 175.
28 A. Hirschman, *Exit, Voice, and Loyalty: Responses to Decline in Firms, Organizations, and States*, Cambridge, MA: Harvard University Press, 1970.
29 The occupational groups included individual labor, people in the commercial and service sector, people in the science, technology, and education sectors, cadres in administrative and non-administrative public agencies, and workers. See Feng Tongqing, "Zhongguo xinshiqi gongren jieji neibu liyi gejiu baogao" (Report on the Interest Differentiation Within the Chinese Working Class), in Li Peilin (ed.), *Zhongguo xinshiqi jieji jieceng baogao* (Social Stratification During the Market Transition in China: An Analysis of Ten Issues), Liaoning: Liaoning renmin chubanshe, 1995, pp. 133–88.
30 Zhu Guanglei, *Dangdai zhongguo shehui gejieceng fenxi* (An Analysis of Social Strata in China), Beijing: Gonren chubanshe, 1998, p. 66.
31 The ACFTU, *1997 Zhongguo zhigong zhuangkuang diaocha*, p. 1417.
32 J. You, *China's Enterprise Reform: Changing State/Society Relations after Mao*, London: Routledge, 1997.
33 By 1997, the number of people working in the non-state sector accounted for more than 21 percent of the total number of workers in urban China. *Chinese Labor Statistics 1998*, p. 247.
34 The ACFTU, *1997 Zhongguo zhigong zhuangkuang diaocha*, p. 1241.
35 Y. J. Bian, *Work and Inequality in Urban China*, Albany, NY: State University of New York Press, 1994.
36 But this practice was gradually stopped after the 1990s. *Gongren ribao*, September 11, 1999.
37 Interview, China, 2001, no. 6.
38 In a factory of Sichuan province in 1995, a female worker bought a shift from one of her colleagues. As this female worker worked for over 16 hours everyday, she was so exhausted in the work that she fell to the machine and was mortally wounded. *Jiefang ribao* (Liberation Daily), January 8, 1995.
39 *Zhongguo jingji shibao* (China Economic Times), March 18, 1997.
40 Interview, China, 1999, no. 14.
41 The ACFTU, *1997 Zhongguo zhigong zhuangkuang diaocha*, p. 111.
42 Zhang Xiaoming, "Guoqi, wei bing duo jiangguan er zhan" (State Enterprises are Striving to Recruit More Talents), *Kaifang* (Openness), 1997, no. 3, 52–54.

43 Yu Xuecheng, "Wuhanshi guoyou qiye rencai duiwu jianshe sikao" (Thoughts on the Personnel Training in State Enterprises in Wuhan), *Changjiang luntan* (Changjiang Forum), 1999, no. 3, 12–14.
44 Zhou Wenpo, "Guoqi: yi xian gongren zai liushi" (Within State Enterprises: Production Workers are Leaving), *Zhongguo gongren* (Chinese Workers), 1996, no. 11, 12–13.
45 Interview, China, 1999, no. 6.
46 One survey in Wuhan in the late 1990s suggested that the most serious problem faced by these enterprises was the loss of qualified workers, and almost 50 percent of them were young people with skills. About 23 percent of them left for the coastal areas, and another 48 percent took jobs in non-state enterprises. Yu, "Wuhanshi guoyou qiye rencai duiwu jianshe sikao."
47 In its survey in 1997, the ACFTU found that in one factory, all the cadres were interested in being transferred to public administrative or non-administrative work units that provided stable jobs. The All China Federation of Trade Unions, *1997 Zhongguo zhigong zhuangkuang diaocha*, p. 781.
48 The News Center of Nanjing TV Station, *Shehui da guangjiao* (Societal Panorama), Nanjing: Nanjing daxue chubanshe, 1999, pp. 375–78.
49 Shanghai Trade Union, "Benshi zhigong xiagangdaigong zhuangkuan diaocha" (An Investigation of Laid-Off Workers in Our City), cited in Wang Daben, "Shanghai shi qiye xiagang renyuen jiqi fenliu" (The Laid-Off Workers and Their Reallocation in Shanghai), *Yazhou yanjiu* (Asian Study), 1997, no. 15, 70–88.
50 Chui Yingqi and Miao Guangji, "Xiagang renyuan: hequ hecong" (Laid-Off Workers: Where To Go), *Zhongguo gongren* (Chinese Workers), 1996, no. 3, 12–14.
51 Xie Delu, "Chongqing zhenzhi zhongchang pochan xiaoying fenxi" (An Analysis of the Repercussions of the Bankruptcy of the Chongqing Knitting Factory), *Zhongguo gongye jingji yanjiu* (A Study of Chinese Industrial Economy), 1994, no. 11, 37–41.
52 Punishment also takes other forms. For example, a technician in a factory applied to transfer his job to a joint venture and obtained the approval from the factory. Meanwhile, the factory fired his wife who also worked at the factory and evicted them from the factory-owned apartment within a month. Interview, China, 1999, no. 25; also see Zhang, "Guoqi, wei binduojiangguan er zhan."
53 The Research Group of the Public Security, *Zhongguo tese zhi gongan yanjiu* (A Study of Public Security with Chinese Characteristics), Beijing: Qunzhong chubanshe, 1996, p. 178.
54 Zhang, "Guoqi, wei binduojiangguan er zhan."
55 C. Feng, "Industrial Restructuring and Workers' Resistance in China," *Modern China*, 2003, vol. 29, no. 2, 237–58.
56 *Gongren ribao*, December 21, 1998.
57 $\text{Exp}(-0.3068) = 0.7248$, and $(1/0.7248) = 1.379$.
58 *Chinese Labor Statistics 1999*, pp. 443–44.
59 Tang Yunqi (ed.), *Zhuangui zhong de zhenhan* (Shocks in the Transformation), Beijing: Zhongguo laodong chubanshe, 1998, p. 13.
60 Y. J. Bian, "Guanxi and the Allocation of Urban Jobs in China," *The China Quarterly*, 1994, no. 140, 971–99.
61 The Research Group, "Chengzhen qiye xiagang zhigong zaijiuye zhuangkuang diocha: Kunjing yu chulu" (An Investigation of Laid-Off Workers' Reemployment: Plight and Solutions), *Shehuixue yanjiu* (Sociological Research), 1997, no. 6, 24–34.
62 Sombart, *Why is There No Socialism in the United States?*, p. 115.
63 R. Dahrendorf, *Class and Class Conflict in Industrial Society*, Stanford, CA: Stanford University Press, 1959, p. 60.
64 Hershatter, *The Workers of Tianjin: 1900–1949*, p. 228.
65 Yang Yiyong and Xin Xiaobai, "Xiagang zhigong jiben shenghuo baozhang he zaijiuye de diaocha" (An Investigation of Laid-Off Workers' Basic Allowance and Reemployment), in Lu xin (ed.), *1999 nian zhongguo shehui xingshi fenxi yu yuce*

(An Analysis and Prediction of China's Social Situation in 1999), Beijing: Shehui kexue wenxian chubanshe, 1999, pp. 243–55.
66 The Shanghai City Investigation Group, "Xiagang zai jiuye renyuan zhong cunzai yinxing jiuye" (There Was Hidden Employment Among Laid-Off Employees), *Tongji yanjiu* (Statistical Research), 1999, no. 6, 20–23.
67 In the Shanghai example, the average lay-off period was two and a half years. At the time the survey was conducted, most people could not secure employment for that length of time. About 45 percent were employed for less than half a year, while another 24 percent were employed for more than six months but less than a year. Ibid.
68 *Meiri qiaobao* (Overseas Daily), August 11, 1998.
69 *Gongren ribao*, June 14, 1997.
70 J. Kynge, "Chinese miners riot over severance pay," *Financial Times*, April 3, 2000; Also see W. Hurst and K. O'Brien, "China's Contentious Pensioners," *The China Quarterly*, 2002, vol. 170, 345–60.
71 Yang Yiyong, "Zhongguo yanglao baoxian jijin de shoujiao yu touzi" (Collection and Investment of the Retirement Insurance Fund in China), in Xu Dianqing, Yi Zunsheng, and Zheng Yuyun (eds), *Zhongguo shehui baozhang tizhi gaige* (Social Security Reform in China), Beijing: Jingji kexue chubanshe, 1999, p. 388.
72 *Laodong baozhang bao* (Labor Security News), February 14, 2002.
73 Wu Ji, "Bainian laochang pochan de beihou" (Behind the Bankruptcy of a Factory With a 100-Year History), *Jizhe guancha* (Observations of Correspondents), 1999, no. 1, 14–16.
74 *Gongren ribao* (Workers' Daily), May 9, 1998.
75 The Chinese version of this doggerel is "qingchun xiangei dang, dao lao mei ren yang, xiang cong ernu yao, ernu ye xiagang." Da Tong, 'Dangqian zhigong de sige danxin" (Employees' Four Worries in the Current Period of Time), *Sixiang zhengzhi gongzuo yanjiu* (A Study of Political Work), 1999, no. 4, 17.
76 Hurst and O'Brien, 2002, "China's Contentious Pensioners."
77 Wang Jixuan, *Zhengque chuli woguo zhuanxing qi de renmin neibu maodun* (To Correctly Handle People's Internal Contradictions in the Transitional Period), Beijing: Jingji kexue chubanshe, 1997.
78 *Gongren ribao*, May 9, 1998.
79 Interview, China, 1999, no. 7.
80 *Gongren ribao*, June 5, 1999.
81 *Zhongguo shehui bao* (China Social News), September 23, 1999.
82 *China Daily*, August 30, 1999.

5 Management and worker silence

1 E. Muller, H. A. Dietz, and S. E. Finkel, "Discontent and the Expected Utility of Rebellion: A Case of Peru," *American Political Science Review*, 1991, vol. 85, no. 4, 1261–82.
2 G. Hershatter, *The Workers of Tianjin: 1900–1949*, Stanford, CA: Stanford University Press, 1986, p. 238.
3 G. Eley and K. Nield, "Why Does Social History Ignore Politics," *Social History*, 1980, vol. 5, no. 2, 249–71, cited in Hershatter, *The workers of Tianjin: 1900–1949*, p. 6.
4 J. Davis, "Towards a Theory of Revolution," *American Sociological Review*, 1962, vol. 27, 5–19.
5 F. Piven and R. Cloward, *Poor People's Movements: Why They Succeed, How They Fail*, New York: Vintage Books, 1979.
6 C. K. Lee, "From Organized Dependence to Disorganized Despotism: Changing Labor Regimes in Chinese Factories," *The China Quarterly*, 1999, vol. 152, 44–71.
7 P. Pierson, *Dismantling the Welfare State*, New York: Cambridge University Press, 1994, p. 4.

8 Those used in the Cultural Revolution can be seen as exceptions. Also see H. B. Chamberlain, "Party–Management Relations in Chinese Industries: Some Political Dimensions of Economic Reform," *The China Quarterly*, 1987, no. 11, 31–61.
9 J. You, *China's Enterprise Reform: Changing State/Society Relations after Mao*, London: Routledge, 1997, chapter 2.
10 Chen Dengcai and He Xiaoying (eds), *Qiyelingdao tizhi gaige yu dang de jianshe xinlun* (The Reform of the Leadership System in Enterprises and a New Explanation of Party Construction), Beijing: Zhonggong dangshi chubanshe, 1996, p. 49.
11 *Zhongguo jijian jianchabao* (China Discipline Supervision News), August 8, 1999.
12 Li lieman, "Jianguo yilai guoqi lingdao tizhi yange yu dang de jianshe de huigu yu sikao" (The Change of the Leadership System of State Enterprises and Some Thoughts on Party Construction), *Dangshi yanjiu yu jiaoxue* (Study and Teaching of the Party History), 1988, no. 5, 39–45.
13 *Zhongguo jingji shibao* (China Economic Times), April 22, 1999.
14 Also see Jin Shuyan, "Paichu qiye dangzheng guanxi zhong de leiqu" (Removing the Obstacles to the Development of Party–Management Relations in Enterprises), *Zhengzhi sixiang gongzuo yanjiu* (Research on the Work of Political Thought), 1999, no. 8, 29–30.
15 The Research Group of the Organization Department of Ningxia Party Committee, "Xiandai qiye zhidu jianli zhong fahui qiye dang zuzhi zhengzhi hexin zuoyong de fangfa yu duice sikao" (On the Political Core Function of the Party Organization in Enterprises in the Process of Building Modern Firms), *Ningxia shehui kexue* (Ningxia Social Sciences), 1997, no. 5, 20–25.
16 Feng Tongqing and Xu Xiaojun, *Zhongguo zhigong zhuangkuang* (The Situation of Chinese Employees), Beijing: Zhongguo shehui kexue chubanshe, 1994, pp. 164–65.
17 Hence according to a survey of 100 SOE party secretaries in the late 1990s, only 4 percent believed that the MRS was suitable to large and medium SOEs. Li Lieman, "Guoyou qiye lingdao tizhi yu qiye dangjian wenti" (The Leadership System of State Enterprises and Party Construction), *Zhonggong fujian shengwei dangxiao xuebao* (The Journal of Fujian Party School), 2000, no. 5, 55–60.
18 L. Turner, *Democracy at Work: Changing World Markets and the Future of Labor Unions*, Ithaca, NY: Cornell University Press, 2001, p. 12.
19 R. Laba, *The Roots of Solidarity: A Political Sociology of Poland's Working-Class Democratization*, Princeton, NJ: Princeton University Press, 1991, p. 33.
20 J. Godson, "The Role of the Trade Union," in L. Schapiro and J. Godson (eds), *The Soviet Worker: Illusions and Realities*, London: The Macmillan Press, 1981, pp. 106–29.
21 L. T. Lee, *The Structure of the Trade Union System in China, 1949–1996*, Hong Kong: University of Hong Kong, 1984.
22 The General Office of the All China Federation of Trade Unions (ed.), *Jianguo yilai zhonggong zhongyang guanyu gongren yundong wenjian xuanbian* (Selected Documents About Workers' Movements Issued by the Central Party Committee After the Founding of the PRC), Beijing: Gongren chubanshe, 1989.
23 Ibid., p. 357.
24 The ACFTU, *Zhongguo zhigong duiwu zhuangkuang diaocha 1986* (An Investigation of Chinese Workers 1986), Beijing: Gongren chubanse, 1987.
25 Ibid., p.100.
26 Feng and Xu, *Zhongguo zhigong zhuangkuang* (The Situation of Chinese Employees).
27 A. Chan, "Revolution or Corporatism? Workers and Trade Unions in Post-Mao China," *The Australian Journal of Chinese Affairs*, 1993, vol. 29, 31–61; F. Chen, "Between the State and Labor: The Conflict of Chinese Trade Unions' Double Identity in Market Reform." *The China Quarterly*, 2003, no. 176, 1006–28.
28 As a matter of fact, people of the trade union also have difficulties in dealing with lower-level managerial personnel. As this person admitted, "I am an outspoken person

and sometimes offended people because I tried to say what I thought or because I always wanted to correct the wrongdoing of other people. For example, I intervened in the workshop affairs when they put pregnant women on the night duty, distributed bonuses without an open rule, and ignored labor protection, or when cadres occupied more houses. In so doing, I offended some middle-level cadres." *Gongren ribao*, August 9, 1999.
29 *Gongren ribao*, August 10, 1998.
30 *Gongren ribao*, August 7, 1999.
31 T. Wetson, " 'Learning from Daqing': More Dark Clouds for Workers in State-Owned Enterprises," *Journal of Contemporary China*, 2002, vol. 11, no. 33, 721–34; Chen, "Between the State and Labor 1006–28."
32 The ACFTU, *Zhongguo zhigong duiwu zhuangkuang diaocha 1986* (An Investigation of Chinese Workers 1986), Beijing: Gongren chubanshe, 1987, p. 151.
33 Interview, China, 1998, no. 18.
34 The State Economic and Trade Commission and the Document Research Office of the Central Party Committee, *Shisida yilai dang he guoia lingdaoren lun guoyou qiye gaige he fazhan* (Talks by Central Leaders on the Reform of State-Owned Enterprises after the 14th Party Congress), Beijing: Zhongyang wenxian chubanshe, 2000.
35 M. Kramer, "Polish Workers and the Post-Communist Transition, 1989–1993," *Communist and Post-communist Study*, 1995, vol. 28, no. 1, 71–114.
36 For example, when the Chongqing Knitting Factory was declared bankrupt in 1992, workers were greatly agitated. More than 200 workers forced their manager to go to the local court to withdraw the bankruptcy application because, as they claimed, the reform plans had not been approved by the workers' council. Xie Delu, *Zhongguo zuida pochanan toushi* (A Comprehensive Perspective on China's Biggest Bankruptcy Case), Beijing: Jingji guanli chubanshe, 1993.
37 Tian Zehong, "Guanyu dui pochan qiye zhaokai zhidaihui wenti de sikao" (Some Thoughts on the Convening of the Workers' Council in Bankrupt Enterprises), *Beijing gongren* (Beijing Workers), 1999, no. 1, 3–4.
38 A. Walder, "Workers and the State: The Reform Era and the Political Crisis of 1989," *The China Quarterly*, 1991, no. 127, 467–92; A. Chan and J. Unger, "Voices from the Protest Movement in Chongqing: Class Accents and Class Tensions," in J. Unger (ed.), *The Pro-Democracy Protests in China: Reports from the Provinces*, Armonk, NY: M.E. Sharpe, 1991, pp. 23–45.
39 *Gongren ribao*, June 19, 2000.
40 Indeed, Chinese workers have long realized their position is weak due to the lack of leverage over the enterprise authority. In the 1970s, the Party decided to cease the so-called "four big methods" (i.e., officially allowed voicing of opinions and demands, big posters, and debates) that were the main channels through which the people disciplined cadres in the Cultural Revolution. A survey conducted by a central Party organ and the ACFTU in 1982 revealed that a significant number of workers were upset. They complained that without these channels, they would be unable to keep cadres in check. Some complained that "the 'Four Bigs' is the right Chairman Mao bestowed on us. Now that Chairman Mao is gone, the 'Four Big' is removed." Others held that revoking these methods meant that the central government distrusted workers. The Joint Investigation Group, "Guanyu diyi qiche zhizaochang zhigong zhuangkuang de diaocha baogao" (An Investigation of the Workers of the First Truck Manufacturing Factory), in The Chinese Communist Secretary Office and the All China Federation of Trade Unions (eds), *Dangqian woguo gongren jieji zhuangkuang diaocha ziliao huibian* (A Selection of the Investigation Materials About the Situation of the Working Class in Our Country), Beijing: Zhongyang dangxiao chubanshe, 1983, pp. 23–32.
41 Zhu Guanglei, *Dangdai zhongguo shehui ge jieceng fenxi* (An Analysis of the Social Strata in China), Tianjin: Tianjin renmin chubanshe, 1998, pp. 65, 89.

42 S. Clarke, P. Fairbrother, and V. Borisov, *The Workers' Movement in Russia*, Hants, UK: Edward Elgar Publishing, 1995, p. 400.
43 Ibid., p. 409.
44 F. Chen, "Subsistence Crises, Managerial Corruption and Labor Protests in China," *The China Journal* 2000, vol. 44, 41–63.
45 Piven and Cloward, *Poor People's Movements*, p. 98.
46 Interview, China, 1999, no. 25.
47 Indeed, competition among laid-off workers to avoid being laid off undermines their solidarity. Ling Yubing, "Banzhang, li bugai liu yishou" (Group Leader, You Should Not Keep Your Skill a Secret), *Zhongguo gongren* (Chinese Workers), 1996, no. 11, 63.
48 Interview, China, 1999, no. 27.
49 Interview, China, 1999, no. 23.
50 Interview, China, 1999, no. 16.
51 *Lingdao juece xinxi* (Information for the Decision Making of the Leaders), 1998, no. 2, item 29.
52 *Gongren ribao*, March 18, 1999.
53 J. Oi, *State and Peasant in Contemporary China: The Political Economy of Village Government*, Berkeley, CA: University of California Press, 1989.
54 He Shijian, "Yige bei gongren ganzhou de changzhang" (A Manager Driven Out by Workers), *Fazhi yu xinwen* (Law and News), 1998, no. 49, 48–51.
55 Interview, China, 1999, no. 7.
56 The Investigation System of Chinese Entrepreneurs, "Xianjieduan woguo qiyejia duiwu de xingwei tezheng diaocha fenxi" (An Investigation and Analysis of the Behaviorial Characteristics of the Entrepreneurs in Our Country in the Current Period), *Guanli shijie* (Management World), 1995, no. 3, 153–63.
57 *Zhongguo funu bao* (Chinese Women Daily), February 25, 2002.
58 A talk by a Chinese scholar who participated in the making of the reform plan. Stanford University, November 19, 1999.
59 The Chinese phrase for this reform is "*youhua laodong zuhe.*"
60 Yang Xuqing, Wu Yue, and Chang Ping, *Shui ye bao buzhu tiefanwan* (Nobody Can Keep His Iron Rice Bowl), Chengdu: Sichuan daxue chubanshe, 1993, p. 58.
61 Ibid.
62 *Gongren ribao*, November 3, 1993.
63 In Liaoning province, an investigation revealed that there were 296 violent incidents in the second half of the year. Among the 300 leaders who were hurt, 196 were directors or managers, 71 were workshop managers, and 30 were section directors. *Gongren ribao*, March 24, 1993.
64 Zhang Xinjie (ed.), *Kuashiji de youhuan* (Worries That Persist Into the Next Century), Lanzhou: Lanzhou daxue chubanshe, 1998, p. 114.
65 Chen Shaohui, *Guoyou qiye laodong jiuye tizhi yanjiu* (A Study of the Employment System of State Enterprises), Beijing: Zhongguo jingji chubanshe, 1998, p. 116.
66 *Gongren ribao*, August 17, 1999.
67 About 10 percent reported that layoffs were based on performance, education, skills, and health. And most of the rest reported that they were laid off due to the shortage of production tasks, merger, bankruptcy, privatization, or other reform measures.
68 This form of layoffs is sometimes called internal retirement (*nei tui*). These people are laid off before they reach the retirement age (60 for men, 55 for women cadres, and 50 for women workers) and receive subsidies determined by their firms. Once they reach the retirement age, they register with the firm for benefits offered to formal retirees.
69 Interview, China, 1999, no. 27.
70 Interview, China, 1998, no. 4.
71 Reported in *Neibu canyue* (*Internal References*),1999, no. 32, p. 23.
72 Interview, China, 1999, no. 16.

73 Zuo Fu, *21 shiji shui geili fanchi* (Who Will Feed You in the 21st Century?), Nanchang: Baihuazhou wenyi chubanshe, 1998, p. 111.
74 Interview, China, 1999, no 12.
75 *Gong ren ribao*, October, 8 1998; Cai Yingyang and Zhao Yuelin, "Jiujing shui xiagang" (Who Will be Laid Off), *Shehui* (Society), 1998, no. 11, 46–48.
76 Feng Changyong, "Dengdai zuzhi anpai, buyuan canyu jingzheng" (Awaiting Government Reallocation and Unwilling to Compete), *Neichanxuanbian* (Compilation of Selected Materials), 1998, no. 20, 15–16.
77 Wang Yutan, *Weiren* (As a Human Being), Beijing: Xiyuan chubanshe, 2000, p. 120.
78 A. Walder, *Communist Neo-Traditionalism*, Berkeley, CA: University of California Press, 1986.
79 Some of my interviewees reported that their severance pay was only about 500 yuan for each year served. Interview, China, 1998, no. 5.
80 The company is PetroChina Co. which owns most of Daqing' oil assets and is listed on the New York and Hong Kong stock exchanges. J. Pomfret, "Chinese Oil Country Simmers as Workers Protest Cost-Cutting," *Washington Post*, March 17, 2002; E. Eckholm, "Leaner Factories, Fewer Workers Bring More Labor Unrest to China," *The New York Times*, March 19, 2002; Jin Yan and Tian Lei, "Daqing caiyuan de gaoang chengben" (The High Cost of Retrenchment in Daqing), *Sanlian shenghuo zhoukan* (Sanlian Weekly), 2002, no. 14, 12–17.
81 Interview, China, 1999, no. 18.
82 The dependent variable is dichotomous. If it is the government or its organs, it is coded as "1," otherwise "0." $N = 158$, coefficient $= 0.5766$, standard error $= 0.2207$, odds ratio $= 1.78$.
83 D. Donald, *Soviet Workers and the Collapse of Perestroika: The Soviet Labor Process and Gorbachev's Reforms, 1985–1991*, New York: Cambridge University Press, 1994, p. 95.
84 Yu Xiu, *Zaoyu xiagang* (Facing Retrenchment), Beijing: Zhonghua gongshanglian chubanshe, 1998, pp. 103–04.
85 She began to find work on her own and succeeded. Ibid., pp. 165–66.
86 Wang Hansheng and Chen Zhixia, "Zaijiuye zhengce yu xiagang zhigong zaijiuye xingwei" (The Reemployment Policies and the Job-Search Behavior of Laid-Off Workers), *Shehuixue yanjiu* (Sociological Research), 1998, no. 4, 13–30.
87 Interview, China, 1999, no. 22.
88 Wu Ji, "Bainian laochang pochan de beihou" (Behind the Bankruptcy of a Factory With a 100-Year History), *Jizhe guancha* (Observations of Correspondents), 1999, no. 1, 14–16.
89 J. Jon, *Making Sense of Marx*, Cambridge: Cambridge University Press, 1985.

6 The government and the prevention of worker resistance

1 G. Ekiert and J. Kubik, "Contentious Politics in New Democracies: East Germany, Hungary, Poland, and Slovakia, 1989–1993," *World Politics*, 1998, vol. 50, 547–81.
2 *Chinese Statistical Yearbook 2000*, p. 424.
3 J. Kynge, "Chinese Miners Riot Over Severance Pay," *Financial Times*, April 3, 2000.
4 *Shengyang wanbao* (Shenyang Evening News), October 27, 2001.
5 Tian Zehong, "Guanyu dui pochan qiye zhaokai zhidaihui wenti de sikao" (Some Thoughts on the Workers' Council in Bankrupt Enterprises), *Beijing gongren* (Beijing Workers), 1999, no. 1, 3–4.
6 Y. Cao, Y. Qiang, and B. R. Weingast, "From Federalism, Chinese Style to Privatization, Chinese Style," *Economics of Transition*, 1999, vol. 7, no. 1, 103–31.
7 *Gongren ribao*, May 14, 1998.
8 X. L. Ding, "The Illicit Asset Stripping of Chinese State Firms," *The China Journal*, 2000, vol. 43, 1–28.
9 *Gongren ribao*, July 31, 1997.

10 Between 1988 and 1998, Chinese citizens reported over 1.47 millions cases of illegal conduct or crimes of public workers. Among the cases investigated by the legal departments during the 10 years, about 70 percent of them involved enterprise leaders. Similarly, among the people punished, enterprise leaders accounted for 70 percent. See *Gongren ribao*, July 25, 1999; Hou, Xiaoqi, "Wei shen me, zen me ban?" (Why and How), *Banyuetan* (Biweekly Forum), 2000, no. 3, 22–25.
11 An investigation of 2,586 money-losing enterprises in 8 provinces by the State Statistical Bureau indicated that only less than 10 percent made loss because of state policies, whereas more than 80 percent lost money because of mismanagement. *Meiri qiaobao* (Overseas Chinese Daily), June 2, 1997.
12 F. Chen, "Subsistence Crises, Managerial Corruption and Labor Protests in China," *The China Journal*, 2000, vol. 44, 41–63.
13 Li Hongjun, "Guoqi gaige zhong 'xinfang' xianxiang de sikao" (Thoughts on the Petitions During the Reform of State Enterprises), *Lilun yu shijian* (Theory and Practice), 1999, no. 2, 32–33. In the protests in Liaoyang of Liaoning province in 2002, workers of different factories demanded to remove and punish corrupt officials and managers. See J. Pomfret, "Thousands of Workers Protest in Chinese City," *Washington Post*, March 20, 2002.
14 The Chinese phrase for the two sentences is "xiagang gongren buyong chou, dangguande jiali sha douyou". Jin Ye, *Jieceng de fubai* (Corruption of Social Groups), Zhuhai: Zhuhai chubanshe, 1998, p. 306.
15 E. Perry, "Shanghai's Strike Wave of 1957," *The China quarterly*, 1994, vol. 137, 1–27.
16 G. Ekiert, *The State Against Society: Political Crisis and Their Aftermath in East Central Europe*, Princeton, NJ: Princeton University Press, 1996, p. 109.
17 The General Office of the All China Federation of Trade Unions (ed.), *Jianguo yilai zhonggong zhongyang guanyu gongren yundong wenjian xuanbian* (Selected Documents About Workers' Movements Issued by the Central Party Committee After the Founding of the PRC), Beijing: Gongren chubanshe, 1989, p. 1036.
18 Ibid.
19 Ibid.
20 Perry, "Shanghai's Strike Wave of 1957."
21 M. Manion, "Reluctant Duelists: The Logic of the 1989 Protest and Massacre," in M. Oksenberg, L. Sullian, and M. Lambert (eds), *Beijing Spring, 1989: Confrontation and Conflict: The Basic Documents*, Armonk, NY: M.E. Sharpe, 1990, pp. xiii–xliii.
22 C. Cheng, *Behind the Tiananmen Massacre: Social, Political, and Economic Ferment in China*, Boulder, CO: Westview Press, 1990.
23 The State Education Commission, *Jingxin dongpo de wushiliu tian* (The Soul-Stirring 56 days), Beijing: Dadi chubanshe, 1989.
24 See Huntington, Samuel, *The Third Wave: Democratization in the Late Twentieth Century*, Norman, OK: University of Oklahoma Press, 1991.
25 S. Fish, *Democracy from Scratch*, Princeton, NJ: Princeton University Press, 1994; For a discussion of the case of China, see A. Walder, "When State Unravel: How China's Cadres Shaped Cultural Revolution Politics," in K. Brodsgaard and S. Young (eds), *State Capacity in East Asia: Japan, Taiwan, China, and Vietnam*, Hong Kong: Oxford University Press, 2000, pp. 157–84.
26 For a discussion on China, see B. Bakken, "State Capacity and Social Control in China," in K. Brodsgaard and S. Young (eds), *State Capacity in East Asia: Japan, Taiwan, China, and Vietnam*, Hong Kong: Oxford University Press, 2000, pp. 185–202.
27 Lohaman suggests that the collapse of East Germany is due to the fact that more and more people received the signal which indicated the popular discontent with the regime. S. Lohmann, "The Dynamics of Information Cascades: The Monday Demonstration in Leipzig East Germany, 1989–1991," *World Politics*, 1994, vol. 47, 42–101.
28 The Document Research Office of Chinese Communist Party Committee, *Shisi da yilai guoyou qiye gaige he fazhan dashi jiyao* (A Record of the Important Events of

the Reform of State-Owned Enterprises After the 14th Party Congress), Beijing: Zhongyang wenxian chuabanshe, 1999, p. 163.
29 In 2001, the central government took harsh measures to deal with the media that did not follow the party line. See C. Hutzler, "Beijing Tells Media to Toe Party Line," *The Asian Wall Street Journal*, July 31, 2001.
30 The talk by the governor of Jilin province, Hong Hu, was reported on the website of the Jilin provincial government, http://www.jl.gov.cn/jlzb/zb200109/zb2001-09-01.htm (accessed April 10, 2001).
31 For example, Robert Bates' study of governments in tropical Africa suggests that governments tend to deal with each social group based on their political influence. R. Bates, *Markets and States in Tropical Africa: The Political Basis of Agricultural Policies*, Berkeley, CA: University of California Press, 1981.
32 M. Oksenberg, "Occupations and Groups in Chinese Society and the Cultural Revolution," in *The Cultural Revolution: 1967 in Review*, Ann Arbor, MI: University of Michigan Center for Chinese Studies, 1968, pp. 1–39.
33 *Shehui kexue daobao* (Social Science News), August 21, 1999.
34 The All China Federation of Trade Unions, *1997 Zhongguo zhigong zhuangkuang diaocha* (1997 Investigation of Chinese Employees), Beijing: Xiyuan chubanshe, 1999, p. 78.
35 A survey of 2,674 bureaucrats of 9 ministries found that about 67 percent were allocated new jobs in other public sectors or were paid to study in universities, and another 19 percent were granted early retirement. The Research Group of the Bureaucratic Reform, "Jigou gaige yu renyuan fenliu: shi buwei diaocha baogao" (Organizational Reform and the Reallocation of Employees: An Investigation of Ten Ministries), *Jingji gongzuozhe xuexi ziliao* (Study Materials for Economic Workers), 1999, no. 15, 2–9.
36 F. Piven and R. Cloward, *Poor People's Movements: Why They Succeed, How They Fail*, New York: Vintage Books, 1979, p. 76.
37 Also see D. Solinger, *Contesting Citizenship in Urban China: Peasant Migrants, the State, and the Logic of the Market*, Berkeley, CA: University of California Press, 1999.
38 The Beijing Labor Bureau, "Jiakuai shishi 'zaijiuye gongcheng,' duoqudao anzhi xiagang zhigong." (Speeding up the Implementation of Reemployment and Reallocating Laid-Off Workers Through Multiple Channels), in The Research Office of the Beijing Party Committee and Beijing Labor Bureau (eds), *Zaijiuye gongzuo de yanjiu yu shijian* (Studies On and the Practices of Reemployment), Bejing: Jingji guanli chubanshe, 1998, pp. 69–83.
39 *Hubei ribao* (Hubei Daily), May 21, 1998. In some cities, the local government even required peasants to pay certain fees that were then used to pay laid-off workers. Private talk with Chinese scholars, July 21, 1999.
40 In China, the importance of legitimacy is exemplified in the 1989 Tiananmen incident in which those who worked for the Party and government organs also took to the streets. The State Education Commission, *Jingxin dongpo de 56 tian* (The Soul-Stirring 56 Days), p. 138.
41 A. Oberschall, "Opportunities and Framing in the Eastern Europe Revolts of 1989," in D. McAdam, J. D. McCarthy, and M. N. Zald (eds), *Comparative Perspectives on Social Movements*, Cambridge, UK: Cambridge University Press, 1996, pp. 172–99.
42 Chen, "Subsistence Crises, Managerial Corruption and Labor Protests in China." This is also true for other social groups in China. For example, some peasants claimed that in their village, about a thousand villagers formed an "Anti-Corruption Group." But their goal—"to severely punish corrupt cadres by relying on the leaders headed by President Jiang Zemin at the central level and the masses at the bottom"—is within the boundary of state tolerance. Zhao Shukai, "Shequ chongtu he xinxing quanli guanxi" (Conflicts Within Rural Communities and New Patterns of Power

Relationship), *Zhongguo nongcun guancha* (Observations of Rural China), 1999, no. 6, 19–22.
43 Zuo Fu, *21 shiji shui geili fanchi* (Who Will Feed You in the 21st Century?), Nanchang: Baihuazhou wenyi chubanshe, 1998, p. 111.
44 These strategies were reminiscent of what students had adopted in the early period of the 1989 Tiananmen incident when they did not intend to offend the government. Their slogans include "Support the Communist Party," "Uphold Socialism," "Support the Four Cardinal Principles," "Sincere Talk," "Eliminate Corruption, Down with the Merchant Officials," "Oppose Turmoil," and the like. The Education Commission, *Jingxin dongpo de wushi liutian* (The Soul-Stirring 56 Days), p. 53.
45 Citizens do report. The legal departments admit that among the cases investigated, about 80 percent of them were reported by citizens. *Gongren ribao*, July 25, 1999.
46 C. Tilly, *From Mobilization to Revolution*, New York: Random House, 1978, p. 228.
47 K. Opp and W. Ruehl, "Repression, Micromobilization and Political Protest," *Social Forces*, 1990, vol. 69, 521–47.
48 R. Laba, *The Roots of Solidarity: A Political Sociology of Poland's Working-Class Democratization*, Princeton, NJ: Princeton University Press, 1991, p. 37.
49 E. Rosenthal, "Workers' Plight Brings New Militancy in China," *New York Times*, March 10, 2003.
50 Ekiert, *The State against Society*, p. 115.
51 Ibid., p. 325.
52 Reported in *Gaige neican* (Reference of Reform), 1999, no. 6, p. 43.
53 *Renmin ribao* (Overseas Edition), February 16, 1998.
54 ACFTU, *1997 Zhongguo zhigong zhuangkuang diaocha* (1997 Investigation of Chinese Employees), p. 371.
55 Some local governments that lack resources to help workers have tried to silence laid-off workers by identifying and punishing a few corrupt managers. Interview, China, 1999, no. 5.
56 This was claimed to be the case in the United States in the 1930s. Piven and Cloward, *Poor People's Movements*, pp. 48–49.
57 Wu Bangguo, "Qieshi zuohao guoyou qiye xiagang zhigong jiben shenghuo baozhang he zaijiuye gongzuo" (To Do a Good Job of Providing Minimum Allowance for Laid-Off Workers and Helping Them Secure Reemployment), *Qiushi* (Seeking the Truth), 1998, no. 13, 2–7.
58 *Gongren ribao*, April 22, 1998.
59 *Gongren riabo*, August 12, 1999.
60 For a discussion of the attribution error, see, among others, E. E. Jones, "The Rock Road From Acts to Dispositions," *American Psychologist*, 1979, vol. 34, 107–17.
61 The Ministry of Organization of the CCP Central Committee, *2000–2001, Zhongguo Diaochao baogao* (2000–2001 China Investigation Report), Bejing: Zhongyang bianye chubanshe, 2001, p. 148.
62 Cheng Xuebin, "Chengzhen geren shouru caijiu de xingcheng ji fazhan qushi" (The Formation of the Income Gap Between Urban Citizens and its Development Tendency), in the Research Group of the Research Office of the State Council (ed.), *Chengzhen jumin shouru chaju yanjiu* (A Study of the Income Gap Among Urban Citizens), Beijing: Zhongguo yanshi chubanshe, 1997, pp. 76–86.
63 Zhang Chunlin, "Tiaochu 'lushan' shi zhenmian" (To Gain the Truth), *Xinwen jizhe* (Journalists), 2000, no. 5, 56–57.
64 Ibid.
65 For example, a person received training as a technician at the expense of his firm in 1993. He left and started his own business despite the firm's reluctance to let him go. As his sister-in-law was a vice county magistrate, this worker fared very well. Ironically, he was elected a model of self-employed laid-off workers and received a reward. *Gongren riabo*, May 11, 1999.

66 Zhang Chunlin, "Tiaochu 'lushan' shi zhenmian" (To Gain the Truth).
67 *Gongren ribao*, March 27, 1999.
68 Interview, 1998, China. no. 17.
69 M. Blecher, "Hegemony and Workers' Politics in China," *The China Quarterly*, 2002, no. 170, 283–303.
70 E. Hung and S. Chiu, "The Lost Generation: Life Course Dynamics and Xiagang in China," *Modern China*, 2003, vol. 29, no. 2, 204–36.
71 Ekiert, *The State against Society*, p. 101.
72 S. Tarrow, *Power in Movement: Social Movements, Collective Action and Politics*, New York: Cambridge University Press, 1994, p. 95.
73 J. Schumpeter, *Capitalism, Socialism and Democracy*, New York: Harper, 1950, p. 270.
74 S. Popkin, "Public Choices and Peasant Organization," in Clifford R. Russell and Norman K. Nickolson (eds), *Public Choice and Rural Development*. Washington, DC: Resources for the Future, 1987, pp. 256–57.
75 Also see Chen, "Subsistence Crises, Managerial Corruption and Labor Protests in China."
76 B. Klandermans, "Mobilization and Participation: Social–Psychological Expansions of Resource Mobilization Theory," *American Sociological Review*, 1984, vol. 49, 583–600.
77 Interview, China, 1998, no. 26.
78 The dependent variable is dichotomous (i.e., participation or non-participation in collective action). Coefficient = 0.4122, standard error = 0.1786, odds ratio = 1.510.
79 The local government responded by arresting a number of participants and publishing an official editorial in the *Mianyang Daily* accusing hostile foreign and domestic forces of stirring up trouble. No information on the college student who posted the notice was available. This was reported by some of our interviewees. It was also available on the website www.hrichina.org (accessed January 2, 2001).
80 The Beijing Labor Bureau, "Jiakuai shishi 'zaijiuye gongcheng,' duoqudao anzhi xiagang zhigong," p. 135.
81 The government asked the bank to lend enough money to the factory to cover back wages. When the news reached other factories, they, too, demanded and received loans. "We Want to Eat," *Far Eastern Economic Review*, vol. 160, no. 26, June 26, 1997, 14–16.
82 T. J. Shi, *Political Participation in Beijing*, Cambridge, MA: Harvard University Press, 1997.
83 E. Eckholm, "Where Workers, Too, Rust, Bitterness Boils," *The New York Times*, March 20, 2002.
84 The Ministry of the CCP Organization, *2000–2001 China Investigation Report*, p. 290.
85 The Research Group of the Public Security, *Zhongguo tese zhi gongan yanjiu* (A Study of Public Security with Chinese Characteristics), Beijing: Qunzhong chubanshe, 1996, p. 114.
86 Ji Zhengfeng, "Yufang he chuzhi qunti xing shijian de duice xuanze" (The Choice of Modes of Reaction to Mass Action), *Lilun yu shijian* (Theory and Practice), 1999, no. 16, 30–31.
87 *Renmin ribao*, December 27, 1999.
88 *Gongren ribao*, November 4, 1998.
89 The National Complaints Bureau, *Zhongguo xinfang xiezhen* (A Record of People's Letters and Visits in China), Beijing: Gongren chubanshe, 1998, p. 103.
90 *New York Times*, May 1, 1989, pp. 1,7, cited in D. Chong, *Collective Action and the Civil Rights Movement*, Chicago, IL: University of Chicago Press, 1991, p. 131.
91 N. D. Kristof, "Organization Woes Slow China's Student Protesters," *New York Times*, May 1, 1989; cited in Chong, *Collective Action and Civil Rights Movements*, p. 131.
92 Chen, "Subsistence Crises, Managerial Corruption and Labor Protests in China."

93 Sometimes, the government uses more subtle means. For example, a few laid-off workers of a factory decided to organize an appeal when an inspection team of the higher-level authority was scheduled to come to their city. But it happened that the city government learned of their plan. Representatives from the city complaint bureau worked hard to persuade them to give up their plan by seeking help from family members and relatives of the few organizers. The son of a main organizer was a teacher in a local school. Following the bidding of the government, the schoolmaster told this teacher to persuade his father to give up the appeal. The worker agreed because the school would not let his son return to work until the government obtained his promise. Interview, China, 1999, no. 22.

94 Jiang Xueqin, "Fighting to Organize," *Far Eastern Economic Review*, September 6, 2001.

95 Piven and Cloward, *Poor People's Movements*, p. xii.

96 W. Gamson, "The Success of the Unruly," in D. McAdam and D. A. Snow (eds), *Social Movements*, Los Angeles, CA: Roxbury Publishing Company, 1997, pp. 357–64.

97 Similarly in Russia in the early 1990s, "Most strikes were short-lived and over issues which workers perceived to be specific to their factory of their shop, even if, in reality, the same grievances were being expressed by workers elsewhere." D. Filtzer, *Soviet Workers and the Collapse of Perestroika: The Soviet Labor Process and Gorbachev's Reforms, 1985–1991*, New York: Cambridge University Press, 1994, p. 115.

98 Lee, "The Revenge of History."

99 Eckholm, "Where Workers, Too, Rust, Bitterness Boils."

100 For the importance of alternative authorities for the emergence of revolution, see Tilly, *From Mobilization to Revolution*.

101 Within China, the Chinese government succeeded in repressing the Falungong sect in the early 2000s. See J. Pomfret and P. Pan, "Torture Is Breaking Falungong," *Washington Post*, August 5, 2001.

102 Oberschall, *Social Conflict and Social Movements*, p. 75.

103 Wang Daben, "Shanghai shi qiye xiagang renyuen jiqi fenliu" (Laid-Off Workers and Their Reallocation in Shanghai), *Yazhou yanjiu* (Asian Study), 1997, no. 15, 70–88.

104 Xie Delu, *Zhongguo zuida pochanan toushi* (A Comprehensive Perspective on China's Biggest Bankruptcy Case), Beijing: Jingji guanli chubanshe, 1993, p. 54.

105 Cao Siyuan (ed.), *Jianbing yu pochan caozuo shiwu* (Practical Procedure for Merger and Bankruptcy), Beijing: Gongshang chubanshe, 1997, p. 305.

106 Xie, *Zhongguo zhuida pochanan toushi*, p. 77.

107 Ibid.

108 J. Rawls, *A Theory of Justice*, Oxford: Oxford University Press, 1973, p. 143.

109 ACFTU, *1997 Zhongguo zhigong zhuangkuang diaocha*, p. 1054.

110 Li Zuoming, "Cong xiagang nugong dao zhongguo guaqi di yi ren" (From a Laid-Off Woman to China's First Person Who Paints With a Knife), *Falu yu shenghuo* (Law and Life), 1999, no. 4, 14–17.

111 But he was not unsympathetic. Instead he admitted that he would have given the workers some money had he had any. This city could not even pay its cadres and teachers on time because of financial difficulties. Interview, China, 1999, no. 38.

112 Lu Aihong, *Xiagang, zenmeban, zenmekan* (Layoff: How to Handle It), Beijing: Jingji kexue chubanshe, 1998, p. 6.

113 Lu Xin, Lu Xueyi, and Shan Tianlun (eds), *1999 nian zhongguo shehui xingshi fenxi yu yuce* (1999: An Analysis and Prediction of Chinese Society), Beijing: Shehui kexue wenxian chubanshe, 1999, p. 248.

114 A. Kiernan, "State Enterprises in Shenyang: Actors and Victims in the Transition," *China Perspectives*, 1997, vol. 14, 26–32.

115 Chen Lu and Yang Lianyun, "Xiagang zhigong zai jiuye nandian wenti de diaocha fenxi yu duice jianyi" (An Analysis of the Difficult Problems in the Reemployment

of Laid-Off Workers and Countermeasures), *Qiushi* (Seeking the Truth), 1999, no. 3, 19–22.
116 Interview, China, 1999, no. 17.

7 The collective action of Chinese laid-off workers

1 Y. S. Cai, "Relaxing the Constraints from Above: Politics of Privatizing Public Enterprises in China," *Asian Journal of Political Science*, 2002, vol. 10, 94–121.
2 Indeed, in his study of Chinese mayors, Pierre Landry finds that economic performance is not associated with promotion. See P. Landry, "Marketization and the Political Fate of Chinese Mayors," paper presented at the annual meeting of the American Political Science Association, Boston, MA, 2002.
3 Qiu Lu, "Guoqi gaige weihe ruci jiannan" (Why It Is So Difficult to Reform State Enterprises), *Bainian chao* (A Century Stream), 1999, no. 2, 4–14.
4 For a discussion on the appeals system, see Y. S. Cai, "Managed Participation in China," *Political Science Quarterly*, 2004, vol. 119, no. 3, 425–51; L. M. Luehrmann, "Facing Citizen Complaints in China, 1951–1996," *Asian Survey*, 2003, vol. 43, no. 5, 845–66.
5 *Gongren ribao*, December 2, 1998.
6 Jiang Xiaoming, "Cao Guoying: Guanjian yaoyou ganqing" (Cao Guoying: The Fundamental Issue is Passion), *Xinwen zhoukan* (China News Weekly), April 1, 2002, pp. 32–33.
7 The National Complaints Bureau, *Zhongguo xinfang xiezhen* (A Record of People's Letters and Visits in China), Beijing: gongren chubanshe, 1998.
8 Interview, China, 1999, no. 17.
9 For example, a survey of 1,510 households from 6 cities conducted in 1997 found that almost 93 of them reported that "power supersedes law." Wang Chunguang, "1997–1998: Zhongguo shehui wending de diaocha" (1997–1998: An Investigation of China's Social Stability), in Lu Xin, Lu Xueyi, and Shan Tianlun (eds), *Zhongguo shehui xingshi fenxi yu yuce* (1998: An Analysis and Prediction of the China's Social Situation), Beijing: Shehui kexue wenxian chubanshe, 1998, pp. 121–47.
10 The National Complaints Bureau, *Zhongguo xinfang xiezhen*.
11 Ibid., p. 458.
12 K. O'Brien, "Neither Transgressive nor Contained: Boundary-Spanning Contention in China," *Mobilization: An International Journal*, 2003, vol. 8, no. 1, 51–64.
13 According to the 2000 yearbooks of 11 provinces, including Henan, Shandong, Jiangsu, Hebei, and Sichuan, the average number of participants in a collective appeal ranges from 17 to 31.
14 The Chinese phrase for this is "*xiao nao xiao jiejue, daonao da jiejue, bunao bu jiejue.*" See Dong Qingmin, "Renmin neibu tufaxin qunti maodun de tedian ji chuli yuanze" (The Characteristics of Collective Actions and the Strategies of Response), *Lilunqianyan* (Theoretical Frontiers), 1999, no. 13, 7–9.
15 Reported in *Neican xuanbian* (Internal References), 1998, no. 16, pp. 22–23.
16 The term is from R. Mnookin and L. Kornhauser, "Bargaining in the Shadow of the Law: The Case of Divorce," *Yale Law Journal*, 1979, vol. 88, 950.
17 The General Office of the ACFTU (ed.), *Jianguo yilai zhonggong zhongyang guanyu gongren yundong wenjian xuanbian* (Selected Documents About Workers' Movements Issued By the Central Party Committee After the Founding of the PRC), Beijing: Gongren chubanshe, 1989.
18 Zhang Zuoji (ed.), *Zhongguo laodong tizhi gaige yanjiu* (A Study of the Reform of the Labor System in China), Beijing: Zhongguo laodong chubanshe, 1994.
19 Some people have proposed that the government should add this right to the Constitution and the Labor Law in order to handle this issue in an institutionalized way. The State Labor Bureau did make some regulations with respect to the proper

handling of strikes. See Zhao Dechun, "Xianfa zhong ying zengjia yixiang bagong de quanli" (The Right of Strikes Should be Added to the Constitution), *Jingji yanjiu ziliao* (Materials for Economic Research), 1999, no. 3, 55–56; Zhang, *Zhongguo laodong tizhi gaige yanjiu*, p. 110.
20 The National Complaints Bureau, *Zhongguo xinfang xiezhen*, p. 58.
21 *Beijing Fazhi bao* (Beijing Legal News), August 9, 1999.
22 Huang Daosheng, "Ruheyufang yueji shangfang" (How to Prevent Appeals to Higher-Level Authorities), *Jiangsu jijian* (Jiangsu Discipline Inspection), 1999, no. 10, 17.
23 The National Complaints Bureau, *Zhongguo xinfang xiezhen*, pp. 81, 86–87.
24 *Zhongguo gaige bao* (China Reform News), March 11, 1999.
25 *Zhongguo Qingnian bao* (Chinese Youth Daily), August 31, 2001.
26 Li Maoguan and Tian Baichun, "Bian qunzhong 'shangfang' wei ganbu 'xiafang'" (From People's Appeals to Cadres' Visits to People), *Qiushi* (Seeking the Truth), 1999, no. 14, 43–45.
27 Gao Jianyan, Li Chunsheng, and Huang Bicheng, "Baijia changzhang, qineng jinchan tuoqiao" (Corrupt Manager, You Have No Chance to Evade Responsibility), *Fazhi yu xinwen* (Law and News), 1999, no. 4, 2–4.
28 Yu Xiu, *Zaoyu xiagang* (Facing Retrenchment), Beijing: Zhonghua gongshanglian chubanshe, 1998, pp. 236–37.
29 Dong Qingmin, "Renmin neibu tufaxin qunti maodun de tedian ji chuli yuanze."
30 The National Complaints Bureau, *Zhongguo xinfang xiezhen*, p. 111.
31 The four cities are Beijing, Haerbin, Wuhan, and Guangzhou. The State Planning Commission, "Shijizhijiao de zhongguo shehui xingshi" (The Social Situation in China at the Turn of the Century), *Jingji gongzuozhe xuexi ziliao* (Studying Materials for Economic Workers), 2000, no. 23, 2–11.
32 With this mode of settlement, workers who were to leave their firms received compensation for their past contributions to the firms, which was not regulated by government policies. Li Zhenghua and Wang Qi, "Shanghai qiye maodun duoshu mei zouru falu qudao" (Most Disputes in the Enterprises in Shanghai Were Not Solved Through the Legal System), *Neican xunabian* (Selected Materials), 1999, no. 7, 22.
33 For example, before the eve of the 1998 Spring Festival, the central Party Committee and the central government jointly issued an exceptionally urgent (*teji*) directive demanding local Party committees and governments to distribute poverty-alleviation subsidies to poverty-stricken workers with "a strong sense of political responsibility." *Zhongguo qiye zhenggong xinxi bao* (Political Work Information of Chinese Enterprises), June 3, 1998.
34 For example, peasants in one village once sent four video tapes showing the illegal occupation of their village land to four top central leaders, but they were all returned for unknown reasons. Ren Yanfang, *Minyuan* (People's Complaints), Bejing: Zhongguo wenlian chubanshe, 1999, p. 92.
35 *Gongren ribao*, May 10, 1996.
36 N. Frohlich, J. A. Oppenheimer, and O. R. Young, *Political Leadership and Collective Goods*, Princeton, NJ: Princeton University Press, 1971, p. 48.
37 Ibid., p. 43.
38 D. Chong, *Collective Action and the Civil Rights Movement*, Chicago, IL: University of Chicago Press, 1991, p. 122.
39 E. Perry and X. Li, *Proletarian Power: Shanghai in the Cultural Revolution*, Boulder, CO: Westview Press, 1997.
40 It has also been found that in China, peasant leaders also tend to be the elite among peasant communities. Yu Jianrong, "Liyi, quanli he zhixu" (Interests, Power, and Order), *Zhongguo nongcun guancha* (Observations of Rural China), 2000, no. 4, 70–76.
41 *Gongren ribao*, March 19, 1998.
42 Interview, China, 1999, no. 31.

43 Zuo Fu, *21 shiji shui geili fanchi* (Who Will Feed You in the 21st Century?), Nanchang: Baihuazhou wenyi chubanshe, 1998, p. 111.
44 D. Bernheim, "A Theory of Conformity," *Journal of Political Economy*, 1994, vol. 102, no. 5, 841–77.
45 Chong, *Collective Action and Civil Rights Movements*, p. 125.
46 Bernheim, "A Theory of Conformity."
47 Chong, *Collective Action and Civil Rights Movements*, p. 126.
48 Philip P. Pan, "Three Chinese Workers: Jail, Betrayal and Fear," *Washington Post*, December 28, 2002. In this event, 4 worker leaders were arrested. Reportedly, 2 of them were released later without being imposed legal punishment. The other 2 (Yao Fuxin and Xiao Yunliang) were accused of "overthrowing the government" in 2003 and were sentenced to 7 and 4 years in prison. Reported at www.chinesenewsnet.com (accessed May 10, 2003).
49 This is based on a logistic regression using a sample size of 172 workers who participated in collective action. The dependent variable is success or failure, and the independent variable is the number of participants (i.e., the unit is 10 people). Coefficient is 0.3224, the odds ratio is 1.38, and the standard error is 0.1474.
50 They also reported that "more participants can strengthen the bargaining position in that we can figure out more reasons to negotiate with the leaders." Interview, China, 1999, no. 22.
51 The ACFTU, *1997 Zhongguo zhigong zhuangkuang diaocha* (1997 Investigation of Chinese Employees), Beijing: Xiyuan chubanshe, 1999, p. 97.
52 F. Chen, "Industrial Restructuring and Workers' Resistance in China," *Modern China*, 2003, vol. 29, no. 2, 237–58.
53 E. Ostrom, "A Behavioral Approach to Rational Choice Theory of Collective Action," *American Political Science Review*, 1998, vol. 92, no. 1, 1–22.
54 Ibid.
55 Xie Delu, "Chongqing zhenzhi zhongchang pochan xiaoying fenxi" (An Analysis of the Repercussions of the Bankruptcy of the Chongqing Knitting Factory), *Zhongguo gongye jingji yanjiu* (A Study of Chinese Industrial Economy), 1994, no. 11, 37–41.
56 J. Kynge, "Chinese Miners Riot over Severance Pay." *Financial Times*, April 3, 2000.
57 These cadres and workers were also irritated by the government's discriminatory policy. At that time, lower-level cadres and workers suspected that the government would assign jobs to the few top cadres in the factory, which turned out to be true. But the government did not assign them jobs at that time because of a possibly strong reaction from workers. About three months after the bankruptcy, the manager, the Party secretary, and two deputy managers were reallocated. This was also true for the bankruptcy of Chongqing Knitting Factory. The original manager, the Party secretary, and the general engineer were transferred. See Jin Pei, *Hequ hecong* (Where To Go), Beijing: Jinrizhongguo chubanshe, 1998, p. 246.
58 The factory, however, refused to accept the proposal entirely. Instead, it reduced the shares that the workers had to buy by a third.
59 Interview, China, 1999, no. 16.
60 Interview, China, 1999, no. 22.
61 For example, in South Korea in April 1960, citizens of Masan protesting against rigged elections were brutally repressed. On April 11, the body of a protester was discovered in a bay with a police tear gas canister lodged in the left eye socket. Protests in Masan exploded again. "Almost every living soul in Masan seemed to have risen to violent hysteria." Q. Y. Kim, "From Protest to Change of Regime: The 4–19 Revolt and the Fall of the Rhee Regime in South Korea," *Social Forces*, 1996, vol. 74, no. 4, 1179–208.
62 Interview, China, 1998, no. 24.
63 This does not mean that all workers in large SOEs are provided with housing. Since the number of working years is often an important criterion to obtain housing, older people in large enterprises are more likely to obtain housing than those in small enterprises. This

is more the case for laid-off workers because, according to my survey, about 70 percent of them were over 38 years old. Nationwide, more than 67 percent of laid-off workers were over 36 years old as of 1998. *Chinese Labor Statistical Yearbook 1999*, p. 443.
64 For a discussion of the importance of ecology for mobilization, see D. X. Zhao, *The Power of Tiananmen: State–Society Relations and the 1989 Beijing Student Movement*, Chicago, IL: University of Chicago Press, 2001.
65 R. Hardin, "Acting Together, Contributing Together," *Rationality and Society*, no. 3, 365–80.
66 "Beijing Struggle to 'Ride the Tiger of Liberalization,'" *Jane's Intelligence Review*, January, 2001, pp. 26–30.
67 The State Statistical Bureau, *Da toushi* (A Comprehensive Perspective), Beijing: Zhongguo fazhan chubanshe, 1998, p. 31.
68 Between 1995 and 1998, the number of large industrial SOEs increased from 4,685 to 5,343; that of medium SOEs increased from 11,000 to 12,490; and those of small SOEs decreased from 102,315 to 48,058. The State Statistical Bureau, *Da toushi*, (A Comprehensive Perspective), Beijing: Zhongguo fazhan chubanshe, 1998, pp. 214–15; *Chinese Financial Statistical Materials 1999*, p. 499.
69 *Chinese Labor Statistics 1999*, pp. 441, 457.
70 *Chinese Labor Statistics 1998*, pp. 431–33.
71 *Chinese Labor Statistics 1998*, pp. 431–32; *Chinese Labor Statistics 1999*, pp. 441–42.
72 F. Piven and R. A. Cloward, *Poor People's Movements: Why They Succeed, How They Fail*, New York: Vintage Books, 1979.
73 J. Scott, *Domination and the Arts of Resistance*, New Haven, CT: Yale University Press, 1990, p. 192.
74 It has found that the pace of privatization of state and collective enterprises is negatively associated with worker resistance. See Cai, "Relaxing the Constraints from Above."
75 All these efforts have contributed to a decline in the number of unpaid laid-off workers in the country. In 1997, nationwide, among unemployed laid-off workers, about 48.8 percent failed to receive subsistence subsidies, and the figure declined to 18 percent in 1998. *Chinese Labor Statistics 1998*, p. 432; *Chinese Labor Statistics 1999*, p. 442.
76 *Lingdao juece xinxi* (Information For the Decision Making of Leaders), 1999, no. 2, p. 26.
77 Li Congguo, "Cong guoqi sannian tuokun kan quoqi gaige" (Examining the Reform of State Enterprises in Light of the Plan of Solving the Loss-Making Issue Within Three Years), *Liaowang* (Perspective), 2000, no. 8, 2–5.
78 Ibid.
79 J. Kynge, "China Slows Economic Reform amid Protests," *Financial Times*, June 8, 2001.
80 J. Kynge, "Beijing Puts Freeze on State-Group Bankruptcies," *Financial Times*, October 24, 2001.
81 *Wenhui bao* (Hong Kong), December 16, 2002.
82 See the Website of Xinhua News Agencies, http://news.xinhuanet.com/fortune/ 2002–06/01/ content _419770.htm (accessed June 1, 2002).
83 D. McAdam, "Conceptual Origins, Current Problems, Future Directions," in D. McAdam, J. McCarthy, and M. Zald (eds), *Comparative Perspectives on Social Movements*, New York: Cambridge University Press, 1996, pp. 23–40, p. 29.
84 S. Huntington, *Political Order in Changing Societies*. New Haven, CT: Yale University Press, 1968.

8 Conclusion

1 The State Planning Commission, "Shijizhijiao de zhongguo shehui xingshi" (The Social Situation in China At the Turn of the Century), *Jingji gongzuozhe xuexi ziliao* (Studying Materials for Economic Workers), 2000, no. 23, 2–11.

2 M. Golden, *Heroic Defeats: The Politics of Job Loss*, New York: Cambridge University Press, 1997.
3 D. Filtzer, *Soviet Workers and the Collapse of Perestroika: The Soviet Labor Process and Gorbachev's Reforms, 1985–1991*, New York: Cambridge University Press, 1994.
4 R. Laba, *The Roots of Solidarity: A Political Sociology of Poland's Working-Class Democratization*, Princeton, NJ: Princeton University Press, 1991.
5 Ibid., p. 104.
6 T. Ash, *The Polish Revolution: Solidarity 1980–1982*, London: Jonathan Cape, 1983.
7 Interview, China, 1999, no. 34.
8 E. Perry and M. Selden, "Introduction: Reform and Resistance in Contemporary China," in E. Perry and M. Selden (eds), *Chinese Society: Change, Conflict and Resistance*, London: Routledge, 2000, pp. 1–19.
9 This sentence was written by Wendell Phillips, quoted in T. Skocpol, *States and Social Revolutions*, Cambridge, UK: Cambridge University Press, 1979, p. 17.
10 Ibid.
11 M. Kramer, "Polish Workers and the Post-Communist Transition, 1989–1993," *Communist and Post-communist Study*, 1995, vol. 28, no. 1, 71–114.
12 Ibid., p. 87.
13 F. Piven and R. A. Cloward, *Poor People's Movements: Why They Succeed, How They Fail*, New York: Vintage Books, 1979.
14 S. Huntington, *Political Order in Changing Societies*, New Haven, CT: Yale University Press, 1968.
15 The Document Research Office of Chinese Communist Party Committee, *Shisi da yilai guoyou qiye gaige he fazhan dashi jiyao* (A Record of the Important Events of the Reform of State-Owned Enterprises After the 14th Party Congress), Beijing: Zhongyang wenxian chuabanshe, 1999, p. 135.
16 M. McFaul, "State Power, Institutional Change, and the Politics of Privatization in Russia," *World Politics*, 1995, vol. 47, 210–43.
17 Golden, *Heroic Defeats: The Politics of Job Loss*, p. 26.
18 Ibid.
19 E. Mueller and T. O. Jukam, "Discontent and Aggressive Political Participation," *British Journal of Political Science*, 1983, vol. 13, 159–79.
20 P. Pierson, *Dismantling the Welfare State?* New York: Cambridge University Press, 1994, 19.
21 J. Oi., "Realms of Freedom in Post-Mao China," in William Kirby (ed.), *Realms of Freedom in Modern China*, Stanford, CA: Stanford University Press, 2003, pp. 264–84; T. J. Shi, *Political Participation in Beijing*, Cambridge, MA: Harvard University Press, 1997.
22 A. Walder, *Communist Neo-traditionalism*, Berkeley, CA: University of California Press, 1986; L. Cook, *The Soviet Social Contract and Why it Failed: Welfare Policy and Workers' Politics from Brezhnev to Yeltsin*, Cambridge, MA: Harvard University Press, 1993.
23 I. Markovits, "Law and Glasnost: Some Thoughts about the Future of Judicial Review under Socialism," *Law & Society Review*, 1989, vol. 23, no. 3, 399–447.
24 He Pin and Hu Manhong, "Ouxin lixue wei renmin" (Working Wholeheartedly For the People), *Minzhu yu fazhi* (Democracy and Law), 1999, no. 3, 18–20.
25 *Henan nianjian 1999*, p. 62.
26 Reported in *Chinese Youth Daily*, August 31, 2001.
27 D. Porta and H. Reiter, "The Policing of Protest in Western Democracies," in D. Porta and H. Reiter (eds), Policing Protest: *The Control of Mass Demonstration in Western Democracies*, Minneapolis, MN: University of Minnesota Press, 1998, pp. 1–34.
28 See www. Chinesenewsnet.com (accessed April 25, 2001).
29 Workers have also increased the use of law in pursuing their rights. C. K. Lee, "From the Specter of Mao to the Spirit of the Law: Labor Insurgency in China," *Theory and Society*, 2002, vol. 31, no. 2, 189–228.

30 E. Rosenthal, "Workers' Plight Brings New Militancy in China," *New York Times*, March 10, 2003.
31 G. Ekiert, *The State Against Society: Political Crisis and Their Aftermath in East Central Europe*, Princeton, NJ: Princeton University Press, 1996, p. 287.
32 *Lao Dongbao* (Labor News), July 30, 1999.
33 The ACFTU, *1997 Zhongguo zhigong zhuangkuang diaocha* (1997 Investigation of Chinese Employees), Beijing: Xiyuan chubanshe, 1999, pp. 1244–45, 1256.
34 Talk by a Chinese scholar, Stanford University, March 6, 1999.

Appendix: data collection

1 Those questions included in the questionnaire but not used in the study are excluded.

Bibliography

Agresti, A., *An Introduction to Categorical Data Analysis*, New York: John Wiley & Sons, 1996.
The All China Federation of Trade Unions, *1997 Zhongguo zhigong zhuangkuang diaocha* (1997 Investigation of Chinese Employees), Beijing: Xiyuan chubanshe, 1999.
——, *Zhongguo zhigong duiwu zhuangkuang diaocha 1986* (An Investigation of Chinese Workers in 1986), Beijing: Gongren chubanshe, 1987.
——, *Dangqian woguo gongren jieji zhuangkuang diaocha ziliao huibian* (A Compilation of the Investigation Materials of the Working Class of Our Country in the Contemporary Period), Beijing: Zhonggong zhongyang dangxiao chubanshe, 1983.
Aronowitz, S., *False Promise: The Shaping of American Working Class Consciousness*, New York: McGraw-Hill, 1973.
Ash, T. G., *The Polish Revolution: Solidarity 1980–1982*, London: Jonathan Cape, 1983.
Axelrod, R., *The Evolution of Cooperation*, New York: Basic Books, 1984.
Bai Meilin, *Shicheng xinchao* (New Trends in the City of Stone), Nanjing: Nanjing University Press, 1998.
Bao Huasheng, "Heilian yeyao you ren chang" (Some People Have to be the Offenders), *Neican xuanbian* (Selected Materials), 1999, no. 25, 9–11.
Bates, R. H., *Markets and States in Tropical Africa: The Political Basis of Agricultural Policies*, Berkeley, CA: University of California Press, 1981.
The Beijing Labor Bureau, "Jiakuai shishi 'zaijiuye gongcheng,' duoqudao anzhi xiagang zhigong" (Speeding Up the Implementation of Reemployment and Reallocating Laid-Off Workers Through Multiple Channels), in the Research Office of the Beijing Party Committee and Beijing Labor Bureau (eds), *Zaijiuye gongzuo de yanjiu yu shijian* (Studies on and the Practice of Reemployment), Bejing: Jingji guanli chubanshe, 1998, pp. 61–82.
Bernheim, D., "A Theory of Conformity," *Journal of Political Economy*, 1994, vol. 102, no. 5, 841–77.
Bernstein, T. and Lu, L. B., *Taxation Without Representation in Contemporary Rural China*, New York: Cambridge University Press, 2003.
Bian, Y. J., *Work and Inequality in Urban China*, Albany, NY: State University of New York Press, 1994.
——, "Guanxi and the Allocation of Urban Jobs in China," *The China Quarterly*, 1994, no. 140, 971–99.
Blasi, J. R., Kroumova, M., and Kruse, D., *Kremlin Capitalism: The Privatization of the Russian Economy*, Ithaca, NY: Cornell University Press, 1997.

Blecher, M., "Hegemony and Workers' Politics in China," *The China Quarterly*, 2002, no. 170, 283–303.
Booth, W. J., "On the Idea of the Moral Economy," *American Political Science Review*, 1994, vol. 88, no. 3, 653–67.
Braverman, H., *Labor and Monopoly Capital: The Degradation of Work in the Twentieth Century*, New York: Monthly Review Press, 1974.
Briet, M., Klandermans, B., and Kroon, F., "How Women Become Involved in the Women's Movement of the Netherlands," in Katzenstein, M. F. and McClurg Mueller, C. M. (eds), *The Women's Movements of the United States and Western Europe*, Philadelphia, PA: Temple University Press, 1987, pp. 44–64.
Buechler, S. M., "Beyond Resource Mobilization? Emerging Trends in Social Movement Theory," *The Sociological Quarterly*, 1993, vol. 34, no. 2, 217–35.
Cai, Y. S., "Managed Participation in China," *Political Science Quarterly*, 2004, vol. 121, 425–51.
——, "Relaxing the Constraints from Above: Politics of Privatizing Public Enterprises in China," *Asian Journal of Political Science*, 2002, vol. 10, 94–121.
Cai Yingyang and Zhao Yuelin, "Jiujing shui xiagang" (Who Will be Laid Off?), *Shehui* (Society), 1998, no. 11, 46–48.
Calhoun, C., *Neither Gods nor Emperors: Students and the Struggle for Democracy in China*, Berkeley, CA: University of California Press, 1994.
Cao, Y., Qiang, Y. Y., and Weingast, B. R., "From Federalism, Chinese Style to Privatization, Chinese Style," *Economics of Transition*, 1999, vol. 7, no. 1, 103–31.
Cao Siyuan (ed.), *Jianbing yu pochan caozuo shiwu* (Practical Procedure for Merger and Bankruptcy), Beijng: Gongshang chubanshe, 1997.
Chamberlain, H. B., "Party–Management Relations in Chinese Industries: Some Political Dimensions of Economic Reform," *The China Quarterly*, 1987, no. 11, 31–61.
Chan, A., *China's Workers under Assault*, Armonk, NY: M.E. Sharpe, 2001.
——, "Labor Relations in Foreign-Funded Ventures, Chinese Trade Unions, and the Prospects for Collective Bargaining," in Greg O'leary (ed.), *Adjusting to Capitalism: Chinese Workers and the State*, Armonk, NY: M.E. Sharpe, 1998, pp. 122–49.
——, "Revolution or Corporatism? Workers and Trade Unions in Post-Mao China," *The Australia Journal of Chinese Affairs*, 1993, vol. 29, 31–61.
Chan, A. and Unger, J., "Voices from the Protest Movement in Chongqing: Class Accents and Class Tensions," in Jonathan Unger (ed.), *The Pro-Democracy Protests in China: Reports from the Provinces*, Armonk, NY: M.E. Sharpe, 1991, pp. 23–45.
Chen, A., *Restructuring Political Power in China*, Boulder, CO: Lynne Rienner Publisher, 1999.
Chen, F., "Industrial Restructuring and Workers' Resistance in China," *Modern China*, 2003, vol. 29, no. 2, 237–58.
——, "Between the State and Labor: The Conflict of the Chinese Trade Unions' Double Identity in Market Reform," *The China Quarterly*, 2003, no. 176, 1006–29.
——, "Subsistence Crises, Managerial Corruption and Labor Protests in China," *The China Journal*, 2000, vol. 44, 41–63.
Chen Dengcai and He Xiaoying (eds), *Qiyelingdao tizhi gaige yu dang de jianshe xinlun* (The Reform of the Leadership System in Enterprises and a New Explanation of Party Construction), Beijing: Zhonggong dangshi chubanshe, 1996.
Chen Lu and Yang Lianyun, "Xiagang zhigong zai jiuye nandian wenti de diaocha fenxi yu duice jianyi" (An Analysis of the Problems with the Reemployment of Laid-Off Workers and Countermeasures), *Qiushi* (Seeking the truth), 1999, no. 3, 19–22.

Chen Qingtai, Wu Jinglian, and Xie Fuzhan (eds), *Guoqi gaige gongjian 15 ti* (15 Critical Issues in the Reform of State-Owned Enterprises), Beijing: Zhongguo jingji chubanshe, 1999.

Chen Shaohui, *Guoyou qiye laodong jiuye tizhi yanjiu* (A Study of the Employment System of State Enterprises), Beijing: Zhongguo jingji chubanshe, 1998.

Chen Zuxin, "Chengzhen pinkun wenti ji duice" (The Poverty Issue in Urban Areas and Countermeasures), in Research Group of the Research Office of the State Council (ed.), *Chengzhen jumin shouru chaju yanjiu* (A Study of the Income Gap Among Urban Citizens), Beijing: Zhongguo yanshi chubanshe, 1997, pp. 76–86.

Cheng, Chuyuan, *Behind the Tiananmen Massacre: Social, Political, and Economic Ferment in China*, Boulder, CO: Westview Press, 1990.

Cheng, Siwei, *Zhongguo shehui baozhang tixi de gaige yu wanshan* (The Reform and Improvement of China's Social Security System), Beijing: Minzhu yu jianshe chubanshe, 2001.

Chong, D., *Collective Action and the Civil Rights Movement*, Chicago, IL: University of Chicago Press, 1991.

The City Investigation Team of the State Statistical Bureau, "Xiagang zhigong jiuye qingkuang diaocha" (An Investigation of the Reemployment of Laid-Off Workers), *Tongji ziliao* (Statistical Materials), 1998, no. 16, 10–12.

Clarke, S., Fairbrother, P., and Borisov, V., *The Workers' Movement in Russia*, Hants: Edward Elgar Publishing Limited, 1995.

Connor, W., *Tattered Banners: Labor, Conflict, and Corporatism in Postcommunist Russia*, Boulder, CO: Westview Press, 1996.

——, *The Accidental Proletariat*, Princeton, NJ: Princeton University Press, 1991.

Cook, L., "Workers in the Russian Federation: Responses to the Post-Communist Transition, 1983–1993," *Communism and Post-Communism Studies*, 1995, vol. 28, no. 1, 13–42.

——, "Conclusion: Workers in Post-communist Poland, Russia, and Ukraine," *Communism and Post-Communism Studies*, 1995, vol. 28, no. 1, 115–18.

——, *The Soviet Social Contract and Why it Failed: Welfare Policy and Workers' Politics from Brezhnev to Yeltsin*, Cambridge, MA: Harvard University Press, 1993.

Crowley, S., *Hot Coal, Cold Steel*, Ann Arbor, MI: The University of Michigan Press, 1997.

——, "Between Class and Nation: Worker Politics in the New Ukrain," *Communism and Post-Communism Studies*, 1995, vol. 28, no. 1, 43–69.

Cui Yingqi and Miao Guangji, "Xiagang renyuan: he qu he cong" (Laid-Off Workers: Where to Go), *Chengshi diaocha* (City Investigation), 1996, no. 6, 35–38.

Da Tong, "Dangqian zhigong de sige danxin" (Employees' Four Worries in the Current Period of Time), *Sixiang zhengzhi gongzuo yanjiu* (A Study of Political Work), 1999, no. 4, 17.

Dahrendorf, R., *Class and Class Conflict in Industrial Society*, Stanford, CA: Stanford University Press, 1959.

Davis, J., "Towards a Theory of Revolution," *American Sociological Review*, 1962, vol. 27, 5–19.

Davis, M., "Why the US Working Class is Different," *New Left Review*, 1980, vol. 123, 3–44.

Deyo, F. C., *Beneath the Miracle: Labor Subordination in the New Asian Industrialization*, Berkeley, CA: University of California Press, 1989.

Ding, X. L., "The Illicit Asset Stripping of Chinese State Firms," *The China Journal*, 2000, vol. 43, 1–28.

The Document Research Office of Chinese Communist Party Committee, *Shisi da yilai guoyou qiye gaige he fazhan dashi jiyao* (A Record of the Important Events in the

Reform of State-Owned Enterprises After the 14th Party Congress), Beijing: Zhongyang wenxian chuabanshe, 1999.

Dong Qingmin, "Renmin neibu tufaxin qunti maodun de tedian ji chuli yuanze" (The Characteristics of Collective Action and the Strategies of Response), *Lilunqianyan* (Theoretical Frontiers), 1999, no. 13, 7–9.

Drakeford, M., *Social Movements and Their Supporters*, Hampshire: Macmillan Press Ltd., 1997.

Ekiert, G., *The State Against Society: Political Crisis and Their Aftermath in East Central Europe*, Princeton, NY: Princeton University Press, 1996.

Ekiert, G. and Kubik, J., *Rebellious Civil Society: Popular Protest and Democratic Consolidation in Poland, 1989–1993*, Ann Arbor, MI: The University of Michigan Press, 1999.

——, "Contentious Politics in New Democracies: East Germany, Hungary, Poland, and Slovakia, 1989–1993," *World Politics*, 1998, vol. 50, 547–81.

Elster, J., *Making Sense of Marx*, New York: Cambridge University Press, 1985.

——, *Ulysses and the Sirens: Studies in Rationality and Irrationality*, New York: Cambridge University Press, 1979.

The Expert Group of China's Reform and Development, *Xianshi de xuanze* (Realistic Choices), Shanghai: Shanghai Yuandong chubanshe, 1997.

Fan Qin, "Xiagang shishui—woguo xiagang renyuan jiegou fenxi" (Who Were Laid Off?—an Analysis of the Composition of Laid-Off Workers in Our Country), *Zhongguo guoqing guoli* (The Situation and Strengths of China), 1998, no. 5, 20–22.

Feng Changyong, "Dengdai zuzhi anpai, buyuan canyu jingzheng" (Awaiting Government Reallocation and Unwilling to Compete), *Neican xuanbian* (Compilation of Selected Materials), 1998, no. 20, 15–16.

Feng Tongqing, "Workers and Trade Unions under the Market Economy: Perspectives From Grassroots Union Cadres," *Chinese Sociology and Anthropology*, 1996, no. 3 (Spring, the whole special issue).

——, "Zhongguo xinshiqi gongren jieji neibu liyi gejiu baogao" (Report on the Interest Differentiation Within the Chinese Working Class), in Li Peilin (ed.), *Zhongguo xinshiqi jieji jieceng baogao* (Social Stratification During the Market Transition in China: An Analysis of Ten Issues), Liaoning: Liaoning renmin chubanshe, 1995, pp. 133–88.

Feng Tongqing and Xu Xiaojun, *Zhongguo zhigong zhuangkuang* (The Situation of Chinese Employees), Beijing: Zhongguo shehui kexue chubanshe, 1994.

Filtzer, D., *Soviet Workers and the Collapse of Perestroika: The Soviet Labor Process and Gorbachev's Reforms, 1985–1991*, New York: Cambridge University Press, 1994.

Finkel, S. E. and Muller, E. N., "Rational Choice and the Dynamics of Collective Political Action: Evaluating Alternative Models with Panel Data," *American Political Science Review*, 1998, vol. 92, no. 1, 37–49.

Fish, M. S., *Democracy from Scratch*, Princeton, NJ: Princeton University Press, 1994.

Fowkes, B., *The Rise and Fall of Communism on Eastern Europe*, New York: St. Martin's Press, 1993.

Freund, E. M., "Downsizing China's State Industrial Enterprises: The Case of Baosha Steel Works," in O'leary, G. (ed.), *Adjusting to Capitalism: Chinese Workers and the State*, Armonk, NY: M.E. Sharpe, 1998, pp. 48–74.

Friedman, D. and McAdam, D., "Collective Identity and Activism: Networks, Choices, and the Life of a Social Movement," in Morris, A. and Mueller, C. M. (eds), *Frontiers in Social Movement Theory*, New Haven, CT: Yale University Press, 1992, pp. 156–73.

Frohlich, N., Oppenheimer, J. A., and Young, O. R., *Political Leadership and Collective Goods*, Princeton, NY: Princeton University Press, 1971.
Fu Gangzhan, *Zhongguo laodongli shichang fayu de jingji fenxi* (An Economic Analysis of China's Labor Market), Shanghai: Shanghai renmin chubanshe, 1992.
Fukui, K., *Japanese National Railways Privatization Study*, Washington, DC: The World Bank, 1992.
Gallagher, M., " 'Reform and Openness': Why China's Economic Reforms Have Delayed Democracy," *World Politics*, 2002, vol. 54, 338–72.
Gamson, W. A., "The Success of the Unruly," in McAdam, D. and Snow, D. (eds), *Social Movements*, Los Angeles, CA: Roxbury Publishing Company, 1997, pp. 357–64.
Gao Jianyan, Li Chunsheng, and Huang Bicheng, "Baijia changzhang, qineng jinchan tuoqiao" (Corrupt Manager, You Have No Chance to Evade Responsibility), *Fazhi yu xinwen* (Law and News), 1999, no. 4, 2–4.
The General Office of the All China Federation of Trade Unions (ed.), *Jianguo yilai zhonggong zhongyang guanyu gongren yundong wenjian xuanbian* (Selected Documents About Workers' Movements Issued by the Central Party Committee After the Founding of the PRC), Beijing: Gongren chubanshe, 1989.
Godson, J., "The Role of the Trade Union," in Schapiro, L. and Godson, J. (eds), *The Soviet Worker: Illusions and Realities*, London: The Macmillan Press, 1981, pp. 106–29.
Golden, M. A., *Heroic Defeats: The Politics of Job Loss*, New York: Cambridge University Press, 1997.
Goldstone, J. and Tilly, C., "Threat (and Opportunity): Popular Action and State Response in the Dynamics of Contentious Action," in Aminzade, R. R., Goldstone, J., McAdam, D., Perry, E., Sewell, W. H., Tarrow, S., and Tilley, C. (eds), *Silence and Voice in the Study of Contentious Politics*, New York: Cambridge University Press, 2001, pp. 179–94.
Green, J. R., *The World of the Worker: Labor in Twentieth-Century America*, New York: Hill and Wang, 1980.
Greif, A., "Cultural Belief and the Organization of Society: A Historical and Theoretical Reflection on Collectivist and Individualist Societies," *Journal of Political Economy*, 1994, vol. 102, 912–50.
Gu, X., "From Permanent Employment to Massive layoffs: The Political Economy of 'Transitional Unemployment' in Urban China (1993–1998)," *Economy and Society*, 1999, vol. 28, no. 2, 281–99.
Guo Qingsong, "Lun woguo chengzhen shiye renkou de shehui jingji houguo" (On the Social and Economic Consequences of the Unemployed Population in Our Country), *Shehuixue yanjiu* (Sociological Research), 1997, no. 2, 93–102.
Gurr, T., *Why Men Rebel*, Princeton, NY: Princeton University Press, 1970.
Gutman, H., *Work, Culture, and Society in Industrializing America: Essays in American Working-Class and Social History*, New York: Vintage Books, 1976.
Hai Xi, *Zhongguo jingji daliebian* (Great Changes in the Chinese Economy), Guangzhou: Guangdong jingji chubahshe, 1996.
Han Xu, "Gaige guoyou qiye lingdao ganbu gaunli zhidu" (Reforming the Management System of Enterprise Leaders), *Neibucanyue* (Internal References), 1999, no. 32, 8–15.
Hardin, R., *One for All: The Logic of Group Conflict*, Princeton, NY: Princeton University Press, 1995.
——, "Acting Together, Contributing Together," *Rationality and Society*, 1991, no. 3, 365–80.
——, *Collective Action*, Baltimore, MD: The Johns Hopkins University Press, 1982.
Hauslohner, P., "Gorbachev's Social Contract," *Soviet Economy*, 1987, vol. 3, no. 1, 54–89.

He Pin and Hu Manhong, "Ouxin lixue wei renmin" (Working Wholeheartedly for the People), *Minzhu yu fazhi* (Democracy and Law), 1999, no. 3, 18–20.

He Shijian, "Yige bei gongren ganzhou de changzhang" (A Manager Driven out by Workers), *Fazhi yu xinwen* (Law and News), 1998, no. 49, 48–51.

He Songyuan and Shang Zhihong, "Guanzhu pinkun zhigong qunti" (Paying Attention to the Group of Poverty-Stricken Employees), *Qiyegaige yu guanli* (Enterprise Reform and Management), 1998, no. 3, 34.

He Wei, "Siying qiyejia shibushi zibenjia" (Whether Private Entrepreneurs are Capitalists), *Gaige neican* (Internal Reference of Reform), 1998, no. 1, 32–34.

Hechter, M., *Principles of Group Solidarity*, Berkeley, CA: University of California Press, 1987.

Herbst, J., "How the Weak Succeed: Tactics, Political Goods, and Institutions in the Struggle over Land in Zimbabwe," in Colburn, F. D. (ed.), *Everyday Forms of Peasant Resistance*, Armonk, NY: M.E. Shape, 1989, 198–220.

Hershatter, G., *The Workers of Tianjin: 1900–1949*, Stanford, CA: Stanford University Press, 1986.

Hill, S. and Rothchild, D., "The Impact of Regime on the Diffusion of Political Conflict," in Midlarsky, M. (ed.), *The Internationalization of Communal Strife*, London: Routledge, 1992, 189–206.

Hirschman, A. O., *Exit, Voice, and Loyalty: Responses to Decline in Firms, Organizations, and States*, Cambridge, MA: Harvard University Press, 1970.

Hirszowicz, M., *Coercion and Control in Communist Society: The Visible Hand of Bureaucracy*, Sussex: Wheatsheaf Books Ltd., 1986.

Holmes, L., *Politics in the Communist World*, Oxford: Clarendon Press, 1986.

Honig, E., *Sisters and Strangers: Women in Shanghai Cotton Mills, 1919–1949*, Stanford, CA: Stanford University Press, 1986.

Hou, Xiaoqi, "Wei shenme, zenme ban?" (Why and How), *Banyuetan* (Biweekly Forum), 2000, no. 3, 22–25.

Hua Ercheng, *Zhongguo jingji de ruan zhuoluo* (The Soft Landing of the Chinese Economy), Beijing: Zhongguo caizheng jingji chubanshe, 1997.

Huang Chenxi and Wang Daben, "Shanghai shi guoyou qiye xiagang renyuan fenliu anzhi de xianzhuang, wenti yu duice" (The Current Situation and Problems of the Reallocation of Laid-Off Workers in State Enterprises in Shanghai and Countermeasures), *Shichang yu renkou fenxi* (Market and Demographic Analysis), 1999, no. 4, 22–25.

Huang Daosheng, "Ruheyufang yueji shangfang" (How to Prevent Appeals to Higher-Level Authorities), *Jiangsu jijian* (Jiangsu Discipline Inspection), 1999, no. 10, 17.

Hunan Statistical Bureau, "Guoqi zaijiuye fuwu zhongxin jianli yu yunzuo qingkuang" (The Establishment and Operation of the Reemployment Service Centers of State Enterprises), *Tongji ziliao* (Statistical Materials), 1999, no. 13, 13–19.

——, "Zenyang kandai xiagang yu zaijiuye" (How to Look at Layoffs and Reemployment), *Tongji ziliao* (Statistical Materials), 1998, no. 20, 16–22.

Hung, E. and Chiu, S., "The Lost Generaion: Life Course Dynamics and Xiagang in China," *Modern China*, 2003, vol. 29, no. 2, 204–36.

Huntington, S., *The Third Wave: Democratization in the Late Twentieth Century*, Norman: University of Oklahoma Press, 1991.

——, *Political Order in Changing Societies*, New Haven, CT: Yale University Press, 1968.

Hurst, W. and O'Brien, K., "China's Contentious Pensioners," *The China Quarterly*, 2002, vol. 170, 345–60.

The Industrial Research Office of the Chinese Academy of Social Sciences, *Zhongguo gongye fazhan baogao 1999* (China Industrial Development Report 1999), Beijing: Jingji guanli chubanshe, 1999.

The Investigation Group of Beijing Economic Commission, "Gongye xitong fuyu renyuan xiagang fenliu shishi zhaijiu ye de xiangzhuang yu jianji" (The Current Situation of Layoffs and the Reemployment of the Redundant Employees in the Industrial Sector and Some Suggestions), in the Research Office of Beijing Party Committee and Beijing Labor Bureau (eds), *Zaijiuye gongzuo de yanjiu yu shijian* (A Study of Reemployment and the Practice), Beijing: Jingji guanli chubanshe, 1998, pp. 21–42.

The Investigation System of Chinese Entrepreneurs, "Xianjieduan woguo qiyejia duiwu de xingwei tezheng diaocha fenxi" (An Investigation and Analysis of the Behaviorial Characteristics of the Entrepreneurs in Our Country in the Current Period), *Guanli shijie* (Management World), 1995, no. 3, 153–63.

Jenkins, J. C., "Resource Mobilization Theory and the Study of Social Movements," *Annual Review of Sociology*, 1983, vol. 9, 527–53.

Jenkins, J. C. and Perrow, C., "Insurgency of the Powerless: Farm Workers' Movements (1946–1972)," *American Sociological Review*, 1977, vol. 42, no. 2, 249–68.

Ji Zhengfeng, "Yufang he chuzhi qunti xing shijian de duice xuanze" (The Choice of the Modes of Reaction to Mass Action), *Lilun yu shijian* (Theory and Practice), 1999, no. 16, 30–31.

Jia Qinglin, "Dali shisi zaijiuye gongcheng, tuijin shoudu gaige yu fazhan" (Making All Efforts to Promote the Reemployment Work and Promote the Reform and Development of the Capital), in the Research Office of Beijing Party Committee and Beijing Labor Bureau (eds), *Zaijiuye gongzuo de yanjiu yu shijian* (A Study of Reemployment and the Practice), Beijing: Jingji guanli chubanshe, 1998, pp. 4–20.

Jiang Mingan, *Zhongguo xingzheng fazhi fazhan jincheng diaocha baogao* (Investigation Reports on the Progress of Rule of Law in China), Beijing: Zhongguo falu chubanshe, 1998.

Jin Pei, *Hequ hecong* (Where To Go), Beijing: Jinrizhongguo chubanshe, 1998.

Jin Shuyan, "Paichu qiye dangzheng guanxi zhong de leiqu" (Removing the Obstacles to the Development of Party-Management Relations in Enterprises), *Zhengzhi sixiang gongzuo yanjiu* (Research on the Work of Political Thought), 1999, no. 8, 29–30.

Jin Weixin, "Bufen qiye qinfan zhigong quanli shi quntixing shijian zengduo" (The Encroachment of Workers' Interests Led to More Collective action), *Zhengfa cankao* (References of Political and Legal Affairs), 2002, no. 10, 15–16.

Jin Yan and Tian Lei, "Daqing caiyuan de gaoang chengben" (The High Cost of Retrenchment in Daqing), *Sanlian shenghuo zhoukan* (Sanlian Weekly), 2002, no. 14, 12–17.

Jin Ye, *Jieceng de fubai* (Corruption of Social Groups), Zhuhai: Zhuhai chubanshe, 1998.

The Joint Investigation Group, "Guanyu diyi qiche zhizaochang zhigong zhuangkuang de diaocha baogao" (An Investigation of the Workers of the First Truck Manufacturing Factory), in The Chinese Communist Secretary Office and the All China Federation of Trade Unions (eds), *Dangqian woguo gongren jieji zhuangkuang diaocha ziliao huibian* (A Selection of the Investigation Materials About the Situation of the Working Class in Our Country), Beijing: Zhongyang dangxiao chubanshe, 1983, pp. 23–32.

The Joint Research Group, *Qiji shi ruhe chuangzao de* (How Was the Miracle Made?), Shanghai: Fudan daxue chubanshe, 1998.

Jones, E. E., "The Rock Road from Acts to Dispositions," *American Psychologist*, 1979, vol. 34, 107–17.

Kahneman, D. and Tversky, A., "Prospect Theory: An Analysis of Decision under Risk," *Economica*, 1979, vol. 47, 263–91.
Kiernan, A., "State Enterprises in Shenyang: Actors and Victims in the Transition," *China Perspectives*, 1997, vol. 14, 26–32.
Kim, H. and Berman, P. S., "The Structure and Dynamics of Movement Participation," *American Sociological Review*, 1997, vol. 62, 70–93.
Kitschelt, H., "Resource Mobilization Theory: A Critique," in Rucht, D. (ed.), *Research on Social Movements*, Boulder, CO: Westview Press, 1991, pp. 323–47.
Klan, A. R. and Riskin, C., "Income and Inequality in China: Composition, Distribution and Growth of Household Income, 1988–1995," *The China Quarterly*, 1998, no. 154, 221–53.
Klandermans, B., "Mobilization and Participation: Social–Psychological Expansions of Resource Mobilization Theory," *American Sociological Review*, 1984, vol. 49, 583–600.
Kolakowski, L., "Admist Moving Ruins," *Daedalus*, 1992, vol. 121, no. 2, 43–76.
Kong Zhangsheng, "Yanghang kua shengshi fenhang de qianqian houhou" (The Process of the Establishment of Cross-Provinces Branches by the Central Bank), *Dadi* (The Land), 1999, no. 2, 19–21.
Koo, H., "Work, Culture, and Consciousness of the Korean Working Class," in Perry, E. (ed.), *Putting Class in its Place*, Berkeley, CA: University of California Press, 1996, pp. 53–76.
Kopstein, J., "Chipping Away at the State: Workers' Resistance and the Demise of East Germany," *World Politics*, 1996, vol. 48, 391–423.
Kramer, M., "Introduction: Blue-Collar Workers and the Post-Communist Transition in Poland, Russia, and Ukraine," *Communist and Post-Communist Studies*, 1995, vol. 28, no. 1, 3–12.
——, "Polish Workers and the Post-Communist Transition, 1989–1993," *Communist and Post-communist Study*, 1995, vol. 28, no. 1, 71–114.
Kuran, T., "Now out of Never: The Element of Surprise in the East Europe Revolution of 1989," *World Politics*, 1991, vol. 44, no. 1, 7–48.
Kurzman, C., "Structural Opportunities and Perceived Opportunity in Social-Movement Theory: The Iranian Revolution of 1979," in McAdam, D. and Snow, D. (eds), *Social Movements*, Los Angeles, CA: Roxbury Publishing Company, 1996, pp. 66–79.
Laba, R., *The Roots of Solidarity: A Political Sociology of Poland's Working-Class Democratization*, Princeton, NJ: Princeton University Press, 1991.
Lardy, N. R., *China's Unfinished Economic Revolution*, Washington, DC: Brookings Institute Press, 1998.
Lee, C. K., "From the Specter of Mao to the Spirit of the Law: Labor Insurgency in China," *Theory and Society*, 2002, vol. 31, no. 2, 189–228.
——, "Pathways of Labor Insurgency," in Perry, E. and Selden, M. (eds), *Chinese Society: Change, Conflict and Resistance*, London: Routledge, 2000, 41–60.
——, "The 'Revenge of History': Collective Memories and Labor Protests in Northeastern China," *Ethnography*, 2000, vol. 1, no. 2, 217–37.
——, "From Organized Dependence to Disorganized Despotism: Changing Labor Regimes in Chinese Factories," *The China Quarterly*, 1999, vol. 152, 44–71.
——, "The Labor Politics of Market Socialism: Collective Inaction and Class Experiences Among State Workers in Guangzhou," *Modern China*, 1998, vol. 24, no. 1, 3–31.
Lee, H. Y., "*Xiagang*, the Chinese Style of Laying off Workers," *Asian Survey*, 2000, vol. 40, no. 6, 914–37.
Lee, L. T., *The Structure of the Trade Union System in China, 1949–1996*, Hong Kong: University of Hong Kong, 1984.

Leung, T., "Labor Fights For Its Rights," *China Perspectives*, 1998, vol. 19, 6–21.
Li Congguo, "Cong guoqi sannian tuokun kan quoqi gaige" (Examining the Reform of State Enterprises in Light of the Plan of Solving the Loss-Making Issue Within Three Years), *Liaowang* (Perspective), 2000, no. 8, 2–5.
Li Dahong, "Shehui wending: lishun qingxu huajie maodun" (Social stability: To Resolve the Contradictions), *Liaowang* (Perspectives), 1999, no. 10, 52–53.
Li Hongjun, "Guoqi gaige zhong 'xinfang' xianxiang de sikao" (Thoughts on the Petitions in the Reform of State Enterprises), *Lilun yu shijian* (Theory and Practice), 1999, no. 2, 32–3.
Li Lieman, "Guoyou qiye lingdao tizhi yu qiye dangjian wenti" (The Leadership System of State Enterprises and Party construction), *Zhonggong fujian shengwei dangxiao xuebao* (The Journal of Fujian Party School), 2000, no. 5, 55–60.
——, "Jianguo yilai guoqi lingdao tizhi yange yu dang de jianshe de huigu yu sikao" (The Change of the Leadership System of State Enterprises and Some Thoughts on Party Construction), *Dangshi yanjiu yu jiaoxue* (Study and Teaching of the Party History), 1988, no. 5, 39–45.
Li Maoguan and Tian Baichun, "Bian qunzhong 'shangfang' wei ganbu 'xiafang' " (From People's Appeals to Cadres' Visits to People), *Qiushi* (Seeking the Truth), 1999, no. 14, 43–5.
Li Peilin, "Lao gongye jidi de shiye zhili: hou gongyehua he shichanghua" (Dealing with Unemployment in the Old Industrial Bases: Post-Industrialization and Marketization). *Shehuixue yanjiu* (Sociological Research), 1998, no. 4, 1–12.
Li Tongwen, *Zhongguo minsheng baogao* (A Report on the Life of Chinese People), Beijing: Jingcheng chubanshe, 1998.
Li Zhenghua and Wang Qi, "Shanghai qiye maodun duoshu mei zouru falu qudao" (Most Disputes in the Enterprises in Shanghai Were Not Solved Through the Legal System), *Neican xunabian* (Selected Materials), 1999, no. 7, 22.
Li Zuoming, "Cong xiagang nugong dao zhongguo guaqi di yi ren" (From a Laid-Off Woman Worker to the First Person Who Paints With a Knife in China), *Fazhi yu jingji* (Law and Economy), 1999, no. 6, 33–34.
Liao Mingtao and Hua Shanqing, "Jiti laodong zhengyi he tufa shijian de zhuyao tedian he chuli yanjiu" (A Study of the Main Characteristics and Settlement of Collective Labor Disputes and Mass Action), *Shanghai gongyun* (Workers' Movements in Shanghai), 1998, no. 3, 12–14.
Lichbach, M., *The Rebel's Dilemma*, Ann Arbor, MI: The University of Michigan Press, 1995.
——, "Rethinking Rationality and Rebellion," *Rationality and Society*, 1994, vol. 6, no. 1, 8–39.
Ling Yubing, "Banzhang, li bugai liu yishou" (Group Leader, You Should Not Keep Your Skill a Secret), *Zhongguo gongren* (Chinese Workers), 1996, no. 11, 63.
Linz, J. and Stepan, A., *Problems of Democratic Transition and Consolidation: Southern Europe, South America, and Post-Communist Europe*, Baltimore, MD: Johns Hopkins University Press, 1996.
Liu, A., *Mass Politics in the People's Republic: State and Society in Contemporary China*, Boulder, CO: Westview Press, 1996.
Liu Jiesan and Wang Xueli, "Zhigong gongzi wai shouru yu guanli" (Employees' Extra Income and Management), in the Research Group of the State Council (ed.), *Chengzhen jumin shouru chaju yanjiu* (A Study of the Income Gap Among Urban Citizens), Beijing: Zhongguo yanshi chubanshe, 1997, pp. 21–34.
Liu Yong, *Disanci shiye gaofeng: xiangang, shiye, zaijiuye* (The Third Peak of Unemployment: Layoffs, Unemployment, and Reemployment), Beijing: Zhongguo shuji chubanshe, 1998.

Liu Zhiqiang, "Jiaqiang he gaishan dang dui qiye de zhengzhi lingdao" (Strengthening the Party's Leadership in Enterprises), *Lilun dongtai* (The New Development of Theories), 1997, no. 13, 13–15.

Lohmann, S., "The Dynamics of Information Cascades: The Monday Demonstration in Leipzeig East Germany, 1989–1991," *World Politics*, 1994, vol. 47, 42–101.

Lu Aihong, *Xiagang, zenme ban, zenme kan* (Retrenchment: How to Look At It and Handle It), Beijing: Jingji kexue chubanshe, 1998.

Lu Xin, Lu Xueyi, and Shan Tianlun (eds), *2000 nian: zhongguo shehui fenxi yu yuce* (2000: An Analysis and Prediction of Chinese Society), Beijing: Shehui kexue wenxian chubanshe, 2000.

——, *1999 nian zhongguo shehui xingshi fenxi yu yuce* (1999: An Analysis and Prediction of Chinese Society), Beijing: Shehui kexue wenxian chubanshe, 1999.

Ludlam, J., "Reform and the Redefinition of the Social Contract under Gorbachev," *World Politics*, 1991, vol. 43, no. 2, 284–312.

Luehrmann, L. M., "Facing Citizen Complaints in China, 1951–1996," *Asian Survey*, 2003, vol. 43, no. 5, 845–66.

Ma Cheng, *Xiagang zhihou* (After Retrenchment), Beijing: Minzhu yu jianshe chubanshe, 1988.

McAdam, D., *Political Process and the Development of Black Insurgency 1930–1970*, Chicago, IL: The University of Chicago Press, 1999.

——, "Conceptual Origins, Current Problems, Future Directions," in McAdam, D., McCarthy, J., and Zald, M. (eds), *Comparative Perspectives on Social Movements*, New York: Cambridge University Press, 1996, pp. 23–40.

——, "Tactical Innovation and the Pace of Insurgency," *American Sociological Review*, 1983, vol. 48, 735–54.

McAdam, D., Perry, E., Sewell, W. H., Tarrow, S., and Tilley, C. (eds), *Silence and Voice in the Study of Contentious Politics*, New York: Cambridge University Press, 2001. pp. 179–94.

McCarthy, J. and Zald, M., "Resource Mobilization and Social Movements: A Partial Theory," *American Journal of Sociology*, 1977, vol. 82, no. 6, 1212–41.

McFaul, M., "State Power, Institutional Change, and the Politics of Privatization in Russia," *World Politics*, 1995, vol. 47, 210–43.

McGraw, K. M., "Managing Blame: An Experimental Test of the Effects of Political Accounts," *American Political Science Review*, 1991, vol. 85, no. 4, 1133–57.

Manion, M., "Reluctant Duelists: The Logic of the 1989 Protest and Massacre," in Oksenberg, M., Sullian, L. and Lambert, M. (eds), *Beijing Spring, 1989: Confrontation and Conflict: The Basic Documents*, Armonk, NY: M.E. Sharpe, 1990, pp. xiii–xliii.

Markovits, I., "Law and Glasnost: Some Thoughts about the Future of Judicial Review under Socialism," *Law & Society Review*, 1989, vol. 23, no. 3, 399–447.

The Ministry of Organization of the CCP Central Committee, *2000–2001, Zhongguo Diaochao baogao* (2000–2001 China Investigation Report), Bejing: Zhongyang bianye chubanshe, 2001.

Montgomery, D., "To Study the People: The American Working Class," *Labor History*, 1980, no. 21, 485–512.

Moore, B., *Injustice: The Social Bases of Obedience and Revolt*, White Plains, NY: M.E. Sharpe, 1978.

Mueller, E., "The Psychology of Political Protest and Violence," in Gurr, T. (ed.), *Handbook of Political Conflict*, New York: Free Press, 1980, pp. 69–99.

Mueller, E. N. and Jukam, T., "Discontent and Aggressive Political Participation," *British Journal of Political Science*, 1983, vol. 13, 159–79.
Muller, E. N., Dietz, H., and Finkel, S., "Discontent and the Expected Utility of Rebellion: A Case of Peru," *American Political Science Review*, 1991, vol. 85, no. 4, 1261–82.
The National Complaints Bureau, *Zhongguo xinfang xiezhen* (A Record of People's Letters and Visits in China), Beijing: Gongren chubanshe, 1998.
Nelson, D., "Worker-Party Conflict in Romania," in White, S. and Nelson, D. (eds), *Communist Politics: A Reader*, Hampshire: Macmillan Education, 1986, pp. 280–91.
The News Center of Nanjing TV Station, *Shehui da guangjiao* (Societal Panorama), Nanjing: Nanjing daxue chubanshe, 1999.
North, D., "Economic Performance through Time," *The American Economic Review* 1994, vol. 84, 359–68.
Oberschall, A., "Opportunities and Framing in the Eastern Europe Revolts of 1989," in McAdam, D., McCarthy, J., and Zald, M. (eds), *Comparative Perspectives on Social Movements*, New York: Cambridge University Press, 1996, pp. 172–99.
——, *Social Conflict and Social Movements*, Englewood Cliffs, NJ: Prentice-Hall, 1973.
O'Brien, K., "Neither Transgressive nor Contained: Boundary-Spanning Contention in China," *Mobilization: An International Jounal*, 2003, vol. 8, no. 1, 51–64.
——, "Rightful Resistance," *World Politics*, 1996, vol. 49, no. 1, 31–55.
Oegema, D. and Klandermans, B., "Why Social Movement Sympathizers Don't Participate: Erosion and Nonconversion of Support," in McAdam, D. and Snow, D. (eds), *Social Movements*, Los Angeles, CA: Rozbury Publishing Company, 1997, pp. 174–89.
Oestreigher, R. J., *Solidarity and Fragmentation: Working People and Class Consciousness in Detroit 1875–1900*, Urbana, IL: University of Illinois Press, 1986.
Oi, J., "Realms of Freedom in Post-Mao China," in Kirby, W. (ed.), *Realms of Freedom in Modern China*, Stanford, CA: Stanford University Press, 2003, pp. 264–84.
——, *State and Peasant in Contemporary China: The Political Economy of Village Government*, Berkeley, CA: University of California Press, 1989.
Oksenberg, M., "Occupations and Groups in Chinese Society and the Cultural Revolution," *The Cultural Revolution: 1967 in Review*, Ann Arbor, MI: University of Michigan Center for Chinese Studies, 1968, pp. 1–39.
Oksenberg, M., Sullivan, L., and Lambert, M. (eds), *Beijing Spring, 1989: Confrontation and Conflict: The Basic Documents*, Armonk, NY: M.E. Sharpe, 1990.
Olson, M., *The Logic of Collective Action*, New York: Schocken, 1965.
Ostrom, E., "A Behavioral Approach to Rational Choice Theory of Collective Action," *American Political Science Review*, 1998, vol. 92, no. 1, 1–22.
Pei, M. X., "Citizens Versus Mandarins: Administrative Litigation in China," *The China Quarterly*, 1997, no. 152, 832–62.
Perry, E., "Challenging the Mandate of Heaven: Popular Protest in Modern China," *Critical Asian Studies*, 2001, vol. 33, no. 2, 163–200.
——, "Shanghai's Strike Wave of 1957," *The China Quarterly*, 1994, vol. 137, 1–27.
——, *Shanghai On Strike*, Berkeley, CA: University of California Press, 1993.
Perry, E. and Li, X., *Proletarian Power: Shanghai in the Cultural Revolution*, Boulder, CO: Westview Press, 1997.
Perry, E. and Selden, M., "Introduction: Reform and Resistance in Contemporary China," in Perry, E. and Selden, M. (eds), *Chinese Society: Change, Conflict and Resistance*, London: Routledge, 2000, 1–19.

Pierson, P., *Dismantling the Welfare State*, New York: Cambridge University Press, 1994.
Piven, F. and Cloward, R., *Poor People's Movements: Why They Succeed, How They Fail*, New York: Vintage Books, 1979.
Popkin, S., "Public Choices and Peasant Organization," in Russell, C. and Nickolson, N. (eds), *Public Choice and Rural Development*, Washington, DC: Resources for the Future, 1987, pp. 236–57.
Porta, D. and Reiter, H., "The Policing of Protest in Western Democracies," in Porta, D. and Reiter, H. (eds), *Policing Protest: The Control of Mass Demonstration in Western Democracies*, Minneapolis, MN: University of Minnesota Press, 1998, pp. 1–34.
Posusney, M. P., "Irrational Workers: The Moral Economy of Labor Protest in Egypt," *World Politics*, 1993, vol. 46, no. 1, 83–120.
Qiu Lu, "Guoqi gaige weihe ruci jiannan" (Why It Is So Difficult to Reform State Enterprises), *Bainian chao* (Century Stream), 1999, no. 2, 4–14.
Rawls, J., *A Theory of Justice*, Oxford: Oxford University Press, 1973.
Ren Yanfang, *Minyuan* (People's Complaints), Bejing: Zhongguo wenlian chubanshe, 1999.
The Research Group, "Chengzhen qiye xiagang zhigong zaijiuye zhuangkuang diocha: Kunjing yu chulu" (An Investigation of Laid-Off Workers' Reemployment: Plight and Solutions), *Shehuixue yanjiu* (Sociological Research), 1997, no. 6, 24–34.
The Research Group of Laid-off Workers and Their Employment, "Xiagang zhigong de shenghuo zhuangkuang jiqi shehui zhichi" (The Living Condition of Laid-Off Workers and Their Social Support), *Xiaofei jingji* (Economy of Consumption), 1997, no. 1, 48–51.
The Research Group of the Bureaucratic Reform, "Jigou gaige yu renyuan fenliu: shi buwei diaocha baogao" (Organizational Reform and the Reallocation of Employees: An Investigation of Ten Ministries), *Jingji gongzuozhe xuexi ziliao* (Study Materials for Economic Workers), 1999, no. 15, 2–9.
The Research Group of the Ministry of Organization, *2000–2001 Zhongguo diaocha baogao: xinxingshi xia renmin neibu maodu yanjiu* (2000–2001 China Investigation Report: a Study of People's Internal Contradictions in the New Era), Beijing: Zhongyang bianyi chubanshe, 2001.
The Research Group of the Organization Department of Ningxia Party Committee, "Xiandai qiye zhidu jianli zhong fahui qiye dang zuzhi zhengzhi hexin zuoyong de fangfa yu duice sikao" (On the Core Function of the Party Organization in Enterprises in the Process of Building Modern Firms), *Ningxia shehui kexue* (Ningxia Social Sciences), 1997, no. 5, 20–25.
The Research Group of the Party School of Hangzhou, "Guoqi jingyingzhe de xinli dangan" (Psychological Profiles of the Managers of State Enterprises), *Guancha yu sikao* (Observation and Thinking), 1999, no. 5, 10–14.
The Research Group of the Public Security, *Zhongguo tese zhi gongan yanjiu* (A Study of Public Security with Chinese Characteristics), Beijing: Qunzhong chubanshe, 1996.
The Research Group of the State Planning Commission, "Shiji zhijiao de zhongguo shehui xingshi" (China's Social Situation at the Turn of the Century), *Jingji gongzuozhe xuexi ziliao* (Study Materials for Economic Workers), 2000, no. 2, 2–11.
Ruan Ying, "Wuhanshi zaijiuye gongcheng baogao weihe yidu bei foujue" (Why the Report on the Reemployment Work of Wuhan was Not Approved), *Minzhu yu fazhi* (Democracy and Law), 1997, no. 12, 16–17.
Sable, C. F., *Work and Politics: The Division of Labor in Industry*, Cambridge, MA: Cambridge University Press, 1982.
Saich, T., "The Rise and Fall of the Beijing People's Movement," in Jonathan Unger (ed.), *The Pro-Democracy Protests in China*. Armonk, NY: M.E. Sharpe, 1991, 8–34.

Schechter, D., *Falun Gong' Challenge to China*, New York: Akaschic Books, 2001.
Schumpeter, J., *Capitalism, Socialism and Democracy*, New York: Harper, 1950.
Scott, J., *Domination and the Arts of Resistance*, New Haven, CT: Yale University Press, 1990.
——, *The Weapons of the Weak: Everyday Forms of Peasants Resistance*, New Haven, CT: Yale University Press, 1985.
——, *The Moral Economy of the Peasant: Rebellions and Subsistence in Southeast Asia*, New Haven, CT: Yale University Press, 1976.
The Shanghai City Investigation Group, "Xiagang zai jiuye renyuan zhong cunzai yinxing jiuye" (There Were Hidden Employment Among Laid-Off Employees), *Tongji yanjiu* (Statistical Research), 1999, no. 6, 20–23.
Shi, T. J., *Political Participation in Beijing*, Cambridge, MA: Harvard University Press, 1997.
Shuai Bin, "Xiagang zhigong zai da menwai paihuai" (Laid-off Workers Lingered Outside the Door), *Zhongguo gongren* (Chinese Workers), 1999, no. 8, 12–13.
Skocpol, T., *States and Social Revolutions*, Cambridge, UK: Cambridge University Press, 1979.
Solinger, D., "Labor Market Reform and the Plight of the Laid-off Proletariat," *The China Quarterly*, 2002, no. 170, 304–26.
——, "Why We Cannot Count the 'Unemployed'," *The China Quarterly*, 2001, no. 167, 671–88.
——, "The Potential for Urban Unrest: Will the Fencers Stay on the Piste?," in David Shambaugh (ed.), *Is China Unstable?* Armonk, NY, New York: M.E. Sharpe, 2000, pp. 79–94.
——, *Contesting Citizenship in Urban China: Peasant Migrants, the State, and the Logic of the Market*, Berkeley, CA: University of California Press, 1999.
——, "The Chinese Work Unit and Transient Labor in the Transition from Socialism," *Modern China*, 1995, vol. 21, no. 2, 155–83.
Sombart, W., *Why is there no Socialism in the United States?* London: Macmillan Press, 1976.
Song Xiawu, Zhang Zhongjun, and Zhen Dingquan, *Zhongguo shehui baozhang zhidu jianshe 20 nian* (The 20 Years of the Construction of Social Security in China), Zhengzhou: Zhongzhou guji chubanshe, 1999.
The State Economic and Trade Commission and the Document Research Office of the Central Party Committee, *Shisida yilai dang he guoia lingdaoren lun guoyou qiye gaige he fazhan* (Talks by Central Leaders on the Reform of State-Owned Enterprises After the 14th Party Congress), Beijing: Zhongyang wenxian chubanshe, 2000.
The State Education Commission, *Jingxin dongpo de wushiliu tian* (The Soul-Stirring 56 Days), Beijing: Dadi chubanshe, 1989.
The State Planning Commission, "Shijizhijiao de zhongguo shehui xingshi" (The Social Situation in China at the Turn of the Century), *Jingji gongzuozhe xuexi ziliao* (Studying Materials for Economic Workers), 2000, no. 23, 2–11.
The State Statistical Bureau, *Xin zhongguo tongji ziliao huibian* (A Collection of China's Statistics), Beijing: Zhongguo tongjin chubanshe, 1999.
—— *1998 Zhongguo fazhan baogao* (1998 China Development Report), Beijing: Zhongguo tongji chubanshe, 1998.
——, *Da toushi* (A Comprehensive Perspective), Beijing: Zhongguo fazhan chubanshe, 1998.
Steinfield, E. S., *Forging Reform in China: The Fate of State-Owned Industry*, New York: Cambridge University Press, 1998.

Sun Yong, "Shuilai baowei yinhang" (Who Can Protect the Banks?), *Zhongguo qiye jia* (Chinese Entrepreneurs), 1997, no. 4, 33–36.

Tan Biyuan, Ke Shanfan, and Li Hongshan, "Zhigong guanzhu de ridian, nandian wenti jiqi duice" (The Problems that Workers are Concerned With and Solutions), *Neibu wengao* (Internal Manuscripts), 1998, no. 14, 16–19.

Tang, W. F. and Parish, W., *Chinese Urban Life under Reform: The Changing Social Contract*, New York: Cambridge University Press, 2000.

Tang Yunqi (ed.), *Zhuangui zhong de zhenhan* (Shocks in the Transformation), Beijing: Zhongguo laodong chubanshe, 1998.

Tarrow, S., "States and Opportunities: The Political Structuring of Social Movements," in McAdam, D., McCarthy, J., and Zald, M. (eds), *Comparative Perspectives on Social Movements*, New York: Cambridge University Press, 1996, pp. 41–61.

——, *Power in Movement: Social Movements, Collective Action and Politics*, New York: Cambridge University Press, 1994.

Taylor, M., "Rationality and Revolutionary Collective Action," in Michael Taylor (ed.), *Rationality and Revoltuion*, New York: Cambridge University Press, 1988, pp. 63–97.

——, *The Possibility of Cooperation*, New York: Cambridge University Press, 1987.

Thompson, E. E., "The Moral Economy of the English Crowd in the Eighteenth Century," *Past and Present*, 1971, vol. 50, 76–136.

Tian Zehong, "Guanyu dui pochan qiye zhaokai zhidaihui wenti de sikao" (Some Thoughts on the Convening of the Workers' Council in Bankrupt Enterprises), *Beijing gongren* (Beijing Workers), 1999, no. 1, 3–4.

Tilly, C., *From Mobilization to Revolution*, New York: Random House, 1978.

The Trade Union of Zibo City, "Yingxiang zhigong duiwu wending de yinsu" (Factors Affecting Employees' Stability), *Zhongguo gongren* (Chinese Workers), 1999, 6, 13–14.

Turner, L., *Democracy at Work: Changing World Markets and the Future of Labor Unions*, Ithaca, NY: Cornell University Press, 2001.

Tversky, A. and Kahneman, D., "The Framing of Decisions and the Psychology of Choice," *Science*, 1981, vol. 211, 453–58.

Unger, J., *The Pro-democracy Protests in China: Reports from the Provinces*, Armonk, NY: M.E. Sharpe, 1991.

Walder, A., "Collective Behavior Revisited: Ideology and Politics in the Chinese Cultural Revolution," *Rationality and Society*, 1994, no. 3, 400–21.

——, "Urban Industrial Workers: Some Observations on the 1980s," in Rosenbaum, A. (ed.), *State and Society in China: The Consequences of Reform*, Boulder, CO: Westview Press, 1992, pp. 103–20.

——, *Popular Protest in the 1989 Democracy Movement: The Pattern of Grassroots Organization*, Hong Kong: Hong Kong Institute of Asia Pacific Studies, 1992.

——, "Workers and the State: The Reform Era and the Political Crisis of 1989," *The China Quarterly*, 1991, no. 127, 467–92.

——, *Communist Neo-Traditionalism*, Berkeley, CA: University of California Press, 1986.

Walder, A. and Gong, X. X., "Workers in the Tiananmen Protests: The Politics of Beijing Workers' Autonomous Federation," *The Australian Journal of Chinese Affairs*, 1993, vol. 29, 1–29.

Wang, S. G., "Deng Xiaoping's Reform and The Chinese Workers' Participation in the Protest Movement of 1989," *Research in Political Economy*, 1992, no. 13, 163–97.

Wang Chunguang, "1997–1998: Zhongguo shehui wending de diaocha" (1997–1998: An Investigation of China's Social Stability), in Lu Xin, Lu Xueyi, and Shan Tianlun (eds),

Zhongguo shehui xingshi fenxi yu yuce (1998: An Analysis and Prediction of the China's Social Situation), Beijing: Shehui kexue wenxian chubanshe, 1998, pp. 121–47.

Wang Daben, "Shanghai shi qiye xiagang renyuen jiqi fenliu" (Laid-off Workers and Their Reallocation in Shanghai), *Yazhou yanjiu* (Asian Study), 1997, no. 15, 70–88.

Wang Daming, "Zhengque chuli qunti shijian, quebao wending daju" (Correctly Handling Mass Action and Ensuring Stability), *Qiushi* (Seeking the Truth), 2001, no. 4, 1–3.

Wang Haibo and Dong Zhikai, *Xin zhongguo gongye jingji shi (1958–1965)* (The Industrial History of China 1958–1965), Beijing: Jingji guanli chubanshe, 1995.

Wang Hansheng and Chen Zhixia, "Zaijiuye zhengce yu xiagang zhigong zaijiuye xingwei" (The Reemployment Policies and the Job-Search Behavior of Laid-Off Workers), *Shehuixue yanjiu* (Sociological Research), 1998, no. 4, 13–30.

Wang Jixuan, *Zhengque chuli woguo zhuanxing qi de renmin neibu maodun* (To Correctly Handle People's Internal Contradictions in the Transitional Period), Beijing: Jingji kexue chubanshe, 1997.

Wang Meng, "Chengshi jumin ruhe kan 'yigai'" (How Urban Citizens Think About the Reform of Medical Care), *Gaige yu kaifang* (Reform and Openness), 1999, no. 8, 13–14.

Wang Shuguang, "Zhigong xiagang yu shehui zhian wenti yanjiu" (A Study of Layoffs and Public Security), *Qiusuo* (Exploration), 1999, no. 1, 62–64.

Wang Yutan, *Weiren* (As a Human Being), Beijng: Xiyuan chubanshe, 2000.

Wang Zhifang, "Shiye qunti: buke hushi de shehui anding wenti" (The Unemployed: an Issue of Social Stability that Cannot be Ignored), *Shichang yu renkou fenxi* (Market and Demographic Analysis), 1998, no. 2, 4–7.

Weaver, R. K., "The Politics of Blame Avoidance," *Journal of Public Policies*, 1986, vol. 6, 371–98.

Weller, R. P. and Li, J. S., "From State-Owned Enterprise to Joint Venture: A Case Study of the Crisis in Urban Social Services," *The China Journal*, 2000, vol. 43, 83–100.

Wetson, T., " 'Learning from Daqing': More Dark Clouds for Workers in State-Owned Enterprises," *Journal of Contemporary China*, 2002, vol. 11, no. 33, 721–34.

Wright, T., *The Perils of Protest: State Repression and Student Activism in China and Taiwan*, Honolulu: University of Hawaii Press, 2001.

Wu Bangguo, "Qieshi zuohao guoyou qiye xiagang zhigong jiben shenghuo baozhang he zaijiuye gongzuo" (To Do a Good Job of Providing Minimum Allowance for Laid-Off Workers and Helping Them Secure Reemployment), *Qiushi* (Seeking the Truth), 1998, no. 13, 2–7.

Wu Chenguang, "Fangbao jingcha: saohei jianbing" (Riot Police: The Vanguard of Crushing Crime), *Zhongguo xinwen zhoukan* (Chinese Newsweek), 2001, no. 7, 3–6.

Wu Ji, "Bainian laochang pochan de beihou" (Behind the Bankruptcy of a Factory with a 100-Year History), *Jizhe guancha* (Observations of Correspondents), 1999, no. 1, 14–16.

Wu Junping and Xu Ying, *Woshishui* (Who Am I?), Huhehaote: Neimenggu renmin chubanshe, 1997.

Xiang Huaicheng, *1999, Zhongguo caizheng baogao* (1999, China's Fiscal Report), Bejing: Zhongguo caizheng chubanshe, 1999.

Xie Delu, "Chongqing zhenzhi zhongchang pochan xiaoying fenxi" (An Analysis of the Repercussions of the Bankruptcy of the Chongqing Knitting Factory), *Zhongguo gongye jingji yanjiu* (A Study of Chinese Industrial Economy), 1994, no. 11, 37–41.

——, *Zhongguo zuida pochanan toushi* (A Comprehensive Perspective on China's Biggest Bankruptcy Case), Beijing: Jingji guanli chubanshe, 1993.

Xu Jianchuan, Zhou Dingchun, and Zhao Xuwei (eds), *Xiagang zhigong jiben shenghuo baozhang yu zaijiuye gongzuo shouce* (A Handbook on the Basic Allowance for Laid-Off Workers and Reemployment), Beijing: Zhongguo jiancai chubanshe, 1998.

Xu Tieyuan, Jiang Hui, and Zhang Xinmin, "Shanghai bufen qiye tufa shijian de diaocha fenxi" (An Analysis of Mass Action in Some Enterprises in Shanghai), *Tansuo yu zhengming* (Exploration and Debate), 1995, no. 4, 28–31.

Xue Qina and Xu Wei, "Qiantan qiye pochan yu zhengfu ganyu" (A Preliminary Analysis of Bankruptcy and Government Intervention), *Jingji yu guanli yanjiu* (Research on Economy and Management), 1995, no. 2, 39–40.

Yang Xuqing, Wu Yue, and Chang Ping, *Shui ye bao buzhu tiefanwan* (Nobody Can Keep His Iron Rice Bowl), Chengdu: Sichuan daxue chubanshe, 1993.

Yang Yiyong, "Zhongguo yanglao baoxian jijin de shoujiao yu touzi" (Collection and Investment of the Retirement Insurance Fund in China), in Xu Dianqing, Yi Zunsheng, and Zheng Yuyun (eds), *Zhongguo shehui baozhang tizhi gaige* (Social Security Reform in China), Beijing: Jingji kexue chubanshe, 1999, pp. 388–97.

Yang Yiyong and Xin Xiaobai, "Xiagang zhigong jiben shenghuo baozhang he zaijiuye de diaocha" (An Investigation of Laid-Off Workers' Basic Allowance and Reemployment), in Lu Xin (ed.), *1999 nian zhongguo shehui xingshi fenxi yu yuce* (An Analysis and Prediction of China's Social Situation in 1999), Beijing: Shehui kexue wenxian chubanshe, 1999, pp. 243–55.

Yang Zhanhui, "Guoqi 'liangji fenhua' buke hushi" (The Polarization of State Enterprises Should Not Be Ignored), *Zhongguo guoqing guo li* (The Situation and Strengths of China), 1999, no. 5, 9–11.

Ye Nanke, "Nanjing shimin dui zhiye shengwang de pingjia" (Citizens' Evaluation of the Social Respect for Occupations in Nanjing), *Shehui* (Society), 1997, no. 1, 8.

Ye Xingping and Yi Songguo, "Shenzhen shi 100 zhong zhiye de shehui shengwang" (The Social Respect for the 100 Occupations in Shenzhen), *Shehui* (Society), 1998, no. 11, 24–25.

You, J., *China's Enterprise Reform: Changing State/Society Relations after Mao*, London: Routledge, 1997.

Yu Bin, "Gaozhu 'santiao baozhangxian'" (To build "Three Protection Lines"), *Liaowang* (Perspectives), 1999, no. 37, 27–29.

Yu Fahong and Guo Yue, "Muqian woguo jiuye xingshi yu duice" (The Current Situation of Employment in Our Country and Solutions), *Lingdao juece xinxi* (Information for the Decision Making of Leaders), 2000, no. 31, 2–3.

Yu Jianrong, "Liyi, quanli he zhixu" (Interests, Power, and Order), *Zhongguo nongcun guancha* (Observations of Rural China), 2000, no. 4, 70–76.

Yu Xiu, *Zaoyu xiagang* (Facing Retrenchment), Beijing: Zhonghua gongshanglian chubanshe, 1998.

Yu Xuecheng, "Wuhanshi guoyou qiye rencai duiwu jianshe sikao" (Thoughts on the Personnel Training in State Enterprises in Wuhan), *Changjiang luntan* (Changjiang Forum), 1999, no. 3, 12–14.

Zeng Peiyan (ed.), *1999 Zhongguo guomin jingji he shehui fazhan baogao* (A Report on China's Economic and Social Development in 1999), Beijing: Zhongguo jihua chubanshe, 1999.

Zhan Qinghe and Bai Ningxiang, "Yingdang dui dangqian gongren fei zhengshi zuzhi jinxing yanjiu" (Workers' Informal Organizations Should Be Studied), *Xueshujie* (Academia), 1999, no. 3, 78–83.

Zhang Banghui, Ji Wenru, and Tian Wen (eds), *Qiye jianbing pochan anli* (Cases of Mergers and Bankruptcy), Beijing: Zhongguo wujia chubanshe, 1995.

Zhang Chunlin, "Tiaochu 'lushan' shi zhenmian" (To Gain the Truth), *Xinwen jizhe* (Journalists), 2000, no. 5, 56–57.

Zhang Huiming, *Zhongguo guoyou qiye gaige de luoji* (The Logic of the Reform of State Enterprises in China), Taiyuan: Shanxi jingji chubanshe, 1998.
Zhang Jianhua (ed.), *Zhongguo mianlin de jinyao wenti* (Pressing Problems Faced by China), Beijing: Jingji ribao chubanshe, 1998.
Zhang Wei, "Pochan, guaxiang qiye de dong bei feng" (Bankruptcy: A Measure Applied to Enterprises), *Zhongguo qiyejia* (Chinese Entrepreneurs), 1995, no. 1, 44–46.
Zhang Xiaoming, "Guoqi, wei bing duo jiangguan er zhan" (State Enterprises are Striving to Recruit More Talents), *Kaifang* (Openness), 1997, no. 3, 52–54.
Zhang Xinjie (ed.), *Kuashiji de youhuan* (Worries that Persist into the Next Century), Lanzhou: Lanzhou daxue chubanshe, 1998.
Zhang Zhilin and Feng Lei, "Guanyu guoyou qiye xiagang zhigong wenti de kaocha yu sikao" (Observations Of and Some Thoughts on Laid-Off Workers of State Enterprises), *Jingji gongzuo zhe xuexi ziliao* (Study Materials for Economic Workers), 1999, no. 9, 34–47.
Zhang Zuoji (ed.), *Zhongguo laodong tizhi gaige yanjiu* (A Study of the Reform of the Labor System in China), Beijing: Zhongguo laodong chubanshe, 1994.
Zhao, D. X., *The Power of Tiananmen: State–Society Relations and the 1989 Beijing Student Movement*, Chicago, IL: University of Chicago Press, 2001.
Zhao Dechun, "Xianfa zhong ying zengjia yixiang bagong de quanli" (The Right of Strikes Should be Added to the Constitution), *Jingji yanjiu ziliao* (Materials for Economic Research), 1999, no. 3, 55–56.
Zhao Yining, "Wei shehui ruoshi qunti 'xuezhongsongtan'" (Providing Crucial Help to the Deprived in Society), *Liaowang* (Perspecitve), 2002, no. 15, 11–13.
Zhen Xiang, "Shishi zaijiuye gongcheng" (To Institute a Reemployment System), *Zhongguo gongren* (Chinese Workers), 1996, no. 3, 10–11.
Zheng Haihang, *Guoyou qiye kuisun yanjiu* (A Study of the Loss Making of State Enterprises), Beijing: Jingji guanli chubanshe, 1998.
Zhou, X. G., "Unorganized Interests and Collective Action in Communist China," *American Sociological Review*, 1993, vol. 58, 54–73.
Zhou Wenpo, "Guoqi: yi xian gongren zai liushi" (Within State Enterprises: Production Workers are Leaving), *Zhongguo gongren* (Chinese Workers), 1996, no. 11, 12–13.
Zhou Xian, "Woguo jiuye xingshi he cujin jiuye de jianyi" (The Employment Situation in Our Country and Some Suggestions), *Jingji gongzuo ze xuexi ziliao* (Study Materials for Economic Workers), 1998, no. 19, 16–23.
Zhu Guanglei, *Dangdai zhongguo shehui ge jieceng fenxi* (An Analysis of the Social Strata in China), Tianjin: Tianjin renmin chubanshe, 1998.
Zhu Qingang, "Chengzhen pinkun renkou de tedian, pinkun de yuanyin he duice" (The Characteristics of and the Reasons for Urban Residents' Poverty and Some Solutions), *Shehuixue yanjiu* (Sociological Research), 1998, no. 1, 62–66.
Zuo Fu, *21 shiji shui geili fanchi* (Who Will Feed You in the 21st Century?), Nanchang: Baihuazhou wenyi chubanshe, 1998.

Index

ACFTU *see* All China Federation of Trade Unions
administrative hierarchy of China's political system 7
age: criteria for layoffs 76; and job search 53–55
All China Federation of Trade Unions (ACFTU) 21, 23, 65, 90, 140, 148, 152, 157; General Office of 152, 156, 161; national sampling survey of employees 49
Aminzade, R. R. 138
Anderson, Ken 90
anticorruption measures, demand for 120
appeals (*jiti shangfang*) 33, 127; *see also* collective appeals
Arandarenko, M. 147
arbitration organizations 127
Aronowitz, S. 148
Ash, T. 165
Asian financial crisis 14
Association of Brothers 48
Association of Friends 48
attribution error 89
authoritarian regime: survival of 85; understanding of collective action 36
Axelrod, R. 137

Bai Ningxiang 148
Bakken, B. 156
banking system, reform 14
bankruptcy 83
Bates, R., study of governments in tropical Africa 157
Beijing 23; Labor Bureau 49, 146, 157, 159; municipality 86, 104; Party Committee Research Office 85, 146, 157; Public Security Bureau 75; SOEs policy of Optimal Combination of Labor 75

belief and reaction of government 83–85
benefits: in collective action 37, 45; and individuals' participation 40–42
Berman, P. S. 137
Bernheim, D. 163
Bian, Y. J. 149–50
blame avoidance 88–90
Blasi, J. R. 135
Blecher, M. 4, 136, 145, 159
bonuses 26
Borisov, V. 135, 147, 154
Braverman, H. 48, 148
bribery 83
Brodsgaard, K. 156
Buddhism, god of 28
budget constraints: and end of socialist contract 14–18; and layoffs 15
Buechler, S. M. 144
Bureau of Civil Affairs 98
business activities of laid-off workers 24

Cai, Y. S. 135, 145, 161, 164
Cai Yingyang 155
Cao, Y. Z. 13, 139, 155
Cao Siyuan 160
capacity 85–99
catness 6
catnet 6; of participants 121; undermining 78
Chamberlain, H. B. 152
Chan, A. 142, 152–53
Chang Ping 154
Changchun 25; laid-off workers' attitudes toward collective appeals in 57
Chen, F. 4, 53, 94, 135–36, 144–45, 154, 156, 157, 159, 163
Chen Dengcai 152
Chen Hao 34
Chen Lu 142, 160

Chen Qingtai 143
Chen Shaohui 154
Chen Zhixia 155
Cheng, C. 156
Cheng Xuebin 158
Chinese Communist Party 65
Chinese Labor Statistical Yearbook 1998 53, 131, 140, 164
Chinese Labor Statistics: of 1999 143
Chinese political system, flexibility of 125–28
Chinese–foreigner relations 47
Chiu, S. 4, 136, 144, 159
Chong, D. 42, 107, 109, 137, 142, 162–63
Chongqing Knitting Factory 153; bankruptcy 96
Chongqing municipality 33
Chui Yingqi 150
City Investigation Team of State Statistical Bureau 143
civil demonstrations 95
civil war 114
Clarke, S. 39, 135, 147, 154
Cloward, R. A. 61, 95, 117, 151, 157, 160, 164–65
Colburn, F. D. 139
collective (work unit) 28
collective action of Chinese laid-off workers 45, 101, 161; alternative and nonparticipation 55–60; community pressure to become organizers 109–10; coordination 122–24; cross-firm 36; defined in Chinese trade union statistical yearbook 33; fragmentation and difficulty of 46–48; goal oriented 80; mobilization 6; number of 35; resistance to reform 4; scenarios for 111–15; shared interests and potential of 40, 120–22; spontaneous 114–15; studies of 9; sufficient participants 110–11; under authoritarian regime 2; workers' participation *see* workers
collective appeals 34, 104
collective inaction of laid-off workers 12
communication and preference disclosure 7
Communist Party: absence of political alternatives 95; committee (MICPC) 62; and management 62–64
complaints: bureau 102, 127; system 103
complexity of state–labor interactions 12
confidence 42–45
Connor, W. 138

consensus: between state and citizens in post-communist countries 87; building 110
constraints 85–99; on government 8–10, 101–06; on local officials 127; and management tactics 72–78
Cook, L. 2, 9, 136, 138, 165
coordination 122–24
coordinators or leaders 107
corruption 39, 63, 88, 122; managerial 3, 73, 83, 94, 105–06
costs: and benefit calculation 11; free-riding or defecting 46; and participation 42–45; *see also* benefits
crimes of public workers 156
Criminal Law 93
Crowley, S. 135–36, 147
cultural and social visions, different 47
Cultural Revolution, worker participation 9
Czechoslovakia 87

Dahrendorf, R. 150
Daqing 118
data collection on laid-off workers 131–34; definition of 10–11
Davis, J. 151
Davis, M. 148
democratic systems 126
Department of the Party and Masses Work 66
deprivation: discontent, and collective action 37–39; and resentment, factors related to 45; theory 11, 39
Detroit, workers in 47
Dietz, H. A. 144, 146, 151
Ding, X. L. 155
discontent: or frustration in laid-off workers, survey 38; and participation in collective violence, causal link 32
divide-and-rule, strategy of 47, 71
Document Research Office of Chinese Communist Party Committee 135, 153, 156, 165
Donald, D. 155
Dong Qingmin 162
Dong Zhikai 140
Dorothy, D. 137
Drakeford, M. 144

East Germany, former 39–40
Eckholm, E. 146, 159–60
economic and social status of workers, decline of 49

economic failure: of firms 52; occurrence and magnitude of layoffs 15
economic restructuring in industrial sectors in communist states 1
education 60; and job search 53–55
Ekiert, G. 84, 87, 138, 147, 155–56, 158–59, 166; and Kubik, comparative study of workers' protests in four post-communist countries 39
electoral systems, pressure arising from 125–26
Eley, G. 151
elite congress 67
Elster, J. 147
embezzlement 83
emergence of organizers 107–08
employees: job shifts 52; share-holding system 83; in urban sector 18
employment in private sector, hurdles to 22
Enterprise Law enacted in 1988 63
Ercheng Hua 139
evolution toward more institutionalized state–society interaction 128–30
ex ante–ex post arrangement with laid-off workers 13
ex post job search 53–55

Fairbrother, P. 135, 147, 154
Falungong: punishment of leaders of 94; repression in 1999 and early 2000s 85
family background, criterion for layoffs 77
Fan Qin 16, 139–40
Feng, C. 149–50
Feng Changyong 155
Feng Lei 141
Feng Tongqing 152
Filtzer, D. 78, 138, 165
finance and insurance sector 16
Finkel, S. E. 144, 146, 151
firms: collective resistance arising from reform 125; and laid-off workers, "mutual evasion" 55; normative role of 75
Fish, S. 156
focal issue: as coordination mechanism 120; potential or possible scale of collective action 122
foreign investors 130
former Soviet Union: in late 1980s and early 1990s, common economic concerns 121; state–labor relations in 2; trade union in 65

fragmentation and collective action 46, 110, 148
free riders 45
Frohlich, N. 138, 162
frustration–aggression theory 32
Fujian province, strikes in 48
Fukui, K. 139

Gamson, W. 160
Gao Jianyan 162
Geary, D. 61
gender, and job search 53–55
General Office of the ACFTU *see* All China Federation of Trade Unions
Germany: labor quiescence in 61; steelworkers in 47
Gibson, J. 148
Godson, J. 152
Golden, M. 137, 165
Goldstone, J. 8, 138
Gong, X. X. 138
Government: concessions 8, 114; different measures to weaken laid-off workers' motivation for resistance 100; divide-and-rule strategy 114; laid-off workers' reemployment 23–25; normative role of 75; patience and cost of sustained action 96–97; policies 62, 85–99; prevention of worker resistance 82, 155; redress measures and limitations 18–25; reform policies 124–25; "soft landing" policy after 1993 139
Great Leap Forward, between 1958 and 1960 18
Gurr, T. R. 136, 146
Gutman, H. 148

Harbin 22
Hardin, R. 137, 148, 164
He Pin 146, 165
He Shijian 154
He Xiaoying 152
Heilongjiang province 118; Acheng Sugar Factory 80; mining factory of 59; number of laid-off workers 17
Henan province 24; complaints organization 127; number of laid-off workers 17; one-vote-veto system and responsibility-locating system 104
Herbst, J. 10, 139
Hershatter, G. 47, 55, 148, 150–51
"hidden employment" (*yinxing jiuye*) 56
Hirschman, A. 149
Hong Hu 146

Honig, E. 47, 148
housing 116, 122; reform 143
Hu Manhong 146, 165
Hua Shanqing 145
Huang Bicheng 162
Huang Chenxi 142
Huang Daosheng 145, 162
Huang Weiping 34
Hubei province 74
Hunan: number of laid-off workers 17; Statistical Bureau 141, 143
Hung, E. 4, 136, 144, 159
Hungary 39; 1956 crackdown in 84, 87
Huntington, S. 156, 164–65
Hurst, W. 151
Hutzler, C. 157

income: degree of decrease in 37; level of localities 43
individual/s: action 48–55; behavior 81; and collective action, cost-benefit analysis 40; enterprise-based welfare system in China 122; participation 42–43; propensity to free ride 40; stakes or benefits 41; voluntary participation 41, 120
industrial reform 118
industrial sectors, budget constraints and scale of layoffs 15
industrial SOEs in China by size 18
inflation, high 120
information dissemination 6
Inner Mongolia 35
institutional arrangements and constraints 72–73
insurance: benefits 13; system, inadequate 31
interaction: among workers 40; between laid-off workers and firm 12; between laid-off workers and government 12; between workers and target of their action 40
Investigation Group of Beijing Economic Commission 142
Investigation System of Chinese Entrepreneurs 154

Japanese government, privatization of national railways 13
Ji Zhengfeng 159
Jia Qinglin 141
Jiang Xueqin 160
Jiang Zemin, President 33, 103
Jiangxi, bombing of a primary school in 127

Jilin province 35, 118; number of laid-off workers 17
Jin Shuyan 152
job: in foreign joint ventures 51; search of laid-off workers 53–54; transfers 51
Jon, J. 155
Jones, E. E. 158
Jukam, T. O. 125, 146, 165

Kadar regime 84
Kahneman, D. 136
Karmer, M. 165
Kiernan, A. 99, 160
Kim, H. 137
Kim, Q. Y. 163
Kitschelt, H. 137
Klandermans, B. 137, 159
Kong Zhangsheng 139
Kopstein, J. 136
Kornhauser, L. 161
Kramer, M. 123, 135–36, 153
Kristof, N. D. 159
Kroumova, M. 135
Kruse, D. 135
Kubik, J. 138, 147, 155
Kynge, J. 145, 151, 155, 163–64

Laba, R. 152, 158, 165
labor: contract system 19; market, tight 22; militancy 47; optimal combination of 74–75; oversupply in market 50; protests in three provinces in northeast 118; quiescence 1; unrest in late 1990s 57
Lai Ruoyu 65
laid-off workers (*xiagang zhigong*) 10; "absolute deprivation" for 13; collective action *see* collective action; from different places 43; different responses to retrenchment 11, 33; jobs through government's direct help 25; official count of 18; power of 118; predictors of action 45; by sector 16; *see also* workers
Lambert, M. 138, 156
Landry, P. 161
Lardy, N. R. 139
layoff/s: background in public enterprises 11; impact of 25–30; manner and target of 123; multiple criteria in 76; sequential and proportion-based 71; subsidies 20
leaders in rebellious collective action, emergence of 107
leadership groups (*lingdao banzi*) 72

leaving firms 51–53
Lee, C. K. 135–37, 145, 148, 151, 160, 165
Lee, H. Y. 142
Lee, L. T. 152
legal system 127
Leung, T. 136
Lev, M. 146
Li, X. 138, 162
Li Chunsheng 162
Li Congguo 164
Li Dahong 147
Li Hongjun 156
Li Lieman 152
Li Lisan 65
Li Maoguan 162
Li Peeling 140
Li Peilin 149
Li Pend 103
Li Zhenghua 162
Li Zuoming 160
Liao Mingtao 145
Liaoning province 35, 83, 89, 118; number of laid-off workers 17; SOEs debts in retirement pensions 59
Liaoyang 36, 118; workers' protests in 2002 110
Lichbach, M. 5, 137, 147
lifetime employment system 1, 19
Linz, J. 135
Liu, A. 145
Liu Jiesan 143
Liu Yong 143
local governments: blame avoidance 88; concessions 104; constraints 12, 104; guarantee of payment of retirement pensions 59–60; and political space in China 102; privatisation, role in 83; responsibility for social stability 102; system of "visiting the people" 104
Lohmann, S. 137, 147, 156
Lovas, Istvan 90
Lu Aihong 160
Lu Xin 136, 141, 160–61
Lu Xueyi 136, 141, 160–61
Ludlam, J. 136
Luehrmann, L. M. 161
lump sump severance pay 112
Luoyang of Henan, fire in 127

Ma Cheng 144
McAdam, D. 8, 137–39, 157, 160, 164
McCarthy, J. 138–39, 144, 157, 164
McFaul, M. 165

machinery industry, survey of blue-collar workers 49
maltreatment of employees, private firms 22
management: dominance of 62–67; as helpless patron 78–80; and labor 47, 83; power in Chinese SOEs 70; and worker silence 61, 151; and workers and *ex post* resistance 70–72
manager responsibility system (MRS) 62–63, 152
managers: informed constraints 73–75; role of 63
Manion, M. 156
Mao period, SOEs 14
market economy, transition to a 87
Markovits, I. 165
Marx 61
media, government control over 85
medical care, employees covered by 20
Mianyang, silk factory in 91
Miao Guangji 150
Michael, M. 138
microenvironment of workers 7, 101, 122
minimum allowance 20
Ministry of Labor and Social Security 18, 129
Ministry of Organization of CCP Central Committee 145, 158–59
Ministry of Public Security 35, 75
Mnookin, R. 161
Mo Daquan 58
mobilization 115, 119; and collective action 106–11; developed and less developed areas 44
mode of layoffs 124; and collective action, relationship 123
Model Self-Employed Laid-Off Worker 98
Model Self-Employed Stars 89
Montgomery, D. 148
Moore, B. 47, 148
moral arrangements, dismantling of 2–4
moral order, violation of 29
moral-economy approach 29, 32, 37
motivation 115; for resistance, dispelling 2–4, 87–88
MRS *see* manager responsibility system
Mueller, E. 146, 165
Muller, E. 125, 144, 146, 151
Muslims in Shandong province, repression of 104, 127
"mutual avoidance," importance of 56

Nanchong of Sichuan province 92
National Complaints Bureau 145, 159, 161–62
National Day 114
National Institutional Reform Commission, survey by 30
National Statistical Bureau 20, 25–26
netness 6
Nickolson, N. K. 137, 147, 159
Nield, K. 151
Ningxia Party Committee, Research Group of Organization Department of 152
non-repressive measures 87

Oberschall, A. 157, 160
O'Brien, K. 151, 161
odds of success 7, 61
Oestreigher, R. J. 47, 137, 148
Oi, J. 154, 165
Oil Bureau of Daqing in Heilongjiang province 78
Okesnberg, M. 138, 156–57
Olson, M. 137, 147–48
Opp, K. 158
Oppenheimer, J. A. 138, 162
Optimal Combination of Labor, policy 74–75
organizations in collective action, importance of 6
organizers and collective action 90–93; backgrounds of 108; emergence or absence of 7; inhibiting emergence of 95
Ost, D. 135, 147
Ostrom, E. 163

Pan, P. P. 160, 163
Parish, W. 148
Party see Communist Party
patron–client relations 73; between managers and supporters 77
Peace Sugar Factory 80
peaceful confrontations as war of attrition 97–99
Peasant Workers' Association 48
peasants-turned-workers 18
pension: owed to retired workers 58; system, employees covered by 20
People's Congress of Wuhan in Hubei province 24
perception of costs 12, 42, 45
Perry, E. 6, 9, 47, 135, 137–38, 148, 156, 162, 165; on fragmentation across groups 6; and Li's study of Chinese workers in the Cultural Revolution 107
personal connections 50, 73; as criterion for layoffs 77
PetroChina Co 155
Pierson, P. 126, 151, 165
Piven, F. 61, 95, 117, 151, 157, 160, 164–65
Poland 39, 87; labor movement 121; police department 39; "shock therapy" of post-communist 1; SOEs 1, 123; Solidarity foundation for 121, 128; workers' councils 67
Polish workers: 1970 strike 64; common economic goal 121; silent in post-communist period 123
Political and Legal Commission 93
political influence of Chinese citizens 85
political institutions and economic transition, relations between 2
political participation channels for 119
political space in China 126–28; embedded in political system 9
Pomfret, J. 146, 156, 160
pooled unemployment insurance system 20
Popkin, S. 90, 137, 147, 159
Porta, D. 165
Posuney, M. P. 136
pre-1949 China: Shanghai, workers in 6; workers in Tianjin 55, 61
pre-layoff resistance 11
preference disclosure 6
previous occupation and job search 53–55
previous occupations 60
principal–agent relation between different levels of governments 128
private firms, no labor contract and no welfare provision 22
privatization 83; affected workers, two forms of 83; of small SOEs 2
public insurance organizations 21
public opinion, survey of SOE workers 49
Public Security Bureau of Liaoning province 35
public work units 21
punishing organizers 93

Qiang, Y. Y. 13, 139, 155
Qiu Lu 161
qualified workers, loss of 150

Rawls, J. 160
reemployment: different access to 55; environment, absence of 19; mentality 88; rate of laid-off workers 60
reemployment service centers (RSCs) 13, 31; ability to address, reemployment environment 23; help for laid-off workers 41; local governments 20; as problem 22–23; shortage of funds 21; "three one-third" principle 20
reform: interactive nature of 5; and resistance, dual interaction 4–10
reform of SOEs: adoption of MRS 63; management dominates enterprise affairs 81
Reiter, H. 165
relations-based layoffs 77
religion, sense of 28
Ren Yanfang 162
repression 8; ineffective 86; *see also* Falungong; Tiananmen incident
Research Group of Bureaucratic Reform 157
Research Group of Laid-off Workers and their Employment 144
Research Group of Public Security 150, 159
resource mobilization theory 6, 32
"retaining the large and letting go of the small" (RLS) 124
retrenchment and laid-off workers' responses 32, 144
Roosevelt Administrations 86
Rosenthal, E. 158, 166
RSC *see* reemployment service centers
Rucht, D. 137
Ruehl, W. 158
Russell, C. R. 137, 147, 159
Russia 39, 124; in early 1990s, strikes 160; economic restructuring 1; post-communist 68; privatization 1

Sable, C. F. 47, 136, 148
Saich, T. 139
scale of resistance and reform 115–19
Schumpeter, J. 90, 159
Scott, J. 136, 139, 164
Selden, M. 122, 135, 165
selection of council representatives 67
selective punishment: and risk of action 90; and social stability 95
self-employed laid-off workers 23–24; lack of skills and funds 25
self-interest 108–09

sequential layoffs 123; leaders, and collective action 113–14; survey by ACFTU 111
severance pay 155
Sewell, W. H. 138
Shaanxi province 33; city complaints bureau in 105; city trade union in 68
Shan Tianlun 136, 141, 160, 161
Shandong province 35
Shanghai 23; cases of collective labor disputes 106; City Investigation Group 151; reemployment programs 96; RSCs in 20; Trade Union 150
share-holding system 83
Shenyang 59, 99
Shenzhen, adoption of salary-guarantee system in 129
Shi, T. J. 159, 165
shift selling and buying 60
Shijiazhuang of Hebei, bombing of residential building in 127
Shuai Bin 141
Sichuan province, research report by Party organs in 93
simultaneous layoffs 111, 123; leaders, and collective action 112–13
skills and connections 50, 60
Slovakia 39
Snow, D. A. 160
social stability: during reform period 34; impact of massive layoffs on 115
social unrest in China in selected years, number of instances 34
socialist contract, ending of, and retrenchment 13, 139
SOE (state-owned enterprises): autonomy of management 62–63; gradual or partial mode of reform in 121; keeping unpaid membership in 50–51; lifetime employment welfare benefits to their workers 30; loans, obtaining 139; loss-making 14–15; management and local governments as targets 7; northeast China, study of 10 large 15; reform 117–18
solidarity: and coordination in collective action 5–7; among elites 85
Solinger, D. 19, 135, 137, 139–40, 143–45, 148, 157
Sombart 55, 150
Song Baoan 57, 136
Spring Festival 114, 162

state: capacity in authoritarian regimes 85; controlled media in discussing reemployment 88; owned bike factory in Hebei province 102; responses and prevention of resistance 8
State Complaints Bureau 146
State Economic and Trade Commission 60, 140, 153
State Education Commission 156
State Institutional Reform Committee 56
State Labor Bureau (Ministry of Labor and Social Security) 50, 161
State Labor Science Research Institute of Ministry of Labor and Social Security 141
State Planning Commission 19, 141, 164
State Statistical Bureau, *Dayoushi* 18, 156
statistical analyses of workers' responses 36–45
Steinfield, E. 139
Stepan, A. 135
stratification among Chinese citizens 122
Strike Committee 48
students movement in 1989 *see* Tiananmen incident
subsidies 26; subsistence, laid-off workers 59
Sullivan, L. R. 138, 156
Supreme Court, bankruptcy of SOEs 118
survey questions used 132

"tacit agreement" or moral agreement between state and labor 2
Tainjin working class, before 1949 47
Tang, W. F. 148
Tang Yunqi 150
Tanner, M. S. 34
target: and collective action, power and constraints of reformers 7–8; government as 82–83
Tarrow, S. 9, 33, 45, 138–39, 145, 159; "contentious collective action" 10
tax: collection 24; exemptions 23–24
technical skills, workers with high- or middle-level 51
textile industry 16; of Shanghai 51
Thompson, E. E. 136, 146
threat of punishment by management 67–68
Tian Baichun 162
Tian Zehong 153, 155
Tiananmen incident 9, 63, 68, 85, 95, 102, 157–58; widespread support 120

Tilly, C. 6, 8, 137–38, 148, 158, 160
Trade Union Law 66
trade unions 64–66; lack of independent 121; weakness of 65
trading market for laid-off workers 24
Turner, L. 152
Tversky, A. 136

unemployment insurance 20; pooled or cross-work-unit policy of 19
unemployment subsidies 30
Unger, J. 138–39, 153
United States: absence of positive relationship between discontent and aggressive political participation 125; during the Great Depression 86; lack of socialism due to mobility 55; members of working class 46; state repression 61
unpaid laid-off workers 58
unpaid retired workers, cause of 57–60

violence 128
voluntary participation in collective action 5
voluntary retirement, early 1

Walder, A. 136, 138, 146, 153, 155–56, 165
Wang, S. G. 138
Wang Daben 142, 160
Wang Daming 146
Wang Haibo 140
Wang Hansheng 155
Wang Jixuan 151
Wang Meng 142
Wang Qi 162
Wang Xueli 143
Wang Yongcheng 34
Wang Yushan 57, 136
Wang Yutan 155
Wei Lei 34, 146
Weingast, B. R. 13, 139, 155
welfare system 143; benefits paid to high-income families 26; mechanisms 20; provisions, problems with 19–20, 116
Wetson, T. 153
women mill workers in Shanghai 47
Women's Association 98
wood processing and transportation sector 16
work-unit system 15; socialism, end of 29; welfare system 19

workers: collective action 2, 33–36; confidence, multiple strategies 8; council 66–67, 121; declined status and *ex ante* job search 48; depression and resentment 28–30; differentiation of skills among 47; discontent and deprivation, factors related to 36–38; economic plight 26–28; *ex ante* resistance 68–69; incentive to resist 42; mobilization, factors 7; participation in collective action 42, 44; reaction to reform measures 4, 26, 32; salaries 15; variations in protests 39; weak position in relation to management 67–68; *see also* laid-off workers; layoff/s
Wright, T. 138
Wu Bangguo 143, 158
Wu Chenguang 146
Wu Ji 151, 155
Wu Jinglian 139, 143
Wu Junping 149
Wu Yue 154
Wuhan 59, 86

Xiang Huaicheng 141
Xie Delu 150, 160, 163
Xie Fuzhan 143
Xu Jianchuan 142
Xu Xiaojun 152
Xu Ying 149

Yang Lianyun 142, 160
Yang Xuqing 154
Yang Yiyong 151
Yangjiazhangzhi 112

Ye Nanke 149
Yining, Zhao 135
Yong, O. R. 162
Yong, S. 156
You, J. 149, 152
Young, O.R. 138
Yu Bin 140
Yu Jianrong 162
Yu Xiu 155, 162
Yu Xuecheng 150

Zald, M. N. 138–39, 144, 157, 164
Zhan Qinghe 148
Zhang Chunlin 142, 158–59
Zhang Huiming 139
Zhang Jianhua 149
Zhang Xiaoming 149
Zhang Xinjie 154
Zhang Zhilin 141
Zhang Zuoji 161
Zhao, D. X. 137, 139
Zhao Dechun 162
Zhao Xuwei 142
Zhao Yuelin 155
Zhao Ziyang, premier 74
Zhejiang province a factory collective action 115
Zhen Xiang 144
Zhou, X. G. 9, 137
Zhou Dingchun 142
Zhou Enlai 140
Zhou Wenpo 150
Zhu Guanglei 149, 153
Zhu Qingang 141, 143
Zhu Rongji, Premier 118, 124, 129
Zuo Fu 155, 158, 163

eBooks – at www.eBookstore.tandf.co.uk

A library at your fingertips!

eBooks are electronic versions of printed books. You can store them on your PC/laptop or browse them online.

They have advantages for anyone needing rapid access to a wide variety of published, copyright information. eBooks can help your research by enabling you to bookmark chapters, annotate text and use instant searches to find specific words or phrases. Several eBook files would fit on even a small laptop or PDA.

NEW: Save money by eSubscribing: cheap, online access to any eBook for as long as you need it.

Annual subscription packages

We now offer special low-cost bulk subscriptions to packages of eBooks in certain subject areas. These are available to libraries or to individuals.

For more information please contact webmaster.ebooks@tandf.co.uk

We're continually developing the eBook concept, so keep up to date by visiting the website.

www.eBookstore.tandf.co.uk